time
to
breathe

Navigating life and
work for energy, success
and happiness

time

to

breathe

DR BILL MITCHELL

GREEN TREE
LONDON · OXFORD · NEW YORK · NEW DELHI · SYDNEY

GREEN TREE

Bloomsbury Publishing Plc
50 Bedford Square London WC1B 3DP UK

BLOOMSBURY, GREEN TREE and the Green Tree logo are trademarks of
Bloomsbury Publishing Plc

First published in Great Britain, 2020

A catalogue record for this book is available from the British Library

Library of Congress Cataloguing-in-Publication data has been applied for

ISBN: TPB: 978-1-4729-7298-9; eBook: 978-1-4729-7300-9;
ePdf: 978-14729-7299-6

2 4 6 8 10 9 7 5 3 1

Typeset in Minion Pro by Deanta Global Publishing Services, Chennai, India
Printed and bound in the UK by CPI Group (UK) Ltd. Croydon, CR0 4YY

To find out more about our authors and books visit www.bloomsbury.com
and sign up for our newsletters

Contents

1

Introduction

There are many reasons why you might have picked up this book.

Are you struggling to make life work for you, feeling overwhelmed no matter how much you are doing – and never feeling on top of all the demands on your time?

Do you feel that any reasonable balance to your life – just time for yourself – has completely drifted away as you struggle to keep on top of work demands and family pressures?

Have you drifted into habits like rushing home to see your children, making supper and then working for another couple of hours before you go to bed later than you would have liked, exhausted?

Have you been feeling that life is a struggle, that you are always tired, moody and irritable – and less connected to the people in your life you care about?

I work as a clinical psychologist in London. The people I see come from all walks of life, but most are struggling with their work lives. They tell me about relentless pressures and constant change, leaving them feeling insecure; about working with difficult, over-demanding people in jobs that never end, with no clear boundaries to allow them to let go. Their home lives can also be demanding, coping with young children and often with others who are dependent on them. Most of these people are also very demanding of themselves, conscientious and anxious about letting themselves or others down. It is very easy for work and family demands to take up all the space so that any balance to life disappears; any time for yourself just isn't there.

It is amazing to think that in 1930 the economist John Maynard Keynes predicted that by 2030 living standards would have risen to allow people to work a 15-hour week, so that we'd all be able to devote the rest of our time to non-work interests. For most of the people I see, the reality could not be more different from Keynes' prediction. Many find that even by adding an extra 15 hours to a normal working week, they are still struggling to stay on top of everything they feel they have to do.

But we all *need* balance for energy; and if our energy drops, our mood, our work effectiveness, our happiness can all be compromised, and we find ourselves drifting along a gradual pathway that can eventually lead to ill health – either physically or mentally. Depression, anxiety and burnout are the result. Countless numbers of people are already on this pathway: tired, not sleeping well, anxious and irritable, and often unaware of how long it has been since they felt really good about life.

My job is essentially to help people get back on track; to be more self-aware than they were before and to be mindful of a handful of things they need to do to keep the pressures in balance. At the end of the day, we all need a balancing system that is as strong or stronger than whatever pressures we are under. This balancing system, essentially our resilience, is not a quality we have but a set of skills we need to learn and maintain, to help protect our energy and mental fitness.

This book introduces you to the key building blocks that make up this balancing system. Today, more so than ever before, we need a refresher on the skills we require to navigate the complexities of our lives. You may well identify with many of the characters you will meet in this book, all of whom are struggling to make life work for them. You will come to recognise red flags to warn you that you have drifted off-track as well as the routines in your balancing system that are non-negotiable, while other things might drift away; and you will learn about what you can do to create boundaries and take control of your life. You will also find out about the subtle power of mental habits we all need to challenge in order to unlock the flexibility to make any of this work for us, rather than being held back by feelings of guilt or threat.

Everything in this book is practical, backed up by the evidence that supports the skills that contribute to our mental well-being. The ideas in this book are tested daily in the clinical work I do with my clients, who are looking for tools to navigate their lives better. And, to be honest, they are backed up in my own life, which has had its challenges – and without following the ideas I am advocating here, I might well have drifted down a pathway taking me to an unhappy, tired-out place.

This book will also make you think about what you pass on to others. If you are managing or supervising others, you create a microculture that has an impact on the mental well-being and happiness of your team, as well as on their work effectiveness. If you are a parent, the ideas in this book can be turned into healthy conversations with your children to help them navigate the conflicting pressures they are under.

Read on to build the foundations for a healthier, happier, more energised and balanced life – regardless of the type of work you are doing.

2

Drifting off-track

Hannah wakes at 5 a.m. The last she remembers, it was 3.30 a.m.; she must have fallen asleep again. How many hours has she had? Four, maybe four and a half, better than some nights. Then the feeling of nausea starts, that horrible anxious feeling, the heart beating faster. The sense of dread about what lies ahead, still dark but no point in trying to get back to sleep. Some mornings she gets up and starts working – always more to do, it never ends. How long has it been like this? How long since she slept well, since she got up feeling good about the day ahead? She can't remember – possibly two years, certainly not since she took this job. At one time, having a senior job in an agency would have been the ultimate goal. She has been in advertising for over 20 years and with this agency for eight. How has it become such a struggle? Where has the enjoyment gone? She has always worked long hours, even as an account manager, but now she is rarely home before 9 or 10 at night. And even after doing an 11- or 12-hour day, she never feels on top of it. She had gone to the GP a week ago, worried about how tired she felt. Her blood tests had come back normal, but she shouldn't feel this tired. He had offered her sleeping pills or an antidepressant. But she can't go down that road; she has always coped with demanding jobs, but now the pressure seems relentless. He recommended she see a psychologist.

Hannah walks in, smartly dressed, engaging smile, a sadness in her eyes, a hint of a Scottish accent.

'Tell me about yourself,' I say.

'My name is Hannah, I work in advertising, and I don't feel I'm coping that well any more. I feel tired all the time. I feel numb – I've lost the joy I used to get from my work and my home life. I feel guilty for feeling this way – I work for a great company, I'm married to Jack and we have two lovely kids, but I feel overwhelmed and trapped.'

Through any conventional lens, Hannah has a good life, but it has slipped so far out of balance that she no longer prioritises any time for herself. Although her relationship with Jack is holding together, they are both too busy to find the time to keep the relationship as close and fulfilling as it used to be. Her hours at work are long, but most of the time she feels she is just going from one crisis to the next and she rarely feels she has achieved what she wanted to get done. Work spills into her home life and she rarely has a holiday when work doesn't interfere. Her boundaries in life have gone. She has also drifted into ways of thinking that undermine her – she feels guilty for not seeing more of her children, guilty for not being more supportive of her team, and she is beginning to feel she is failing everyone at work and at home.

Keith

It would be a mistake to assume that stories like Hannah's apply only to those in senior management positions or those who work in finance or professional services firms.

Keith is an IT manager in a utility company. He has worked there for 15 years. He likes the company – he joined as an apprentice, he enjoys a challenging job, he gets on well with people, he progressed and was promoted to this role a year ago. He likes the people he works with and he has a good relationship with his manager, Jess.

Up to recently, he felt the job was manageable. He has always got to work early, and he would get home early enough to see his two young boys, to help with homework and be involved in the bedtime routines. He has been married to Anne, a teacher in a local primary school, for eight years. They have a good, warm relationship.

Keith was promoted to this role at the time the company was going through a major restructure. Some of his colleagues lost their jobs but Keith took on a role that had previously been done by two people. He was proud of where he had got to and the pay rise that went with the job could allow him to take on some of the house renovations he and Anne had wanted to do for some time.

But within a few months it was clear that the new job was tougher than Keith had anticipated. He discovered various issues that the previous manager had not dealt with. They were long-standing problems, but just ignoring them would mean that any projects his team took on would carry risks and could be compromised. He felt a strong sense of urgency to fix these problems, but he was also committed to delivering several projects with a team that wasn't as experienced as he would have liked. There just was not the time to get everything done. He talked to his manager, Jess, about the legacy problems. She was less concerned about them and urged Keith to address them eventually, but to focus on the other projects for now. But Keith knew that any projects he delivered would be compromised and could cause further problems unless those issues were resolved.

He found himself worrying about his work when he was at home. He was trying to fix the work problems and deliver the other projects, but they were running into trouble with inconsistent internal clients changing what they wanted at the last minute. He was working later, getting home preoccupied, finding it difficult to relax in the evenings. He was often feeling anxious when he woke in the morning, anticipating the day: the meetings, the problems, the unanticipated crises.

In the past he had taken pride in being on top of his emails, but in this job the email volume was constant. He kept his work phone with him wherever he went. He responded to it at home, which annoyed his wife. He tried to keep his weekends free, but he got into the habit of working for a few hours on Sundays to clear emails. He felt that no matter how much he did, he was never on top of the demands.

In the last few months he had been feeling overwhelmed by work demands. Although he met with Jess regularly, he felt he couldn't talk to her about how he was feeling. Jess was working over a number of sites and he didn't want to burden her. But he recognised he was struggling. He was starting to become indecisive; he was avoiding difficult tasks. He had been irritable with a colleague recently, which was really unlike him. He had even started taking the odd day off because he couldn't face going in to work.

Keith had never felt this way before. He had always coped and enjoyed his job. His health had always been good. For the past four months, his wife had been worried about him – his poor sleep and his irritability at home. She urged him to see his GP.

Keith was hanging on for his holiday, hoping the break would make him feel more relaxed, but after a few days away he came down with a stomach bug. Within a few days of coming back from holiday, he felt exhausted again. Things came to a head when a project that had been particularly challenging ran into difficulties. A key member of Keith's team went off sick and he took over some of that person's responsibilities in the run-up to delivering the project.

Before a recent meeting, Keith woke in the middle of the night feeling unusually anxious. His heart was racing and he could not get back to sleep. That morning, he felt nauseous and light-headed. He thought he was coming down with something, but he had to go in for the meeting. Walking to the meeting, he felt faint and shaky; while he was waiting to present his update, his heart started beating very rapidly and he felt breathless. He excused himself and went to see his doctor that evening. The doctor prescribed an antidepressant and signed Keith off for three weeks. He was very unwilling to take time off – there was too much to do, and his team would be left unsupported – but he dreaded going into work in case he had a recurrence of what happened in that meeting.

He had a meeting scheduled with his manager that morning. He was tempted to cancel but he went in. Jess could see he wasn't his usual self. She urged him to talk about how he had been feeling. He found himself being more open with her than he had been before. She was sympathetic and spent an hour with him, helping him to think through a more practical approach to the pressures he was struggling with. She briefly mentioned that she had gone through something similar a few years before and that she had learned from the experience. He left the meeting feeling stronger, with a plan to help him get through the next few weeks.

Nadia

It is certainly not only people in managerial positions who are struggling with work demands.

Nadia is in her late twenties. She has an outgoing, friendly personality, conscientious, with a tendency to feel anxious about letting people down. Nadia works in a sales team for an energy company. She has worked there for over eight years. The job involves responding to telephone and email enquiries, sending out estimates, calling potential customers and sending out renewal notices. The job is constantly busy, but the team is friendly. Since the company merged a few years ago, there have been constant changes – a new IT system was introduced, and regulatory changes add to the pressures. On top of all of this, Nadia's workload has increased as a result of the company reducing its administrative assistants, who had supported the sales team.

Nadia's work performance has always been good, but she now feels constantly under pressure. She has become anxious that she will not respond quickly enough or will miss a renewal and she will be criticised or, worse, disciplined. She worries that she might lose her job. She likes to get everything done before she leaves work and she hates leaving things unfinished. She typically works an extra hour most days and never takes a lunch break.

Nadia's home life is also pressurising. She has two young children and has recently gone back to work following maternity leave. Her mother, who lives a few streets away, has developed a heart complaint. Nadia likes to pop in and check on her after she has put her children to bed.

Nadia has been feeing over-pressurised, anxious and guilty about letting people down. She rarely gets to bed before midnight; she is up most nights with her younger child. She rarely gets more than five hours' sleep. Her mood has dropped, she no longer gets enjoyment in the things she used to do, and she often feels tearful. Most of the time she just feels exhausted.

Then, one day she dealt with a call from a customer who was complaining about poor service from the company – an enquiry that had not been followed up. Nadia dealt with it professionally, but afterwards broke down in tears. Her supervisor took her for a coffee and listened sympathetically, and for a brief period Nadia felt there was someone who wanted to help her.

How does it happen?

How is it that countless people like Hannah, Keith and Nadia have drifted into a pathway that takes them a very long way from their normally energised effective selves without even having realised where they have got to?

How is it that thousands of people who have previously been robust and resilient end up tired out, joyless and lost, having invested years in getting to what they hoped would be a fulfilling life?

How can we make life work for us rather than feeling we are at odds with our lives?

If you asked them about the pressures they are struggling with, Hannah, Keith and Nadia would tell you about the difficult things they have to contend with in their jobs. They would talk about targets, the constantly rising bar of expectations. No matter how much they are doing, more is expected of them. They might talk about difficult clients or managers and the hours they spend trying to sort out relationship problems. They might talk about the difficulty in getting any balance to their lives, no clear boundaries around the job – email volume that never ends, the constant uncertainty of change.

All of those pressures are real, they are obvious, they are out there. But the most difficult pressures that people like Hannah, Keith and Nadia have to contend with are the pressures that come from within, from their personalities. These pressures are less visible, almost wired in, and it is these that can be the source of many dysfunctional ways of behaving and thinking.

Hannah is not just driven to achieve, she is driven by conscientiousness and responsibility to her clients and to her teams. Sometimes that responsibility goes beyond what is reasonable. She can find herself in a management meeting picking up a problem that needs to be sorted, even though it is not strictly in her area. She is committed to giving the best to her clients, and recognises she can be a perfectionist. There are underlying fears about letting people down or failing in some way.

Keith's conscientiousness and fears about letting people down make it impossible for him not to try to tackle the legacy problems he inherited when he took over this job. Nadia's perfectionism and commitment to her job, combined with her fears of being criticised, make her feel guilty if she has not completed everything before she goes home, even though most of her colleagues carry over some less urgent tasks to the next day.

These qualities – drive, commitment, responsibility, real attention to detail, anxiety about failing – all contribute to success. They are part of the package of achievement. But if they are unbalanced, they can create seriously dysfunctional ways of working and living.

People have always had these qualities, so what has changed? Well, to start with, at one time there were more organisational constraints on these qualities. At one time, Hannah could not have worked the hours she was doing because the office would have closed in the early evening, documents would have been too heavy to carry home, there was not the constancy of email, clients would not have contacted her outside office hours, deadlines were longer. Those factors created a routine and a pace to the working day that acted to contain and constrain commitment, insecurity and over-responsibility. Today we work in a totally unconstrained work environment.

Our present working age has been termed the Third Industrial Revolution. The first, in the 18th and 19th centuries, was driven by steam power, the mines, cotton mills, faster transport and the movement of large numbers of workers from the countryside to cities. The second, at the beginning of the 20th century, was driven by electricity, telephones, air transport and mass production. We are now in the third – driven by IT, telecommunications, access to limitless information and constant availability, working globally across multiple time zones. This Third Industrial Revolution has removed all constraints on how we work. Countless numbers of people I know get home early enough to see their children then start working again for a few hours before bed, and their smartphones go everywhere with them. Many people tell me they check emails if they get up to go to the bathroom in the night, umpteen people have difficulty sleeping and get up at 4 a.m. and start working, and many professionals now work on holidays, answering emails or reviewing work. There is an intensity and constancy to the work pressures that didn't exist in the days of postal mail and fax machines. Add to that the constancy of change and the ambiguity and insecurity that change can bring, regulatory pressures and the bottlenecks that routinely exist on the promotional pathway and it is not difficult to see how personality pressures like insecurity, commitment and perfectionism could get out of control, rather than be held in balance. And it is not difficult to see how if these pressures are not held in balance, people like Hannah, Keith and Nadia, who had no previous difficulties in coping with life, could drift off-track very slowly, moving towards fatigue, anxiety or ill health.

In most areas of human activity, going off-track is immediately identifiable: in golf your ball is suddenly in the long grass, in sailing you are on the wrong tack, when skiing you are lying in deep snow off-piste. However, when it comes to emotional behaviours there is no instant corrective recognition, and we can go a long way off-track before we realise we are not where we thought we were. Many people are completely unaware of how off-track they have gone.

Tom

Tom is driving to work one Tuesday morning. The traffic is heavier than normal – broken traffic lights, long delays, cars nudging forwards. At this rate he will be late for his first meeting and he has four back-to-back meetings, so there is no flexibility. He needs to prepare a client presentation; he meant to do that at the weekend, but didn't get around to it. He reaches for the phone to call his PA, but the battery is dead and he has lent the charger to his son. Frustration mounting, feeling trapped, he starts to feel odd, like he is out of himself. He's a bit light-headed, he can't get a proper breath, his chest hurts – it feels like something awful is about to happen to him. He opens the window, takes some deep breaths – there is a hospital about half a mile away. After what feels like an eternity, he has left his car in a side street and made it to hospital. The pain in his chest is worse, his heart is racing. A nurse sees him, his pulse is 120, his blood pressure is raised. A doctor examines him, he has an ECG, he is told that he has probably had a panic attack; he is given a couple of tranquillisers and advised to see his GP. That evening he feels better, but still shaken up. But it makes him think hard, and he realises he has been on a slow pathway taking him a long way from feeling good about life for many months.

Tom is a director of marketing for a global company; he was promoted to this job two years ago. It has been a struggle, with a major reorganisation affecting his immediate team; it took longer than expected to fill his previous role and he ended up doing two jobs for over a year. He realises that this was when his sleep started to become disturbed. A couple of years earlier, his marriage had started to come apart; they had separated, but it had taken two years to finalise a divorce settlement.

Tom recognised that he had become irritable and moody; he worked most evenings, he was distracted, often too tired to do anything fun. He realised he had cut himself off from his friends; he hadn't socialised for about three months, and he couldn't remember how long it had been since he had looked forward to going to work. Despite all of this, he had had a good year – he had been responsible for a number of innovative projects, and had been well rewarded for his contribution to company growth. It made him wonder: had he successfully disguised how he had been feeling? Had people noticed changes in his behaviour but said nothing?

A gradual decline

Anyone who knows Hannah, Keith, Nadia and Tom would have considered them to be robust people, working for tough, high-performing organisations. They are committed, conscientious, they are rarely sick, they have dealt with upheaval and various setbacks in their lives, they get on well with their colleagues, they can be trusted to deliver.

When robust people go off-track, they drift into a pathway of increasingly severe stress signs, a very gradual process, often taking many months, sometimes years – until it suddenly becomes serious. It can start with feeling increasingly overwhelmed by demands, at work or at home; your normal sense of feeling in control of life has slipped. You can feel more anxious as a consequence. The normal boundaries between your work and home life break down, you can become increasingly preoccupied and worried at home. It is much harder to relax, which can interfere with falling sleep – or, more commonly, waking in the night, feeling anxious and struggling to get back to sleep, becomes the new habit. All of this can make it harder to concentrate or be decisive. Self-doubts take over from your normal confidence. You can feel increasingly tired, irritable and moody, your sense of enjoyment in day-to-day life can drop. You can withdraw at home and struggle to connect with your partner or your family. This can take many months, gradually slipping further into a spiral of low mood, anxiety and reduced effectiveness. Day-to-day resilience is weakened, reducing your capacity to deal with random frustrations of life, which can trigger anger outbursts or tearfulness. You have drifted a very long way from your normally energised, resilient self.

This pathway can be so gradual that many just do not recognise how far they have drifted. Their commitment to their work, their conscientiousness, their fears of letting other people down, combined with the constant pressures to deliver, make it harder for people to take stock of these changes in how they are dealing with day-to-day life. To recognise there is a problem would demand some corrective action, some change, a different approach, and they are often so locked in to how they are trying to deal with the demands that they do not have the personal resources or the energy to change course. Their ability to navigate life with all its challenges and changes is gradually failing them.

Going to extremes

This is not to imply that pressure is detrimental to our psychological well-being. As you know, you can feel tired, moody, and generally less confident because life is not pressuring enough for you right now. We need some pressure to feel energised, engaged, and to get closer to being at our most effective. There is a well-established inverted-U curve between pressure and our energy, our effectiveness and our mental well-being.

When demands are too low, when every day is the same, when we do not feel stretched or challenged, we can get bored, we can feel we are languishing, confidence can drop, we can feel stressed because we are not challenged enough. In some organisations, low pressure – not being busy enough – can create feelings of insecurity or anxiety. In professional service firms, low pressure raises worries about not achieving targets, with all the insecurities that that creates. Many people leave organisations looking for a bigger challenge, essentially looking for more pressure.

Then there is the optimal zone of the curve, where the demands feel manageable – we might feel stretched, but we feel in control of those

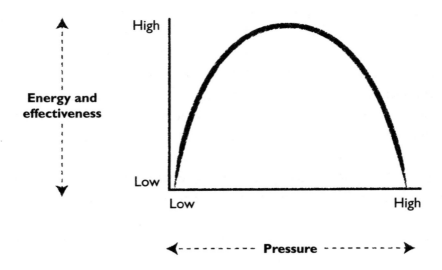

demands and there is a confidence and an energy that flow from that. We feel engaged and purposeful and our emotions feel balanced. We feel generally good about life.

But if the demands become too great, if we feel stretched beyond our ability to control these demands, we can drift into the overwhelmed part of the curve, gradually affecting our energy and confidence, our effectiveness, and our emotional balance – as Hannah, Keith and Nadia and Tom discovered.

Now, obviously there are times when we drift away from the optimal zone of the curve, but we bounce back – there is some degree of elasticity in this. You might have a few days when you feel life has got too demanding, you might feel more irritable and tense, tired, perhaps not sleeping as well as usual, but you come back into the healthy zone when the demands ease off. The self-awareness skill is in recognising when you have gone further into the curve, beyond your normal elasticity. Then you would see more signs that you are struggling, affecting your energy, your emotional balance, your decisiveness, and how you are relating to others. Your normal mental capacity to deal with frustrations and additional pressures is eroding and then one or two additional demands could trigger symptoms of ill health, which could be physical or psychological.

The potential for ill health

At the bottom of this pathway there is a potential to become sick. This could be physical: flu, chest infections, stomach pain, skin disorders. It can sometimes be a condition that makes it impossible for you to carry on at work. This can be a severe chest infection or pneumonia or, as I've seen several times, severe mouth ulcers that make it impossible to speak. Your body is forcing recuperation, which can gradually take you back to overall good health. Others, like Hannah, Keith or Tom, move towards greatly raised anxiety or depression, and some experience such a loss of energy that they burn out. All of these conditions can be hugely disruptive to work and family life. They can lead to a long-term use of medication like antidepressants or time off work. They can lead to a collapse in confidence to the point that many people just walk away from careers into which they have invested years of their lives.

For Keith and Tom, the pathway culminated in greatly raised anxiety and a panic attack, a state of acutely raised adrenal hormones that flooded over them with such intensity that they believed something catastrophic was about to happen to them, like a heart attack or a stroke. An anxiety attack is very physical: raised heart rate or irregular heart rhythm, breathlessness and light-headed feelings, often a sense that you could pass out. Many people call an ambulance or go to hospital because of the intensity of the attack. Although the attack can pass quite quickly, it can leave the person greatly shaken, with a considerable sense of vulnerability that it could happen again, perhaps in some situation where they might lose control and undermine their credibility.

We all have our anxiety baseline, which is part of our evolutionary system that allows us to react defensively in the face of some real threat. That baseline can rise and at its worst can become something called a Generalised Anxiety Disorder, with physiological agitation and constant worries that are hard to subdue. An anxiety attack can lead to the baseline rising. The person is now constantly aware of anxiety, often starting with a sense of dread when they wake in the morning, and having periods of restlessness and panicky feelings, and constant worries out of proportion to the realities of the person's life.

Hannah moved more in the direction of depression. Anxiety and depression have a number of symptoms in common, like sleep disturbance and agitation, but depression is a complete flattening of mood and a loss of drive and motivation. It is much more of an effort to confront life, confidence can collapse and enjoyment in life can go. Depression can bring in feelings of guilt, self-dislike, even worthlessness, which can be very distressing and not easily relieved. Depression distorts memory, making it more likely the person will recall events that reinforce their sense of guilt and failure. It can make decision-making painfully difficult as they agonise over the consequences of making the wrong decision. It can lead to such a blunting in how they feel that they can disengage from people they care about, which inevitably affects others around them. Physically it can lead to changes in weight and a constant feeling of fatigue. Depression is a continuum; it can be relatively mild, not necessarily obvious to others. It can be so severe that the person loses their sense of purpose and can seriously contemplate taking their life. Hannah was a long way from that, but the combination of anxiety and nausea in the mornings together with her loss of energy and a flatness of her mood – the loss of joy – is very typical of many previously robust people who have drifted down the pathway of reduced resilience and energy.

A growing problem

Anxiety and depression, the most common psychological disorders, affect one in six of the population and are more common in women than in men (22 per cent of women and 17 per cent of men in the 35 to 44 age range), according to a 2018 report on mental health statistics for England. According to the World Health Organization (WHO) in their 2017 report 'Depression and Other Common Mental Disorders', the incidence rate of mental ill health has risen considerably: anxiety disorders are affecting 264 million people globally, 4 per cent of the overall population. This has risen by 15 per cent from 2005 to 2015. Over 320 million people worldwide suffer from depression, with the rates higher for women than for men, equivalent to 4.4 per cent of the world's population. The prevalence rates for depression have increased by 20 per cent from 2005 to 2015. According to HSE data published in 2019, work-related stress, anxiety and depression now account for 54 per cent of all working days lost due to ill health in the UK. The cost in terms of revenue alone is enormous; the loss of productivity resulting from anxiety, depression and burnout has been estimated by the *Financial Times* as a $1 trillion problem globally.

Physical illness, anxiety and depression are not the only end points of this slow pathway of increasing stress signs. Some people instead experience a collapse of their energy, both physical and mental, together with a loss of enjoyment in work that used to give them a strong sense of purpose and fulfilment. Burnout was first described in the 1970s by psychologist Herbert Freudenberger, and then by Christina Maslach and Susan Jackson. It is described as consisting of three dimensions: exhaustion, cynicism and loss of one's sense of efficacy. Many people with burnout, in addition to fatigue and loss of engagement and detachment from a job that used to give them a great deal of meaning, can experience physical symptoms, including headaches or muscle pain, that can become very pronounced when they try to push themselves. Concentration can be badly affected, even when it comes to reading newspapers, and paradoxically, even though they are exhausted, they have difficulty sleeping.

Burnout is particularly common in caring professions like healthcare, social work and teaching, but it is certainly common in a wide range of professional groups. In my experience, many people with burnout are inaccurately diagnosed with depression and subsequently prescribed antidepressants.

Conscientiousness, overcommitment and fears of letting themselves or others down drive people into a pathway that can lead to one of these end points. When there are no constraints in how we work, these characteristics can lead to extreme behaviours that many would find hard to believe. I once counselled a young man who worked habitually beyond midnight but who would also set his alarm every hour in the night so as to check and respond to emails. Or I remember a patient who worked in a professional services firm, who after many months of excessive work hours had a panic attack in the office. Fearful that she might be having a heart attack, an ambulance was called. Sitting in the back of the ambulance not knowing what was happening to her, she continued to complete a detailed email to a colleague about a matter she was working on.

None of those conditions develop suddenly. They are the end point of a gradual process of changes in how we behave and feel, but many people lack an awareness of where they are on the continuum that goes from optimum mental well-being – feeling energised, engaged, effective in what we do, enjoying our work lives, feeling reasonably in control of the demands on them – down to, potentially, ill health, constant fatigue, overwhelmed and struggling.

Noticing the red flags

To balance the tendency to ignore or rationalise the increasingly obvious signs that we are drifting off-track, all we need is one red flag, one clear sign that reliably tells us 'I am not my usual self, I have drifted'. The red flags could be:

- I am sleeping less well; I am waking more often and it takes longer to get back to sleep; my head is busy when I wake in the night; it is taking longer to get off to sleep; I am waking earlier than usual.
- I have become irritable, less patient, less tolerant, I feel more easily frustrated than I usually do.
- I have become withdrawn; I am less approachable; I am less engaged with others. I don't have the energy to see people.
- I feel generally more anxious, more worried that something will go wrong.
- I am finding it harder to enjoy the sort of things I used to get a lot of pleasure from – work, family, friends, my free time. I feel I am getting less from it.
- I feel more tired than usual; tired when I get up in the morning, too tired to do much in the evening – mentally tired. It has all become an effort.

These are all early signs. They are a long way from symptoms of anxiety, depression or ill health, but any one of these red flags could tell you that you have drifted into the spiral that could slowly take you to a bad destination.

Failure to recognise the signs of drifting off-track will make it more likely that other dysfunctional habits will develop as ways of compensating for how we are struggling with the demands we have put ourselves under. In my experience, when highly motivated, conscientious people start to struggle with greater demands, they automatically give more time to the job and cut back on activities that are necessary for preserving their mental energy and psychological resilience. This usually occurs incrementally over time – as a subtle drift away from those behaviours rather than a conscious decision, which in turn can make it less likely that they will get back to those behaviours when the demands ease off.

Which zone are you in?

Where are you on the pathway? In the good zone?

- Feeling in good energy
- Sleeping pretty well
- Feeling the demands are manageable
- Feeling generally optimistic and positive
- Looking forward to things

- Feeling engaged and purposeful
- Able to bounce back from a bad day
- Emotions feel balanced
- Feeling pretty confident

Are there red flags appearing?

- Feeling more tired than usual
- Sleeping less well
- Feeling irritable and moody
- Less confident
- Not looking forward to things – everything feels an effort

- Demands feel overwhelming
- More emotional, close to tears some of the time
- Becoming more withdrawn
- Feeling anxious and worried about things

How long has it been since you were in the good zone?

3

Running on empty

If you asked Hannah, Keith, Nadia or Tom how they have been feeling, they would all say they feel really tired. Loss of energy – sometimes to the point of feeling exhausted – is a key red flag in the slow pathway that takes people from feeling generally good about life, confident and engaged, all the way to ill health, physically or mentally.

The importance of energy

Energy is crucial for psychological well-being. Energy underpins every aspect of our work performance, our creativity, our ability to problem-solve, and it is critical for sustaining good relationships, for a satisfying family life, for having fun. It is crucial for our health, both physically and mentally; for our resilience, which protects us from stress; for the psychological qualities that enable us to deal with change and disruption. If our energy goes, all these things are undermined: our work performance suffers, our health can be undermined, stressful events affect us adversely, even our confidence drops.

Underpinning energy is a complex physiological system that we need to keep in good shape if we are to remain effective and on top of the demands we face professionally and in our home lives. Two interconnected systems have a major impact on energy: the cortisol adrenal system and the balance of neurotransmitters in our central nervous system.

Cortisol

Cortisol is a hormone released from the adrenal gland. Its primary function is to preserve energy. Under normal circumstances, our cortisol level is higher in the morning and ideally low by the time we get to bed. Abnormally low levels of cortisol give rise to feelings of fatigue, difficulty getting going in the morning, concentration loss, real dips in energy later in the day, difficulty summoning the energy to do almost anything in the evening. However, if cortisol rises beyond its normal baseline, it switches on a host of reactions that we associate with stress. It makes us irritable, anxious, we become moody and feel low, it greatly interferes with concentration and our ability to respond effectively to unexpected challenges. Cortisol is highly responsive to any set of circumstances that we perceive to be threatening, circumstances that might overwhelm us or leave us feeling that we do not have sufficient control to deal with them. It is released as part of your body's Hypothalamus-Pituitary-Adrenal (HPA) response to stress, mobilising energy resources to enable us to deal with the increased demand, but it can have a number of damaging effects, particularly in situations of prolonged stress.

Cortisol rising can spill over into the night and seriously interfere with sound sleep. Raised cortisol also has a number of potentially damaging effects on our physical health. It reduces our immune response, making us more prone to infectious illness. It raises blood pressure and cholesterol, and allergies become more pronounced. Cortisol interferes with blood sugar regulation, which can in turn interfere with stable energy and in the long term raises the probability of developing diabetes. Prolonged elevation of cortisol interferes with memory and learning and even leads to weight gain.

In recent studies with City traders, cortisol was found to rise in a direct correlation with increased market volatility – to a maximum of 68 per cent above their normal level. In a subsequent study, when participants were given injections of hydrocortisone that artificially raised their cortisol levels by 68 per cent, they became far less effective in decision-making in an experimental task that simulated making decisions under market conditions. The participants became defensive decision-makers, more anxious about making the wrong decision, potentially allowing a bad situation to continue without taking decisive action.

One particularly damaging effect of prolonged cortisol release is that it damages critical brain centres that are involved in switching the cortisol system down. When cortisol disrupts these brain centres, it creates a vicious circle of unregulated cortisol release, creating conditions of chronic stress. These centres include the hippocampus, which is involved in storage of memory, the prefrontal cortex, which has a key role in how we regulate our emotions, and the amygdala, a vital brain region involved in controlling the stress response. All three areas are disrupted by prolonged exposure to cortisol, seriously interfering with their ability to switch the cortisol system down when it is no longer required. This state of chronic unregulated stress response can culminate in sleep disturbance, poor decision-making, inflexible thinking, low mood and agitation, with increasingly disruptive effects on our work performance. What can then happen is that we can go into adrenal exhaustion, resulting in a dramatic drop in cortisol levels, which is experienced as a feeling of physical and mental fatigue.

The neurotransmitter system

Associated with the reactivity of cortisol is our neurotransmitter system. Our central nervous system is made up of millions of nerve endings, which branch at tiny spaces. Into these spaces we release a variety of biochemicals that have a profound effect on how we feel. Collectively known as neurotransmitters, including serotonin, norepinephrine, Gamma-Aminobutyric Acid (GABA), glutamate and dopamine, they are the drivers of mental energy, essential for concentration, memory and problem-solving. They also regulate mood, making it more likely that we will experience pleasurable emotions like enjoyment and anticipation; they protect us from low mood, effectively acting like natural antidepressants. They have a modulating effect on anxiety and are central to the system that regulates sleep. Essentially, neurotransmitters provide a physiological underpinning to the resilience system that allows us to respond effectively to unexpected, potentially threatening circumstances that could knock us off-track.

It is not difficult to see how many of the qualities we need to cope with demanding jobs – clear decision-making, energy, and coolly responding to crises – depend on the optimal functioning of both the cortisol and neurotransmitter systems. Both of those systems are critical to our health, physically and psychologically, and to practically every aspect of our work performance.

Getting the right balance

These systems are dependent on there being a healthy balance in our lives. A handful of behaviours and routines are central to maximising the energy balance, but very often these are the behaviours we drift away from when life becomes more demanding.

Think about yourself here. You are in a full-time job. The demands are constant but you are asked to take on another project, or you have been promoted but no one has been appointed to your old job yet and you end up doing two jobs for the time being. Somehow you have to find more time, so your hours creep up and some of the routines you have in the balance of your life seem less important. Exercise might go – you don't mean it to go forever, just until you get through this project. Your lunch break goes, and you start eating sandwiches and crisps at your desk. Sleep drops from eight hours to six; even family time can drop as you look at how you can fit more in. These are not conscious decisions – this is a drift. But many of those behaviours and routines are necessary for stabilising the physiology of energy and good mental well-being.

However, not everyone allows this drift to happen. Some people recognise that if they stop certain of their routines, they will become tired, less effective and less able to deal with the demands, and they hold on to those routines regardless of how busy or disrupted their life has become. They have some *non-negotiables* in their life. A non-negotiable is something you prioritise on a regular basis because you know that if you stop doing it, you will pay a cost: a cost to your energy, your mood, your effectiveness, your enjoyment in life.

Sally

Sally understands all too well how drifting away from balancing routines and letting work take over can have a serious effect on health and mental well-being. She had joined a mid-sized international company five years earlier at a point when it was going through a rapid expansion. Working in operations, Sally had overseen a number of transformational projects. Bright, dynamic, recognised for her can-do approach to work, she had risen to a managerial level within a few years. She typically worked long hours, but she made it a priority to see her young children before they went to bed and she made time for exercise and yoga a few times a week, often exercising at lunchtime in a gym close to the office.

Then Sally took over the implementation of a major IT programme. Although she had a good team and very capable consultancy support, the project ran into difficulties, seriously overrunning, with costs rising. She was being criticised by her senior colleagues in the US; questions were being asked about her capability. For the first time in her career, she began to feel her work was getting out of control – she was starting to feel overwhelmed. This greatly unsettled her; there were times when she felt panicky before meetings and she often had a sense of dread before she went to work. At other times she felt disoriented and light-headed. By this stage, her hours had increased, her exercise and yoga routines had gone, she was sleeping badly, and it was starting to have an effect on her home life. In the middle of all of this, she had a family holiday planned. She debated cancelling it, but she didn't want to let her children or her partner down and for the last few months she had not seen much of them in the evenings as her work hours had grown. She was feeling guilty enough as it was. She went on holiday, but she ended up working most days on conference calls for four or five hours. Within a few days, Sally had developed a stomach infection and felt wiped out. When she returned from holiday, she felt more exhausted than before she went. It was a real struggle getting up in the mornings, she was having difficulty concentrating at work, and when she got home in the evenings she felt too tired to do anything. She often went to bed as soon as she got in. She was sleeping 10 hours or so at weekends. Then she developed a throat infection that was so bad she could not speak. She was off work for a week or so on antibiotics, but her doctor was also concerned about how exhausted she felt and suggested she complete a cortisol assessment by taking saliva swabs four times between getting up and going to bed. The results showed her cortisol level was so low she was in physiological exhaustion.

Sally had always been a robust, energetic person. Apart from a bout of glandular fever in her teens, she had rarely been ill. But good physical and psychological health depends on the stability of cortisol and the hormones that make up our adrenal system. And for anyone in a demanding, potentially stressful job, having a handful of non-negotiables is a must for preserving energy and well-being.

Sally was off work for about three months, focusing at first on rest, relaxation routines and very moderate exercise. She stopped drinking alcohol and removed sugar, simple carbohydrates and caffeine from her diet. Gradually her energy improved and she made it back to work over a few months of reduced working hours. Looking back, she recognised she had been running on empty but could see no way out without letting everyone down.

Sally had gradually drifted away from everything that has a stabilising effect on the physiological systems that underpin our energy, effectiveness and psychological well-being.

Exercise: a key stabiliser

Let's look at what those stabilisers are. One key stabiliser of this physiological system is moderate aerobic exercise. This doesn't need to be a gym workout, it could be a brisk walk as part of your journey to work. We all know that exercise is good for us, good for our cardiovascular system and good for our weight, but recent research shows how deep the effects of exercise go: for our immune system, for protection against age-related illnesses, cognitive and intellectual functioning, for regulating the stress and neurotransmitter systems, and for the preservation of energy.

A group of scientists led by Steven Moore at the US National Cancer Institute looked at the relationship between physical activity and longevity in a group of over 600,000 adults, followed up over 10 years. They found that for adults over the age of 40 of normal weight, being physically active for around 65 minutes a day adds over seven years to life expectancy in comparison to being inactive and overweight. A recent review of research articles by John Campbell and James Turner from the University of Bath in the UK concluded that regular exercise enhances immunity and even delays the ageing of the immune system, debunking the idea that exercise might suppress immune function. They show that after exercise, the immune system is in a heightened state of immune surveillance and regulation, redeploying immune cells to parts of the body, such as the lungs, that could be vulnerable to infection.

Good health needs healthy cellular reproduction, which in turn needs healthy chromosomes that protect our DNA codes. Tiny structures at the ends of our chromosomes, called telomeres, keep chromosomes in a healthy state. But telomeres can become damaged and shorten as a consequence of chronic stress conditions. Damaged or reduced telomeres can give rise to damaged chromosomes, resulting in cellular ageing. Cells can become senescent and stop reproducing altogether. When that happens, we are much more prone to developing age-related illnesses like cardiovascular disease, type 2 diabetes, various cancers, and inflammatory disorders. Damaged telomeres weaken our immune system and damaged telomeres in the hippocampus are linked to depression. One group that has been studied for telomere health is people who care for others with long-term age-related progressive illnesses. They have been found to have significant telomere shortening, making it more likely that they will also suffer from age-related illnesses.

In 2018, Eli Puterman and colleagues, professors from the University of California, looked at the effect of exercise as a buffer against stress on telomere health. They studied a group of 68 adults caring for elderly people suffering from dementia. The group reported high levels of stress and were physically inactive. Half were assigned to a programme of 40 minutes' aerobic exercise three to five times a week, while the other group did not change their activity levels. At the end of the study, those who had taken part in the exercise programme showed increased cardio-respiratory fitness, reduced body mass index, and reported lower levels of stress. And at a cellular level, those who were exercising had significantly longer telomeres than the inactive group, providing greater protection to their chromosomes. In an earlier study, the same researchers found that women in conditions of high stress had longer telomeres if they were engaged in regular exercise, hence protecting them from cellular ageing (compared to the non-exercisers). Those who were not exercising were not shielded from the damaging effects of stress, evident from their significantly shorter telomeres, hence raising their risk of age-related illnesses.

Exercise and mental health

The impact of exercise on mental health and a more resilient response to stress is also well established. In a 2018 study following nearly 34,000 adults for 11 years at the University of New South Wales in Australia, Dr Samuel Harvey and colleagues collected information on exercise, anxiety and depression. Reporting in the *American Journal of Psychiatry*, they conclude that regular exercise is associated with reduced incidence of depression, when other factors were controlled for. Twelve per cent of future cases of depression could have been prevented if all participants had engaged in just one hour a week of physical activity of any level of intensity. People who exercise regularly have nearly 45 per cent lower odds of having depression than those who are sedentary. On the same note, in 2014, Emma Childs and Harriet de Wit, professors of Psychiatry at the University of Chicago, reported the effect of exercise in building resilience to stress. They induced feelings of stress in their participants by asking them to give a short speech and perform an arithmetical task in front of an assessor, and concluded that while non-exercisers recorded a reduction in their mood after these events, those who exercised regularly didn't suffer in the same way from a drop in their mood. Additionally, according to one US study of over 1.2 million people, reported in *The Lancet*, individuals who exercised had 43 per cent fewer days of poor mental health a month compared to those who didn't exercise, when other characteristics were controlled for (two days of poor mental health for people who exercised, compared to nearly three and a half days for people who didn't exercise). Forty-five minutes at least three times a week produced the most benefit to their mental health.

This improved mental health is likely due to the effects of exercise on neurotransmitter levels. A recent study carried out by scientists at the Center for Neural Science in New York found that after a single bout of exercise, all three mood-enhancing neurotransmitters – norepinephrine, dopamine and serotonin – were boosted. There was also an increase in chemicals known as neuromodulators; these include something called endogenous opioids, which create positive mood changes. Exercise creates three main effects: sharper mental functioning, better mood and reduced stress levels. Vigorous aerobic exercise also produces an increase in two other neurotransmitters, glutamate and GABA, in a part of the brain that is associated with the regulation of heart rate, cognitive function and emotion – the anterior cingulate cortex. Both glutamate and GABA are reduced in brain regions associated with emotional regulation in patients suffering from depression, and often increased when the patients recover – providing additional support for the view that exercise can protect against depression as well as playing a part in recovery. The hippocampus is a crucial brain region involved in emotional regulation, anxiety and memory. The hippocampus is critical to the control of cortisol, but as we have seen, heightened cortisol over a long period of time depresses the functioning of cells in the hippocampus, leading to chronic elevations of cortisol. So a healthy hippocampus is pretty important for good mental health and cognitive functioning. Exercise not only aids in the balancing of cortisol but stimulates the production of new cells in the hippocampus.

In studies on mice, running reduced anxiety responses, and this is likely because running increases GABA activity in the hippocampus, which has an overall calming effect. In one study in 2013, Timothy Schoenfeld and colleagues from Princeton University stressed mice by putting them in ice-cold water for five minutes, and then examined what happened in the hippocampus, comparing mice who had been exercising in the past six weeks and sedentary mice. Both groups showed emotional excitation in response to the cold water, but the runners showed a greater activation of GABA, returning them to a calmer state more quickly. Similarly, looking at the effects of exercise on activity in the hippocampus of mice in 2019, Christina Chatzi and colleagues from Oregon Health and Science University found that exercise had increased connections between brain cells in the hippocampus and increased activity between the brain cells. In other words, exercise stimulated something known as neurogenesis and neuroplasticity. This means they saw a growth of both new brain cells and the connections between them. Neuroplasticity strengthens the ability of the hippocampus to learn and process information. Therefore, while prolonged stress decreases neuroplasticity, weakens our synapses and thus reduces our learning capacity, exercise acts as a neural protection from this damage, protecting our cognitive function and enabling us to perform at a higher capacity when under stress.

Researchers Kazuya Suwabe and colleagues from the University of Tsukuba reported similar results in 2018 in a group of young adults: just 10 minutes of mild exercise led to improved recall on a memory and recognition test; the hippocampus was examined using a high-resolution functional MRI technique within a few minutes of exercise, and they saw increased neural activity between the hippocampus and other cortical areas, leading to enhanced function and memory improvement.

A key biochemical benefit of exercise also lies in its role with the production of a chemical called brain-derived neurotrophic factor (BDNF), which stimulates brain cell growth and protects brain cells from the damaging effects of cortisol. This is supported by recent evidence from a review of 14 clinical trials in 2017 by Joseph Firth and colleagues, professors of Psychiatry at the University of Manchester, who concluded that exercise protects against the reduction in hippocampal volume that is normally seen with age, as a result of increased levels of BDNF.

There are several neurochemical theories about the origin of depression, and it is likely that there are many roads that lead to depression, rather than one that encompasses all the factors associated with depression. There is the neurotransmitter deficit road, which has led to drugs like the selective serotonin reuptake inhibitors (SSRIs) for the treatment of depression. There is an argument that depression is associated with low levels of BDNF and reduced hippocampus function and volume, backed up by studies that report reduced BDNF levels in depressed patients. There is also a theory that depression is caused by inflammation in the brain and a failure to regulate cortisol.

Exercise as treatment

Depression is treated by medication that targets neurotransmitters and by psychological therapies. Antidepressants lead to remission in about 30 per cent of patients and partial benefit in another 30 per cent, and psychological therapies have roughly similar effects, with no particular psychological therapy being superior to others. The combination of medication and psychological therapy is the recommended approach, but physical exercise has a significant antidepressant effect through its impact on neurotransmitters, on BDNF, on the protection of the hippocampus and other brain regions known to regulate our emotional responses through stimulating the growth of new neurons and their interconnection with other brain cells, and regular exercise has anti-inflammatory effects on the brain. People who regularly exercise show approximately 45 per cent lower odds of having depression symptoms, compared with sedentary people.

Looking at the effect of exercise on depression, a 2013 review of 39 trials concluded that exercise has a similar effect to pharmacological treatment and psychological therapy in reducing depression symptoms, particularly in those with mild to moderate depression.

Would Sally have allowed herself to stop her regular exercise routines as part of her general drift away from everything that acted to balance her life if she had fully understood what exercise does, not just for our physical and mental health but also for keeping us at our best, for protecting our energy, mental sharpness, concentration, focus and memory?

If Sally had made exercise a non-negotiable, something that she anchored every week – and 20–30 minutes three times a week would have been enough – would that have protected her from drifting down the curve that eventually took her to burning out?

One of the reasons it might have done is that making exercise a priority makes it easier to protect other stress-protective routines, like sleep, maintaining a good diet, and keeping our alcohol consumption low. Dropping exercise often leads to the others being compromised.

Diet

Exercise is not the only thing that helps to stabilise the physiology of energy and mental functioning. Sleep, our diet, routines that help us to relax, even our social life and the quality of our core relationships have an impact on these physiological systems.

What we eat has an impact on our energy, but it also has a stabilising effect on our concentration, our mood, our problem-solving ability and how we deal with unexpected challenges. But it is interesting to see how many of us often drift away from a good diet when demands start to become overwhelming.

Diet affects energy, mood, work performance and concentration through blood sugar stability. Blood sugar varies with what we eat. Breakfast is a driver of energy, but if breakfast consists of cereal or toast and jam, blood sugar rises rapidly and insulin comes in to bring it down, then it under-shoots and we are left with a dip in blood sugar again. If breakfast consists of protein – eggs, yogurt, fish or complex carbohydrates like porridge – blood sugar rises more slowly and is more stable. As blood sugar drops, we are more likely to become distracted and irritable. If lunch is protein-based – fish, chicken, meat, cheese – blood sugar will be more stable, meaning a more productive afternoon. To make matters worse, heightened cortisol adversely affects blood sugar, and if neurotransmitter levels drop in our central nervous system, we are more likely to crave sugars and carbohydrates.

Some people are more aware of how sensitive their bodies are and for them their diet is a non-negotiable, regardless of what is going on in their life; they make conscious decisions around stabilising blood sugar, a good breakfast, some protein at lunchtime, low sugar and carbohydrate, not skipping meals, fruit and nuts as snacks, and keeping soft drinks and alcohol low – rather than going for the office biscuit tin.

Let's go further. Certain foods are associated with better mental health. Through nutrient profiling, Laura LaChance and Drew Ramsey, researchers within the Department of Psychiatry at the University of Toronto in 2018, identified foods that are the most rich in the 12 key nutrients known to contribute to the prevention of and recovery from depression. Watercress, spinach, lettuce, peppers, kale and oysters were some of the highest-scoring foods. Some foods also stimulate the release of brain-derived neurotrophic factor (BDNF) – that same chemical we heard about earlier that is stimulated by exercise, and which protects the brain from the damaging effects of cortisol, increases the growth of brain cells and stimulates neuroplasticity. These include olive oil, green tea and blueberries (among other fruits and vegetables). Other foods reduce systemic inflammation in the body (just as some foods can cause inflammation) – and inflammation is now being seen as a major cause of depression. Anti-inflammatory foods include ginger, turmeric, tomatoes and leafy greens, whereas sugar and simple carbohydrates fuel chronic inflammation. There is also growing evidence that the population of microbes that live in our gut, called the microbiome, has a considerable impact on our general health and also on our emotional well-being, the regulation of mood and cognitive functioning.

In a 2019 longitudinal study of 50,000 UK residents, Neel Ocean and colleagues from the University of Leeds looked at the relationship between fruit and vegetable consumption and measures of psychological health. They reported that only 50 per cent of people consume at least one portion of vegetables daily and only 46 per cent consume at least one portion of fruit. They found a significant relationship between the amount of fruit and vegetables eaten and psychological health and a measure of life satisfaction. Well-being increases in a direct relationship with the amount of fruit and vegetables consumed. The positive effects of fruit and vegetables on mental health could be due to their antioxidant effect and reduced inflammation, which has an effect on mood, as well as possible links between the complex carbohydrates in fruit and vegetables and serotonin production, enhancing mood.

Specifically looking at the impact of a healthy diet on clinical depression, Felice Jacka and colleagues at the Deakin University in Australia conducted a 12-week study assessing the difference between a group who received nutritional counselling plus a recommended diet, and a group in a 'social support' condition with other people, where they discussed general topics of interest together. The recommended diet consisted of whole grains, vegetables (six per day), fruit (three per day), nuts, lean red meat, chicken, eggs and olive oil and reducing sugar, refined cereals, fried food, fast food and processed meats. They report that at the end of the 12-week period, there was a significant reduction in the depression scores in their diet group and a relatively small improvement in the social support group. At 12 weeks, 32.3 per cent of the diet group achieved remission criteria in comparison to 8 per cent in the social support group. Foods rich in fibre promote gut microbiome health, which is associated with better mental health through the production of neurotransmitters. Generally, fibre is lacking in Western diets, which reduces the diversity of gut bacteria.

Foods for neurotransmitter health

What's important? Neurotransmitter-stimulating foods and amino acids

- Berries, especially blueberries (boost dopamine production)
- Lemons
- Spinach
- Buckwheat (boosts tryptophan production)
- Broccoli and cauliflower (rich in choline)
- Turkey (boosts serotonin production)
- Eggs
- Omega 3 fats, found in oily fish, like mackerel and salmon
- Walnuts and almonds
- Crab
- Fermented foods like kimchi (boost GABA production)

Foods for energy

What's important? Iron-rich foods, low glycaemic index foods, fibre, protein and complex carbohydrates

- Brown rice
- Sweet potatoes
- Lentils
- Chickpeas
- Quinoa
- Oats
- Eggs
- Fish, especially salmon, mackerel and tuna
- Red meat (organic, preferably, to avoid ingestion of antibiotics and growth hormones)
- Green, leafy vegetables, such as spinach and kale – iron-rich, required for the production of red blood cells to combat fatigue
- Bananas
- Avocados
- Nuts (avoid salted or sweetened nuts as these will

destabilise your insulin levels)
- Seeds, including flaxseeds (whole or milled), pumpkin seeds, sunflower seeds, and chia seeds (soaked in water, milk or yogurt for a few minutes beforehand)
- Beans (black beans are usually easier to digest than kidney beans)
- Yerba mate, drunk as a tea, is also a healthy source of caffeine, stimulating release of adrenaline alongside countless antioxidants

What should I avoid? Foods that trigger a surge (and subsequent plunge) in blood sugar levels, including refined, simple carbohydrates and sugar.

- Cakes, sweets, biscuits
- Bagels, white bread
- Plain pasta, pizza
- Alcohol, sugary drinks and 'energy' drinks

If you are having any of these foods, eat fibre alongside it (in the form of any vegetables or any of the examples above) to slow the spike in insulin, lessening the resulting crash in energy.

Foods for a strong immune system

What's important? Anti-inflammatory, anti-viral, free-radical-fighting foods, and antioxidants

- Garlic (an anti-viral)
- Red peppers
- Citrus fruits
- Carrots
- Berries (especially blueberries for their high polyphenol and flavonoid content, to fight cell damage)

- Beetroots
- Artichokes
- Green tea
- Pomegranates
- Turmeric (dried or fresh)
- Ginger (dried or fresh)
- All dried spices, including cumin, cinnamon, sage, celery seed
- Yogurt
- Extra virgin olive oil
- Dark chocolate (over 80 per cent cocoa)

For good psychological well-being, energy and stable mood, it is worth cutting back on alcohol (which often drifts up as other routines drift out), foods containing sugar and simple carbohydrates and processed foods. Sweet foods and comfort foods often increase when life becomes overly demanding, to give us an artificial energy boost – but we certainly pay a cost later as energy crashes.

Alcohol directly affects brain chemistry, having an impact on serotonin and dopamine, in particular affecting stability of mood, mental energy and anxiety levels. Alcohol acts as a depressant on central nervous system functioning, particularly in the withdrawal period. It affects brain centres that are involved in emotional regulation, such as the amygdala and the prefrontal cortex. The HPA system is also affected by alcohol consumption, leading to increased cortisol output, which can be elevated even beyond the level seen in response to various stressful circumstances. In one study, researchers looked at the alcohol concentrations and cortisol levels of subjects who were intoxicated or withdrawing and compared the cortisol levels with those who were abstinent. Both the intoxicated and withdrawing groups had increased cortisol levels, compared to the abstinent group. The initial relaxing effect of alcohol is probably produced by an increase in serotonin and dopamine, but both neurotransmitters then drop, leading to a lowering of mood and increased anxiety. Alcohol also disrupts blood sugar regulation, which is why it interferes with good-quality sleep.

We sleep because we release melatonin, which comes from serotonin, a neurotransmitter. Serotonin can be optimised by an evening meal rich in tryptophan, which is in poultry, seafood, bananas and dairy produce, but we need carbohydrate to optimise the effect. So an evening meal of stir-fried chicken and a small serving of rice or pasta would give us a better night's sleep than a steak. But making good decisions, including prioritising a healthy diet, takes time and focus, and if our work is increasingly demanding, this is often overlooked – so we lose another healthy routine, which would help to stabilise our energy and combat stress.

Another area, and probably the one that is most affected by this gravitational drift, is in what we do to wind down, to relax, to decompress from the constant intensity of day-to-day life.

Anna

Anna works in a corporate PR firm that has seen considerable growth in the number of clients it services and its profitability. Anna has a large portfolio of clients and she has a number of internal roles, including a people-management role. The clients are demanding, the email flow is constant, but Anna's personality demands are greater – her perfectionistic tendencies, her fears of letting people down and her competitive need to achieve add up to a relentlessly intense day; she is constantly in sixth gear. She has two young children, a boy and a girl under five. She tries to prioritise her time with her children as much as she can, leaving work by 5.30 to have a couple of hours with them before they go to bed. Most nights she works again after the children have gone to bed, sometimes for an hour or so but often through to midnight. There is a relentless intensity to everything she does; even her weekends are pressurised.

Occasionally this leads to adrenalisation effects – heart racing, feeling breathless or light-headed and frequently not sleeping well. She occasionally feels so alert when she wakes in the night that she gets up and works. She knows she is running close to the wire and that everything she used to do to decompress on a regular basis has drifted out of her life, like yoga and her gym classes. Anna's approach to life is quite typical of people who go on to develop chronic fatigue conditions or burnout, as increased adrenalisation (caused by high levels of adrenaline released from the adrenal glands) compensates for the lack of relaxation time and good-quality sleep, potentially leading to adrenal fatigue.

Just as many people find it difficult to exercise without having a personal trainer, others find it hard to get close to some state of relaxation without going to a class: yoga, Pilates, meditation, mindfulness. But for Anna this would mean encroaching on the time she gives to her children, which would make her feel guilty.

Finding time to relax in structured ways through meditation, yoga, mindfulness and exercise has been associated with physiological changes such as reductions in blood pressure, cortisol and adrenaline and increases in our immune function, as well as increased concentration, memory and creativity. Structured relaxation is associated with increased neural activity in the right hemisphere of the brain, which stimulates creative problem-solving – the ability to see a novel solution that would not come about from trying to assimilate more information or from analytical problem-solving. Studies have found that mindfulness – the ability to focus your mind on your breathing in the present moment, centring your thoughts on acceptance of transient thoughts and states of mind – has been associated with reduced anxiety and depression and more positive emotions.

But there is no reason to believe that other day-to-day activities woven into the structure of our routines should not have a similar effect, provided we can approach them in an unhurried way, rather than rushing to get on to the next thing, and provided we are able to draw our minds into the activity and resist distractions. With this approach, activities such as listening to music without doing anything else, reading a novel, having a bath, cooking, or reading your children a story could all have similar rebalancing effects to structured relaxation classes – and would be far easier for people like Anna to embrace than trying to fit classes into an over-pressurised day.

Many people confuse relaxation and distraction. Some say they play computer games, browse social media or watch TV, but this is not the same as relaxing. Relaxation is about creating the neural and physiological wind-down effect that we require. Reading and meditation calm the mind and our physiology, in contrast to staring at a screen, which keeps this system alert, impacting sleep quality and our mood. If we come home in an agitated frame of mind, watching TV can keep us agitated.

Learn to breathe

Anna would also benefit from learning diaphragm breathing techniques. This could be applied to almost any situation to bring down unpleasant feelings of anxiety or agitation. When cortisol rises, our breathing almost automatically increases and tends to be focused on the upper chest. Breathing can increase to a breath every two or three seconds, which can create an imbalance in carbon dioxide to oxygen, leading to further feelings of stress, anxiety, light-headedness and agitation. Learning to centre the breathing from the diaphragm and slow it to approximately a breath every eight to 10 seconds, with a slow out-breath, can reduce this physiological over-arousal and create a relative sense of calmness and greater mental control. Usually this can be achieved within 10 minutes and many people feel positive effects within five minutes. Again, it works better if you can adopt an unhurried attitude and prevent yourself from becoming distracted by other things, which could further stimulate you.

This technique can also help you get back to sleep, especially if you try it alongside visualising some peaceful imagery. Our sleep is often disrupted when cortisol or adrenaline levels rise – we either have difficulty getting off to sleep or, more frequently, wake up after a few hours feeling alert, with our heads busy. And of course for many busy people, like Anna, sleep is cut back when life gets busier – working later and getting up earlier to get more done. Some people give up trying to get back to sleep when they predictably wake in the night, and get up and work for a few hours before going back to bed for an hour or two before the alarm goes off.

The importance of sleep

Sleep is pivotal to our physiological balance – just as sleep is easily disturbed by raised cortisol and adrenaline or by reduced levels of serotonin, it is also necessary for keeping this physiological system in balance. Getting less than six hours' sleep, for example, can lead to cortisol levels rising.

Good-quality sleep is necessary for our physical health and our psychological well-being. We are more creative, more resilient and more able to exercise good judgement when our sleep is of good quality. 'Better well rested than well briefed', as the former assistant to the British Prime Minister Jim Callaghan famously remarked.

We need at least seven hours' sleep a night for good physical health and psychological functioning. Less than six hours and sleep can destabilise cortisol in the same way that exposure to prolonged stress can. According to a 2016 report from the RAND corporation, the UK economy loses £40 billion a year, 1.9 per cent of GDP, due to sleep deprivation, and people who sleep less than six hours a night have a 13 per cent increased mortality rate compared to those sleeping seven hours.

The effects of sleep loss on cognitive functioning are also well researched. When people sleep only four hours a night for two weeks, their performance scores are similar to those participants who were kept up for three straight days and nights. Sleep debt makes us less attentive, it takes longer to react to challenging circumstances and reaction times are more variable than when we are well rested.

Many people in high-performing organisations regularly work over 12 hours a day and continue into the night when they are working on transactions or projects that are being driven by tight deadlines. Sleeping five to six hours a night becomes their routine, with a catch-up at the weekends.

But it is not just the over-pressurised professionals who are down to five or six hours a night. Nadia comes home from her telesales job to cook for her family and get them to bed before rushing round to see her mother, who has been unwell for several months. She gets home around 10.30 or 11 p.m., collapses exhausted in front of her TV for an hour or so of time for herself, and gets to bed around midnight or later for a night that is regularly disrupted at least twice by her young daughter.

Philippe

Philippe, a partner in a consulting practice, told me how he had learned about the importance of sleep at an earlier point in his career. When he was a junior consultant, not long out of university, motivated to succeed and be recognised by his managers, he had ended up involved in too many assignments. He had been asked to give a presentation to a group of senior colleagues, most of whom he did not know. He had put a lot of work into the presentation, but unfortunately the day before the meeting he had to travel to Glasgow for a meeting with one of his clients. He got home late, he shared a takeaway supper and a bottle of wine with his flatmate, and then instead of going to bed, he spent a couple of hours working on his presentation. In all he got about four hours' sleep, got up the next morning, had a couple of cups of coffee and walked into the room to give his presentation. One of his bosses asked him a question that he was not expecting before he started. Philippe stumbled through an answer, but his confidence was knocked. He struggled through, but he realised he had come across badly.

Years later, Philippe told me he had pondered on what had gone wrong. Would this have happened if he had made different decisions? Did he need to go to Glasgow? Could he have dealt with the meeting on a conference call? If he had done some exercise the day before and had seven hours' sleep with nothing to drink the night before, the outcome could have been completely different.

The key message is that if we are going to sustain our energy and our ability to function at our best, as well as our emotional and physical well-being, into the long term, we need to prioritise activities and routines that stabilise the physiology that underpins those qualities: the cortisol adrenal system, neurotransmitter function and the strength of our immune response.

Many of the behaviours that can achieve this are linked to our evolutionary past. We are *meant* to be active, we are *meant* to get eight hours' sleep, not six, we are *meant* to eat natural, fresh food, not processed, artificially sweetened food. And recent research indicates that we are *meant* to spend some time regularly in nature.

Walking in nature

Walking and being in nature should not be underestimated for their stabilising effects on our physiology and mental health. To those who are into more vigorous aerobic exercise, like running or cycling, walking is almost looked down on as second best, but walking, particularly walking in nature rather than on a treadmill or through busy streets, gives us other benefits. I see walking as akin to meditation. It can help us make sense of difficulties, settle our minds, be creative. Walking is meditation on the move.

Nietzsche walked between four and six hours a day. It freed him from the oppression of the city and alleviated the chronic headaches that plagued him for years. His walks were meditations: 'I am walking a lot through the forest and having tremendous conversations with myself.' He walked, absorbed in his thoughts, jotting down ideas for some of his greatest works. Rousseau claimed that he was incapable of thinking or finding inspiration unless he was walking: 'Recovering the sensation of just being – freeing yourself from busyness.' Research studies have shown that walking in natural settings has considerable psychological and physiological benefits. Melissa Marselle and colleagues from Edge Hill University in the UK, in a 2014 study reported in *Ecopsychology*, found that group walks in nature were associated with lower ratings of depression and perceived stress, and enhanced mental well-being. In their view, walks in natural settings mitigate the effects of stressful experiences.

Raymond De Young, from the University of Michigan, also argues that effective functioning requires mental vitality to keep us focused and prevent distractions. Pressures of life reduce this mental vitality, leading to signs of mental fatigue, including distractibility, instability, impatience and impulsivity. He advocates walks, particularly in rural settings, to restore our mental vitality – but even a walk in a city park would have similar benefits.

In 2011, Lee Crust and colleagues from the University of Lincoln collected the experiences of a group of six walkers on long-distance walks taking several days, ranging from 84 to 192 miles, in the UK. The investigators accompanied the walkers and recorded their conversations as well as interviewing them at the end of the walks. Participants described increased feelings of emotional well-being and opportunities for reflection and clearer thinking, times when they were completely immersed in the walk in a way that is similar to meditation and what others have described as flow – losing a sense of time with complete absorption in what you are doing – and feelings of pride, satisfaction and joy at the end of the walk. One walker reported, 'In terms of doing something for me in my life, that is the best thing I have ever done.' They reported being mentally refreshed, with a clear, relaxed mind. It gave many an opportunity they did not normally have to reflect on their lives and find new perspectives for dealing with life's challenges.

It does appear to be the connection with nature rather than simply walking itself that brings the benefits. Jenny Roe and Peter Aspinall, two Edinburgh-based researchers, compared the effects of one-hour group walks, either in open countryside or in an urban setting, on two groups of subjects with good and poor mental health. The participants completed rating scales on mood, energy, general happiness and measures of reflection, including personal efficacy. For those without mental health symptoms, the rural walks produced positive changes in all of those measures, whereas the urban walk did not. Those with symptoms of psychological ill health showed a greater improvement on the rating scales with the rural walks and obtained some benefit from walking in an urban setting.

One reason why walking might make us feel good is that it appears to change our physiology, blocking the tendency to ruminate. Rumination is an unproductive, circular form of thinking, which can lock us in to feelings of guilt or regret, and is associated with depression and other psychological conditions. It has been linked to an area of the brain called the subgenual prefrontal cortex (sgPFC). In 2015, Gregory Bratman and colleagues from Stanford University, studying a group of 38 participants with no history of mental disorder, found reduced neural activity in the sgPFC after a 90-minute walk in a natural setting, together with lower levels of rumination. A 90-minute walk in an urban setting (a busy street with a steady flow of traffic), however, had no effect either on neural activity or on levels of rumination. Walking also leads to a number of cognitive benefits that may give us an advantage in dealing with the challenges of life and keeping us closer to our best mentally.

Walking also increases our creativity. Marily Oppezzo and Daniel Schwartz from Stanford University found that subjects generated more creative responses in a creativity test after a walk outdoors compared to subjects who walked on a treadmill or who completed the task while sitting. Walking produces more novel and high-quality thoughts and 'opens up the free flow of ideas'.

Walking appears to have a protective effect, maintaining the stability of our mood in circumstances where our mood could drop. Researchers Jeffrey Miller and Zlatan Krizan from Iowa State University report the mood-lifting effects of just a 12-minute walk around campus buildings, with higher ratings of vigour and attentiveness. They also put their subjects into a condition that was designed to lower their mood by telling them that they would have to write an essay and discuss its contents after the walk. Compared to students who spent their time sitting, those on the walk showed no reduction in their mood.

In older adults, walking has been found to increase the size of the anterior hippocampus and to increase BDNF, leading to memory improvements and to a reverse in cognitive decline in older adults who had not exercised, in as little as six months of walking. The volume of grey matter in the brain, which is a measure of cognitive functioning, also increased as a result of regular walking, in a longitudinal study of over 200 older adults followed up over nine years.

Just being in nature can have a beneficial effect on our physical and psychological health and our mental fitness. Regular contact with nature has a beneficial effect on depression and anxiety symptoms, diabetes and obesity, cardiovascular disease and longevity. MaryCarol Hunter and colleagues from the University of Michigan encouraged 36 participants living in urban settings to take a nature break for at least 10 minutes, at least three times a week. They measured two stress markers, cortisol and amylase, which is highly sensitive to stress, over an eight-week period. They reported a 21 per cent drop in cortisol and a 28 per cent drop in amylase, with the greatest effect occurring with a

20- to 30-minute nature break. A 20-minute walk in a forest has been shown to reduce salivary cortisol and reduce prefrontal activity, indicating a calmer physiological state as measured in a group of students in Tokyo, and reported by Bum-Jin Park from the Chungnam National University and colleagues in the *Journal of Physiological Anthropology*.

Gardening

The benefits of being in nature may go some way to explaining why gardening is so popular. It has been estimated that 40 per cent of the UK population enjoy gardening as a hobby, one in three in the US and one in four in Japan. Gardening gives time to many of the physical and psychological benefits that we get from being in nature – vigour, increased life satisfaction, positive mood, cognitive functioning, and reductions in anxiety, depression and stress ratings. In 2017, Masashi Soga and colleagues from the University of Tokyo analysed the results of 22 studies into the effects of gardening. They reported reductions in anxiety, depression and anger ratings, and improved general health, mood and energy. They also reported reduced feelings of loneliness, and reduced cortisol measures.

One particularly interesting area of physiological research shows how gardening and being in contact with soil can have an anti-inflammatory effect on the brain and stimulate the production of serotonin, promoting mental health and resilience to stress. Christopher Lowry and colleagues from the University of Colorado Boulder have identified a bacterium with anti-inflammatory, immune-enhancing and stress-resilience properties that resides in the soil and feeds on decaying organic matter. The bacterium is known as *M. vaccae* and Lowry and colleagues have demonstrated that it has anti-inflammatory effects and boosts the production of serotonin in animal studies. So when we are getting our hands dirty doing the weeding, we might inadvertently be absorbing minute quantities of this bacterium, which could have beneficial effects on our physical and emotional health.

All of this suggests that from an evolutionary point of view we are meant to be living a life that is more in contact with nature – both walking in nature and working with nature. It has long been known that children who were brought up on farms have a different immune system from children brought up in urban settings, as a result of exposure to a wider range of microorganisms that are protective of certain illnesses, including allergies and asthma. Christopher Lowry's research adds another dimension to the protection that contact with nature gives us for both our physical and mental health.

Exercise, a good diet, ways of winding down, sleep routines, and spending time in natural settings (and that doesn't mean moving to the Scottish Highlands – most of the studies are in urban parks, for roughly 20 minutes) have a stabilising effect on the physiology of energy, our immune system and good mental well-being. We do not need to do all of these but having one or two a week that we prioritise, regardless of how busy our life has become, will help to keep that physiology stable.

Be conscious of the drift

Next we need to be very conscious of how easy it is for other demands to take over and how we then drift away from these stabilising activities. In Sally's case, the drift had been gradual. She used to go to the gym twice a week and did a regular yoga class, she got around seven hours' sleep, and she prioritised her diet – she tried to make good decisions, despite all the contradictory advice that pours out of the nutrition industry. She had muesli and a banana for breakfast, soup and a sandwich for lunch, she avoided snacks between meals, and she had a cooked meal in the evening, usually fish or chicken with vegetables. She kept her alcohol low and restricted coffee to one or two a day. She tried to keep her weekends free; she enjoyed working in her garden and going for walks with her children in Richmond Park or cycling with them along the river towpaths close to her home. Then, when her work demands increased, she started coming into work earlier to get a couple of hours of work in before her first meeting and she often didn't get home until eight or nine at night. Without making any conscious decision whatsoever, she stopped exercising and going to yoga and her diet changed. Breakfast became a rushed slice of toast and coffee, she sometimes skipped lunch or snatched a sandwich between meetings, she started drinking more coffee and her cooked meal in the evening gave way to packaged food in the microwave. She started snacking on biscuits and her alcohol intake increased to around half a bottle of wine in the evening. Her sleep became broken, averaging five to six hours a night – and there were no conscious decisions about any of this. She tried to keep her weekends free and to see her children a couple of nights before they went to bed, but she was feeling increasingly tired, often too tired even to have a conversation with her husband.

The loss of energy and psychological well-being in people who have previously coped well could be seen as a total loss of balance, when practically everything we need for good mental health is gradually lost as other priorities take over. Ultimately, this leaves us increasingly vulnerable to one or two additional pressures, triggering ill health. Burnout could be seen as the body's revenge for neglect and poor choices.

But Sally is certainly not alone. Working long hours in our crowded, polluted cities, exercising in gyms without natural light, snatching packaged food for a five-minute lunch or a microwaved evening meal, relying on screens for our leisure time, we have become disconnected from what our bodies and minds need – we are physiologically and mentally out of balance.

It is also not difficult to see how, as work demands take up more and more of the space, the time we have for our relationships can easily be eclipsed. But if the relationship with our partner disconnects or falls apart, there are almost immediate effects on mental and physiological functioning.

Tips for improving sleep

Sleep is about our physiology: lower physiological arousal, optimal levels of serotonin and melatonin and not disrupting our circadian rhythm – the sleep-wake cycle. It works better if you go to bed around the same time every night.

- Create **an email boundary** at least one and a half hours before bed. The blue light from your device is picked up by light-sensitive cells in the retina that disrupt melatonin. But it's not just about the light, it is about not letting some random irritating email mess up your mood and your sleep.
- A **diet that contains tryptophan** gives you a better sleep by boosting serotonin and melatonin. Tryptophan is in turkey, chicken, seafood, dairy products and bananas, and is more effective when eaten with some complex carbohydrates (such as brown rice or whole-wheat pasta).
- **Alcohol** disrupts sleep.
- **Caffeine** can disrupt sleep for around 10 hours so is best avoided in the afternoon.
- Have **a relaxing routine** before you switch off the light. A bath gives you better sleep. Is watching the news really the best option?
- Doing **a slow breathing routine**, imagining a peaceful image, just before you go to sleep helps.
- Sleep is about **mental habits**: Some people approach the bed with an expectation of relaxation and a good night's sleep. Others anticipate frustration at a disturbed night tossing and turning in the bed. If you wake in the middle of the night, you are at a mental crossroads.
  - One path is **the frustration pathway**: 'Why have I woken? Why can't I sleep through like I used to do? If I can't get back to sleep, I won't be able to function tomorrow. I have an important meeting – I have to get to sleep.' You are not going to get to sleep on the frustration pathway.

- ○ Try **the acceptance pathway**: 'I'm in bed, it's cosy and warm, there are no demands on me right now – tomorrow will be OK, I'd rather be in bed than getting up to go to the airport. I'm going to relax and relaxation is as good as a light sleep.'

- Now that's a better path. Then try this exercise – it is a script you say to yourself that helps to **block out intruding thoughts**.
  - ○ 'Focus on the support of the pillow, the warmth of the duvet, the comfort of the bed – there are no demands on you right now. Let the tensions go, relax your arms . . . your shoulders . . . your eyes . . . your legs . . . Focus on your breathing – slowly in, and slower out, feeling yourself relax as you breathe out.' Repeat the slow breathing exercise five or six times. Let your mind go to a peaceful scene – imagine yourself there, let yourself be immersed in the image. Let everything else go.
  - ○ Now count slowly backwards from 20 (20 seconds or so between the count). Repeat relaxing phrases: 'Feeling relaxed, breathing slowly, let the tensions go.' Focusing on the image. 'Feeling heavy . . . heavy and sleepy. Breathing slowly.'
  - ○ Keep going until you fall asleep. Do this consistently. What you will find is that the exercise **conditions you to sleep** and you will get back to sleep faster, with an expectation that it will work.

- I have done this for years. I started doing it when my children were little and I was up with them in the night. Now if I wake in the night feeling alert – and I'm not a good sleeper in hotels – I will go into this exercise and I will get right back to sleep. It needs **consistency to build the conditioning habit**: stick to it. But it is great to feel there is something you can do to get back to sleep rather than lying there on the frustration pathway.

4

When relationships disconnect

Tim had known his doctor for over 10 years. Usually he saw him once a year for his medical and occasionally for minor complaints; he never imagined he would be in this situation, having this conversation. Tim hadn't slept for over a week now. He felt wretched, his concentration had gone, he felt anxious and lost, he couldn't face going into work, and it all seemed pointless. As he talked about how he was feeling, he occasionally broke down in tears. His doctor listened sympathetically while Tim talked about how his wife, Charlie, had told him she was leaving – she had been having an affair for over a year with someone she met at work. He had tried to persuade her to stay, tried to understand how it had come to this, but that was met with coldness, a detachment he had not seen in her before. They had been married for over 20 years; they had two sons, one at university, one now working. He thought they had a good life, and they rarely argued. He had been planning to retire in a couple of years. He felt completely devastated – how could this be happening to him?

They had met when he was a junior researcher in the bank. His career had gone well and he was now in a senior job. He travelled a lot – he had worked on overseas assignments – but he always tried to be home for weekends. Charlie had gone through a depression a few years ago. She hadn't talked about it to him – she had been distant, and their sex life had dwindled several years ago, but he regarded her as his best friend. He had a few friends from his university days and some guys from work he went to occasional sports matches with, but

Charlie organised most of his social life. Suddenly he realised how lonely he felt.

His doctor listened patiently. He understood how lost Tim was feeling – but what could he do? He offered him some sleeping pills and suggested he see a counsellor. Tim protested that he had not been given a chance, that he had always done his best for the family. His work hours were long; even when the boys were young, he rarely saw them midweek, but he took them to their sports on Saturdays and tried to be there for parents' evenings and school events. But what could you do if you had an international job? What could you do if you wanted to get ahead in an organisation like his?

How relationships drift

Tim's relationship had died not because he had done a bad thing like had affairs or been abusive, but because of neglect. The naïve assumption is that because a relationship is in good shape right now, it always will be. Relationships deteriorate very slowly, almost imperceptibly, work hours, busyness taking over from the time you used to spend together.

Fatigue and routines undermine the spontaneity and affection and intimacy dwindles. Other priorities – work, children, the complex management of domestic life – take over. Arguments are left unsettled. Couples may remain good friends and share some interests, and children can act as a glue that holds them together, but the energy has gradually gone out of the relationship.

A relationship is fundamentally a deal. It can be an emotional deal: 'We will love one another, take care of one another emotionally, try to make each other happy.' Or it can be a transactional deal: 'You take care of the domestic infrastructure, and I will provide the financial wherewithal to support our joint life.'

Most relationships start out as an emotional deal, but through neglect and drift they can end up as some sort of transactional deal – and the journey between the two can take years. Often there are rows when one partner tries to reverse the drift, tries to shake the other into a recognition of what they are losing. Often those rows work temporarily, leading to agreements to spend more time together, have occasional weekends away, be more attentive, listen more; but then the drift continues and the rows and discussions become less frequent, and a resignation settles in.

Benefits of a good relationship

There is convincing evidence to show that relationship status is linked to physical and psychological well-being. Research summarised by Janice Keicolt-Glaser and Tamara Newton in an article titled 'Marriage and Health: his and hers' and subsequent reports of statistics from England and Wales show that couples who are in stable relationships enjoy better physical and mental health, with men benefiting more than women from a physical health perspective. A study analysing national statistics for England and Wales showed higher mortality rates for single, widowed and divorced males and females compared to those who are married.

The mortality rate among unmarried groups is greater among men. Unmarried men have mortality rates about three times that of married men, and single women have mortality rates about double those of married women. But unsurprisingly it is the quality of the relationship that counts. A study by Julianne Holt-Lunstad from Brigham Young University in 2008 compared blood pressure readings of 204 married and 99 single males and females. Overall, married individuals had healthier blood pressure measures, but high-quality relationships were associated with lower blood pressure, lower stress and lower depression. Contrasting those who were unmarried with those in low-quality relationships, they found that single individuals had healthier blood pressure readings than those in unhappy marriages. They also reported that having a supportive network of friends was not sufficient to buffer the effect of being unhappily married. A later meta-analysis by Theodore Robles and colleagues from the University of California, reviewing 126 studies over 50 years, found that being in an unhappy relationship was associated with poorer physical and mental health than not being in a relationship. Women who report higher levels of satisfaction in their relationships report better sleep and better mood and fewer physician visits than women who were less satisfied with their relationships. Men and women who viewed their relationships positively had lower adrenal and cortisol levels, indicative of lower physiological stress responses.

When the relationship goes wrong

However, if relationships disconnect, become unhappy, or fall apart, the effects on our physiological balance, physical and psychological health can be considerable. Troubled relationships are associated with greater stress responses, and unmarried people are happier than those that are living in unhappy relationships. Marital disagreements can undermine mood and living with persistently critical partners is greatly detrimental to mental well-being, stable mood and confidence. A paper from the Tavistock Institute in London reported that people living in dissatisfied relationships are three times more likely to suffer from depression and two and a half times more likely to suffer from anxiety disorders. Reporting on over 7000 people whom they assessed in their couples' therapy service, 71 per cent were suffering from mild to severe depression. One study from the University of Helsinki, reported in the *Journal of Psychosomatic Research*, noted that women who reported considerable conflicts with their partners and also had conflicts at work had a two and a half times greater risk of work disability related to a variety of health problems over a six-year period. Very interestingly, neither work conflicts nor relationship conflicts were a risk factor for men. In dissatisfied relationships, women typically reported more mental and physical health problems than men.

Some studies have looked directly at the physiological effects of relationship conflict in laboratory settings, where the couple discuss a sensitive, problematic topic. Imagine you and your partner going into a lab where you will be observed while you discuss sensitive unresolved issues, which have been elicited during a previous interview. The discussion will last 30 minutes, which must feel like an eternity to some couples. While you discuss the topic, behaviours like listening, agreeing and disagreeing, interrupting, criticising or approving, or tit-for-tat behaviour are recorded. Blood samples are taken during and after the discussion and analysed for levels of cortisol and other adrenal hormones. Using this format, researchers from Ohio State University found potentially harmful changes in these physiological measures during conflict discussions. These effects were more marked in women than in men. Couples showing more long-term patterns of critical and hostile interaction showed more persistent disruptions to their cortisol, adrenal and immune functions.

In a later study, using the same methodology and measuring physiological and behavioural data, Janice Kiecolt-Glaser and Cynthia Bane from Ohio State University looked at the long-term impact of conflict behaviour in a group of 90 recently married couples over a 10-year follow-up period. They used strict criteria to exclude subjects who had physical or psychological ill health. They found that those engaged in more frequent negative behaviour during the discussion were more likely to have separated 10 years later, or more likely to report the marriage as unsatisfying. The group that subsequently divorced also showed higher adrenaline responses during and after the conflict discussion. Levels of a key stress marker, Adrenocorticotropic Hormone (ACTH), were also more likely to be elevated in women who subsequently divorced. During the conflict discussion, ACTH levels in women were twice as high in those whose marriages were troubled at the 10-year point than those whose marriages were stable.

Women tend to be more tuned in to the emotional climate of their relationships than men are. Tim just did not see how his marriage was disconnecting until it got to a point where it could not be rescued. Women's emotional and physiological systems are more affected by a hostile partner than is the case for men. Women seem to suffer more than men when relationships are going wrong and it may well be the case that men are less attuned to their core relationship drifting off-track until it gets to a really critical point. But when a relationship ends, men tend to do worse than women. Their life expectancy is reduced, and rates of depression increase.

Biochemical changes: the bad . . .

Recent research shows that marital unhappiness and conflict can trigger a cascade of biochemical changes that can profoundly affect the physiological landscape, potentially resulting in numerous physical and psychological consequences. Marital conflict increases inflammatory markers in the body, raising the probability of becoming depressed – and depression also increases body inflammation. Both marital conflict and depression interfere with sleep, and prolonged sleep loss reduces our ability to empathise, making conflict more likely. Elevated inflammatory cytokines are linked to a host of age-related illnesses including cardiac disease, osteoporosis, arthritis, type 2 diabetes and certain types of cancer. The time it takes to heal is significantly longer in couples in hostile relationships. Marital conflict can lead to weight gain as a direct consequence of a drop in metabolic rate following an argument. It has been estimated that marital hostility can lead to a seven-pound weight gain over a year purely as a result of this metabolic change, never mind the comfort eating that can also occur in troubled relationships.

. . . and the good

On the other hand, the stabilising effect of a warm, caring relationship on our physiology is equally striking. People who receive encouragement and validation from their partner showed a faster reduction of cortisol after being exposed to some stressful situation, in comparison to those who received critical or hostile responses. Simply thinking about their partner lowered blood pressure and heart rate in subjects who were exposed to a physically stressful situation.

And then there is the oxytocin effect. Oxytocin, a neuropeptide released from the hypothalamus, creates a wave of warm, connected, loving feelings that are responsible for the bonding that occurs between a parent and a child but also emotionally binds a couple in an intimate relationship. Oxytocin has several stabilising effects on the physiology of stress. It down-regulates the cortisol system, helping us recover faster from stressful experiences. It is associated with greater empathy behaviour and more affectionate communication, helping to keep mood stable and reinforce the quality of supportive relationships. Oxytocin is released by a close physical connection, including warm hugs, stroking and massaging. It increases the intensity of sexual experience and the feelings of contentment following sexual intimacy.

A circle of cause and effect

Clearly there are self-reinforcing circles of cause and effect here, with warm, loving, intimate relationships creating physiological effects that further reinforce connection, empathy and happiness, while unhappy, hostile relationships trigger the release of stress hormones and increase the likelihood of depression and physiological changes, which reduce empathy and connectedness and raise the risks of serious illness.

Of course, all of this can have a seriously detrimental effect on work performance. Many find it hard to motivate themselves when relationships are falling apart, they cope less well with day-to-day work difficulties, concentration is affected, they are more likely to make mistakes, and if they manage others, they can become irritable, impatient and indecisive.

So unhappy relationships are bad for our health, energy, mental well-being, and how we cope with demanding jobs. Unhappy relationships are also an opportunity cost: they take time away from other people or activities that could be more valuable to you. Someone who is not in a relationship is free to engage in all sorts of activities that are good for their mental well-being, such as exercise and a good social life, and can also live with a feeling of general optimism that a good relationship is just around the corner, whereas those who are in an unhappy, hostile relationship can feel trapped and helpless.

Relationship burnout

So how do relationships go from a close connection, mutual happiness and real engagement to unhappiness, underlying resentment, simmering hostility, or disconnection and boredom? What had happened between Tim and Charlie that led her to bring the relationship to an end, while Tim had carried on not seeing or not acknowledging the gradual drift in their relationship?

Ayala Malach Pines, a psychologist and couples' therapist, and author of *Couple Burnout: Causes and Cures*, argues that relationship burnout comes about when people have overinvested in their relationship as a source of meaning in their lives but find that the relationship does not live up to their expectations. She found that women were more prone to relationship burnout than men, with more women reporting that they felt depressed about the relationship and emotionally exhausted with nothing left to give.

While Pines acknowledges that some people end up in unhappy relationships because of unresolved childhood conflict and damaging experiences that ultimately destroy their relationships, this is not the case for most. Sadly many people like Tim just assume that the core relationship in their life will stay in good shape irrespective of how little time and energy they invest in it. They allow work and other commitments to eclipse the time they give to their relationship, believing that their partner will remain warm, tolerant, understanding and considerate. Gradually the closeness they had just slips away, often without them noticing what they have lost.

They also assume that even if something does go wrong in their relationship, other areas of life will carry on unaffected. But our life does not exist in watertight compartments: physical health, mental health, emotions, physiology, work-life, relationships. A relationship going wrong will affect all of those areas. As we have seen, it can lead into depression or anxiety, it can seriously destabilise the physiology that underpins mood, resilience, decisiveness and energy, and seriously interferes with our work capabilities, judgement and motivation. If you are interested in sustaining a meaningful and demanding career, good health and happiness, you need to be serious about keeping your relationship with your partner in very good shape.

Ten tips for keeping a relationship alive

So, what can we do to keep energy, engagement and happiness alive in our relationships, despite all the demands from jobs that never end, children, and all the other commitments we have? Here are 10 tips to keep the energy in your relationship.

1. Create time just for the two of you

Sounds obvious, but life is demanding. Work spills over into our time at home, email volume never stops, children need our time, so do the household chores, admin, and maybe some time to catch up on the news or have a bath. Time just for the two of you becomes family time and social time. Life is busy; life can be exhausting; there's no time and no energy for the two of you.

According to research from Relate, when couples were asked how often they made time to spend together as a couple, around half

(47 per cent) reported that they only found time just for the two of them once a month or less, with 11 per cent reporting that they never found time for the two of them.

Some parents who I have talked to discuss having a balance where they alternate, with one partner getting home from work early enough to relieve the childminder, giving their partner the flexibility to work later. What often happens though is that when the kids are in bed, the parent who came home early then starts working again – often until quite late. The couple can end up hardly seeing one another mid-week. In some cases they go to bed at different times and rarely eat together. Even if there is an intention to have a regular evening together just as a couple, that often doesn't happen. If the weekends are spent on domestic chores, doing things as a family and seeing friends, they can end up having no time alone together at all. Not surprisingly, over some time, the relationship can disconnect. One or both partners can end up becoming irritable, humour and physical closeness diminish, there are fewer hugs, fewer expressions of warmth. This can move to an attitude of helplessness and resentment. But underneath the frustration and disconnection there can often be a sadness about having lost something they once had.

However, it doesn't take much to keep the connection. Committing to getting home earlier one night a week in order to have an evening together, an agreement to go to bed at the same time, to eat together a few times a week or to have a couple of evenings when they were both not working could create the conditions for a closer connection.

Even if you only have one hour between getting home and going to bed, what's the best use of that hour? Is it getting home irritable, collapsing on the sofa, watching anything on television and not talking? Could it be sitting around the table, listening to music, having a chat with your partner and catching up, exchanging a story or two about what happened that day, humorous, connected? Sometimes we can have more connections in one hour than others have in a few hours, distracted and doing separate things.

Trying to get a weekend away, just the two of you, would be great, but realistically how often is that going to happen if you have children? Try creating flexibility for small time slots regularly a few times a week.

2. Be there when you are together

I'm sitting in a cafe in south-west London. I'm with my daughter; we're chatting about her work, friends, the stuff of life, with a coffee and chai latte. The cafe is busy; there's a lively buzz to it. A couple of tables across from us there's a couple who are having a really engaged conversation, eye contact is high, they're smiling a lot, often laughing, they use their hands for emphasis. There's a real energy to their conversation; they are obviously enjoying being together. A few tables over, there's another couple about the same age. They're spending their time connected to their phones, scrolling, texting; occasionally they smile, but the smile is to the phone. They might exchange a few words together, but they don't look up. There's no energy, no connection. What's the point of being there together? Were they once like the first couple – engaged, animated? Are they on their way to a disconnected, unhappy relationship? Do they even recognise that they've lost something?

Technology devices are now a real challenge to relationship quality and connection. Consider that people in the UK are now so addicted to phones that they check them every 12 minutes. A 2016 study looking at the damage caused by phones and other devices to relationship happiness and mental health examined the interference from technology in romantic relationships and whether these day-to-day interruptions related to women's personal and relationship well-being. One hundred and forty-three married or cohabiting couples who had completed an online questionnaire reported that technology devices frequently interrupted their leisure time with their partner, conversations and mealtimes. Overall, participants who reported more interference from technology in their relationships also reported more conflict over technology and lower relationship satisfaction, more depressive symptoms and lower life satisfaction. So for the sake of your relationship, and ultimately for your happiness and mental well-being, put the phone away – connect. Keeping the conversation alive keeps the relationship alive.

3. Chat and laugh together

A relationship is a conversation: a physical, verbal, mental conversation kept alive by warm, loving emotions. But what kind of conversations do you have? Think about three levels of conversation:

Level 1 The couple as co-workers in the big domestic project. This type of conversation is task-focused and ideally cooperative, dealing with short-term plans about what needs to be done. It's about who's taking the children to what events, what you need to get from the shops, practical things that need doing to keep the household working.

Level 2 The couple as best friends. This is fast-moving, often animated, humorous; there's an energy to it. It revolves around topics they both enjoy talking about. It might be light and gossipy, or deeper and reflective – it's the kind of conversation that really good friends have.

Level 3 The couple as a romantic entity. This is warm, intimate, special, affectionate and appreciative.

Now, what proportion of your day-to-day conversation with your partner is in which category? If it's spread over all three, great – you are keeping an energised, lively and warm connection. However, many couples lose levels two and three; most of the conversation is at level one. The good news is that recognising this could lead to some change.

Laughing together keeps an energy and an attraction in the relationship. Couples who laugh together report having better-quality relationships; in a 2015 study, researchers Laura Kurtz and Sara Algoe from the University of North Carolina took 71 couples and video-recorded conversations with them talking about how they first met one another. They measured how often they laughed during the conversation. They found that the proportion of the conversation spent laughing was associated with positive evaluations of relationship quality and closeness.

In all likelihood, laughter was one of the key qualities that attracted you to your partner in the first place. Valuing chatting and laughing together could keep an energy and an attraction in your relationship.

4. Think about the mood you carry home

It is not easy to prevent the day-to-day stress of work from having an impact on your home life. Stress spilling over into the relationship raises the likelihood of marital conflict and conflict is created if both spouses have experienced high levels of stress that day.

Many people tell me that they think about their partner coming home with apprehension. What mood will he or she be in? The mood you carry home can really affect the mood of everyone behind the door. Before you walk in, ask yourself: what mood is walking in? Is it irritability, stress, frustration? Is it tired out? Is it a big smile and a hug? Sometimes, just asking the question can change the mood. And if some days it is stress or irritation walking in, then tell your partner that, then go and have a long shower, change, sit on the bed for a few minutes or do some slow breathing exercises before you connect with the family.

Consider doing some things at work to close the day so you are more likely to have let go of the stress of the day by the time you get home.

Take a few minutes to review the day, balance the frustrations of the events that have got you down with some thoughts about what you achieved despite the frustrations, what you nudged along, who you helped. Spend a few moments thinking about what you are looking forward to when you get home and what you appreciate about your home life. Think about what you could do on your journey home that might help you get there in a more relaxed mood – reading a book or listening to music, even on a crowded train, or building in a walk as part of the journey could all help to get to a better frame of mind by the time you walk into your home.

5. Enjoying simple pleasures

In your time together, keep a balance of energising, stimulating interests that create variety with comfortable routines and simple pleasures. Relationships thrive on variety, and pushing out into new interests. If there is no variety, boredom sets in and boredom is like rust sapping the energy out of the relationship. So what are the things you both really enjoy doing? They could be sports or physical things, cultural interests, fitness, theatre, cooking together, trying out new recipes, exhibitions, visiting new places; opportunities to meet new people. And what are the simple routines that give you both pleasure?

Simple Pleasures: Little Things That Make Life Worth Living is a book with a collection of short chapters written by a variety of people on the theme of how 'the deepest pleasures almost always come from the simplest sources'. The writer Adam Nicolson writes about the joy of walking; Prue Leith, the chef and writer, describes the pleasure of a long, hot bath; the writer and broadcaster Jonathan Dimbleby talks about starting the day by collecting eggs from the hens in his orchard, and sharing them in a family breakfast. Yotam Ottolenghi, the Israeli chef and restauranteur, and self-confessed workaholic, finds cooking to be his source of balance – more relaxing for him than meditation.

What are the simple things that give you pleasure as a couple? Shopping for fresh food at the local market, cooking together, walks in the park? Don't let those simple routines drift out of your life displaced by work overload, emails and other seemingly more important pressures.

6. Keep it physical

In a connected relationship, there is a lot of touching – strokes on the shoulders or arms, hugs, sitting on a sofa massaging your partner's feet, gentle massages, kisses, all adding up to a physical intimacy that can naturally become sexual.

There is lots of evidence showing that maintaining a good sex life is associated with relationship satisfaction, love and commitment for both men and women. Sexual satisfaction is associated with relationship stability and greater overall well-being, and a major determinant of happiness. Your sex life keeps you healthy. Making love once or twice a week boosts the immune system, as measured by salivary immunoglobulin, and has the effect of keeping cortisol stable despite work-related stress.

Maintaining a good sex life has also been linked to job satisfaction and engagement at work. Keith Leavitt from Oregon State University, in a 2017 article, reports that sexual intimacy at home has a positive effect at work the following day, with increased daily job satisfaction measures and job engagement. But work strain spilling into home life reduces the likelihood of engaging in sexual intimacy that day.

When relationships disconnect, physical connection drifts away. Sexual intimacy becomes less frequent, less satisfying, and can eventually disappear. Gradually, spontaneous day-to-day physical connection, which is a constant reminder of closeness and specialness, drifts away and creates a sad, empty chasm that becomes very difficult to bridge. There is an awkwardness where there used to be a naturalness. So keep your relationship physical and spontaneous, and talk about it if it is becoming less physical.

7. If there's a problem, talk about it

According to a University of Winchester study by Stefan Robinson and colleagues in 2017, men are talking more to their friends than to their partners. They apparently get more satisfaction and feel they can be more open with male friends than with their partners. In my view, women are better at confronting relationship problems with their partners than men are. Men tend to be less tuned in to relationship difficulties at an early stage in the drift away from real connection. Women are more likely to complain about lack of time together, not doing things they both enjoy, not talking. Men need to see this as a red flag about the relationship drifting to a disconnected place, rather than seeing it as personal criticism. In Tim and Charlie's example, during the slow process of disconnection leading to Charlie leaving Tim she had tried on numerous occasions to point out to Tim how little time they had spent together and how they had stopped doing the things they used to enjoy; she had failed to tell him how lonely she had been feeling. At times, those discussions had escalated into rows, with Tim becoming angry and defensive, accusing Charlie of expecting too much and not understanding how stressful and exhausting his work was. Eventually she had given up complaining about their relationship and settled into a withdrawn hopelessness that anything would change. For Tim, this created the illusion that all was well between them – 'we hardly ever argued' – until it imploded.

8. Be wary of criticising

Being in a relationship that makes you feel appreciated reinforces your self-esteem and strong self-esteem fosters good mental health. Criticism can undermine self-esteem as well as self-confidence: it can be internalised, leaving the person feeling they have failed and depressing their spirit. Among people who had suffered from depression and relapsed, how they answered the question 'How critical is your spouse of you?' was one of the biggest predictors of who would relapse. Criticism can also make the person defensive, so the connection becomes hostile and unpleasant.

If you feel you have to criticise, criticise the action rather than the person. A criticism that becomes a generalisation is almost certain to backfire into defensiveness, simply because it's unlikely to be true. 'You're always late'; 'I can't trust you to do anything'; 'You're just not practical'; 'You never support me'; 'You don't listen'; 'You're never here when I need you'. Those statements, coming out of frustration, will not achieve the change in the person's behaviour you are hoping for. It's more likely they will make the person feel unfairly criticised and undermined. And of course, nobody is *always* late; the bigger the generalisation, the less likely it is to be accurate.

A relationship is a balanced system and your behaviour towards your partner affects the balance. Your warmth, interest, appreciation, humour and supportiveness will encourage similar behaviour in your partner. If you become critical, undermining, hostile, with times when you withdraw and sulk, you will encourage similar negative behaviour in your partner, because relationships balance. So, criticism, particularly generalised criticism, as an attempt to encourage some positive change is unlikely to succeed unless the emotional context is warm and caring.

That's not to say that you shouldn't have standards about what you expect of the relationship. Within the context of being appreciative about the relationship, you need to express when you feel let down. If she has said she will be home early from work and she hasn't even told you she's going to be late, that's not OK. If he spends most of Sunday on a bike ride, leaving you to look after the children, that's not fair. If you've gone to the trouble of cooking a nice meal and it is not appreciated, that's being taken for granted. If you are out for a meal together, and he is constantly responding to his phone, point out that he is being disrespectful.

This is a balance: pointing out what you expect when your partner falls short of that standard sits in a balance between being critical and undermining about any annoyance on the one hand, and being over-accommodating to the point that you are in danger of losing your identity on the other. And if you can see that he or she has a point and that the criticism is coming from a good heart, from the desire to keep the relationship connected and in good shape, then acknowledge that, and an apology is an acknowledgement of the good intention. Many people find it very difficult to apologise; for some, it feels like a surrender, a loss of pride, and they will argue to the end rather than admit they are in the wrong. But an apology is an acknowledgement that you are both committed to keeping this relationship special and not letting it drift into something where you feel taken for granted.

What can be particularly destructive is being critical of something that leaves your partner feeling helpless. For example, some people are critical and quite intolerant of their partner occasionally working at home, even when they're in a job that involves checking emails or catching up on work some evenings. If your partner cannot accept that your job occasionally involves you working in the evenings, it will make life very unpleasant and could undermine your career. If your partner is unable to be more flexible on this, then maybe you are in the wrong job or the wrong relationship.

9. Try to be supportive without being controlling

This is not easy, particularly if what you hear is a problem that needs solving, and then you readily tell your partner what to do. This can give rise to 'solutions' that appear to be trite, and rarely get to something that the person hasn't thought about. 'You've just got to tell your boss to hire more people' is not the most helpful thing to say when your partner is feeling over-stretched by work demands. Equally, saying something like 'You're just being weak – you have to stand up to your boss' is completely undermining.

On the other hand, if what you hear is someone who needs sympathy and support, you might be able to listen, ask a few questions about what they have done, and offer reassurance or some perspective on the difficulty. You might even frame a suggestion within the context of what you did in a similar situation. The choice in approach could determine the long-term happiness of your relationship.

How a couple deals with difficult issues is a predictor of how a relationship fares over time. Discussing a difficult issue can give rise to feelings of frustration, exasperation and defensiveness. Or it could give rise to feelings of compassion and supportiveness, with a sympathy for your partner's point of view.

Couples who show positive supportive behaviours during videoed discussions of difficult issues are more likely to do well as a couple than couples who show undermining negative behaviour. Justin Lavner and Thomas Bradbury from the University of California, in a 2012 study, addressed the question of why couples who were reportedly happy for several years of marriage had divorced during the 10-year follow-up period. One hundred and thirty-six couples were observed in lab discussions within six months of getting married. Fifteen per cent of the couples had divorced by the 10-year point. Interestingly, self-reported satisfaction with the marriage in the first four years did not distinguish between who divorced and who stayed together. What did distinguish them was the behaviour they displayed when they discussed difficult issues. Disagreeing, blaming, invalidating the other person's point of view, getting angry or showing signs of contempt, self-justification or denying responsibility, or interrupting and blocking of the other person were all predictive of the couple divorcing by the 10-year point.

In another study from the University of Denver, the researchers looked at the premarital roots of marital distress and divorce in the first five years of marriage. They observed 210 couples while they discussed problem areas in their relationships. They found that those couples who divorced were more likely to show negative behaviours, including denial, withdrawing, or escalating the argument.

Gradually, over time, the undermining behaviours come to define the nature of the relationship at difficult times and can reduce the protective effect of more supportive behaviours. It appears that negative behaviours are more of a risk factor for a relationship than positive behaviours are protective. The behaviours that are positive and protective of a relationship include listening, paraphrasing, accepting responsibility, seeking to clarify the issue, looking for solutions, compromising and coming across with appreciation, interest and humour. If you are committed as a couple to maintaining happiness and warmth in your relationship, take joint responsibility for developing a self-awareness of your behaviour, discouraging undermining behaviours and encouraging the constructive protective behaviours.

10. Express appreciation: let go of unhappy memories

A relationship is a couple in time, and how it treats its past determines its success and happiness. The past is made up of good and unhappy memories. How do you treat those memories?

How do you weigh them? Some couples see what there is day-to-day that they appreciate about their partner and those appreciations are consolidated by happy memories of their time together. They have a sense of gratitude for their relationship and they freely express it. A study reported by Ayala Malach Pines, which looked at the characteristics of couples with low burnout scores, found that in comparison with those with high burnout scores, the biggest difference was in their ability to look positively at the relationship, as opposed to looking at particular annoyances or frustrations. But in some relationships, the unhappy memories weigh heavily and overshadow the good memories.

In unhealthy relationships, inducing guilt can become a weapon, and inducing guilt requires memories that are faithful to the idea that you are a victim of someone else's bad behaviour. Many people tell me that as soon as they get into an argument in their relationship, their partner lists the wrongs of the past going back over many years. The times they have felt let down, times their partners have not been there for them, been unsupportive, forgetful, put work or other commitments before them, embarrassed them, ignored them in favour of others and on and on.

This can leave the person feeling crushed and hopeless, left carrying the weight of the past, undermining any joy they might get from their relationship. If guilt is to be used as a weapon, it requires the other person to feel guilty, but in most cases, that person instead simply detaches, becomes exasperated and withdraws from the conversation or gets angry, which can reinforce the victim state of the other: 'You see, you're never willing to discuss anything – you never listen to me.'

If the person were to have a memory failure, the relationship would improve. It is as if they are wearing a lens to amplify the disappointments of the past. To maintain a happy relationship, you need to let go of the unhappy memories. If you have expressed openly how you were left feeling, if your partner has acknowledged how they let you down, if something has been learned from it, let it go.

Other couples look at their relationship through a lens of appreciation, noting and often commenting on what their partner does that makes them feel good – small acts of consideration, warmth, tenderness, things the person has done that make life easier for them. Seeing those things puts frustrations and potential annoyances into a different context, and allows them to be brushed aside.

Cherish the good memories, reminisce, rekindle the happiness they brought you, be grateful for them. Use the good memories to shape the joyful, connected personality of your relationship. As the French philosopher André Comte-Sponville wrote, 'the past is in need of our compassion and gratitude'.

The long view

Proof of the long-term advantages of investing in your relationship comes from a recent publication from the Harvard Study of Adult Development. This is one of the most impressive studies in the history of psychology; John F. Kennedy and one of the first *Washington Post* editors, Ben Bradlee, were included within the original cohort. A longitudinal study started in the late 1930s and, following up a cohort of subjects with interviews and questionnaires every two years, it is a rich mine of data on what predicts mental and physical health, happiness and life satisfaction. What is particularly impressive is the association between happy relationships in middle age and physical and mental health decades later. The study found strong associations between happiness and close relationships including spouses, friends and family; Dr Robert Waldinger, the fourth director of the study, says: 'When we gathered together everything we knew about them at age 50, it wasn't their middle-age cholesterol levels that predicted how they were going to grow old. It was how satisfied they were in their relationships. The people who were the most satisfied in their relationships at age 50 were the healthiest at age 80.'

The evidence is clear: prioritising your relationship protects your physical and mental health, strengthens your ability to perform in a high-pressure career and pays dividends in your happiness and health in the decades to come.

Friendship

And what about friends? Do they have similar effects on our physiological stability as close relationships? Friends keep us well, mentally and physically. The evidence for the impact of friendships on longevity goes back decades. In a longitudinal study reported by Lisa Berkman and Leonard Syme in 1979, which followed a sample of nearly 7000 people over a nine-year period, the researchers found that those who lacked social ties were more likely to die over the follow-up period when other factors like physical health, smoking, obesity, physical activity and alcohol intake were accounted for. Those who had the fewest social connections had mortality rates which were more than twice as high as those with the most social contacts.

More recently, in 2010, in a meta-analytic review from Brigham Young University, assessing 148 individual studies with over 300,000 participants, the researchers found that those with stronger social networks had a 50 per cent reduced mortality rate over a seven-and-a-half year period. This effect is similar to that of stopping smoking and has a higher link to reduced mortality than obesity and physical inactivity. In a 2015 study, the same researchers conducted a meta-analysis, concluding that middle-aged adults who were socially isolated or reported feeling lonely had an increased mortality rate between 26 and 32 per cent, greater than more socially committed adults. Having few friends is roughly equivalent to being obese in terms of its effect on health and longevity.

Good friends are particularly good for your heart. People with few friends who see themselves as lonely have higher blood pressure readings by as much as 30 points in one study. In a study of more than 28,000 men, followed up over 10 years, Patricia Eng and colleagues looked at the impact of social integration on longevity. One hundred and forty-six of the participants in the least socially integrated group died of cardiovascular disease, compared to only 28 in the most socially integrated. The number who died from accidents and suicide was also strikingly greater in the least socially integrated group: 28 cases, compared with 5 in the most socially connected group.

Similarly, in a study of more than 500 women with coronary artery disease, women who reported the lowest levels of social support were twice as likely to die over the study's two-year follow-up period. The women who enjoyed good levels of support and social connections were not only more likely to be alive after two years, they also had lower rates of high blood pressure and diabetes. People with stronger social connections have a stronger immune response to stress.

People with richer social lives, who meet up with friends regularly, report higher life satisfaction. An Italian study of over 50,000 participants collecting information on health, lifestyle and social integration found that those people who meet up with friends regularly, i.e. several times a month, reported higher life satisfaction. Those who meet up with friends only a few times a year, or did not have friends, had life satisfaction scores 27 per cent lower than those who met with friends regularly.

The strength of your relationships with your colleagues at work also impacts your health. A 20-year follow-up study of healthy employees assessed, among other things, the degree of social support they received at work. Those reporting high levels of peer social support had a significantly lower mortality risk, particularly in those aged mid-30s to mid-40s at the start of the study.

So, what is it about friendship that creates those beneficial effects on physical and mental health and general happiness? Friends give us support and acceptance; they are there for us regardless of what has happened in our lives. At times, they give us practical help if we need it; they give us perspectives that might reduce the impact of stressful events on us; they give us warmth and hugs. Hugs have a very beneficial effect on our health. In a study at Carnegie Mellon University, over 400 healthy adults were tested to determine whether hugs protected stressed people from getting sick. The subjects were intentionally exposed to the cold virus, a standard way of examining the strength of one's immune response. They found that those who reported high levels of social support were less susceptible to getting sick with the cold virus and that getting hugs regularly was responsible for one-third of the effect of social support.

And of course, friends make us laugh. Laughter has amazing physiological effects, similar to the effects of exercise. JongEun Yim from Sahmyook University summarises the benefits of laughter in a 2016 article. Laughter releases endorphins in the brain, lifting mood and energy; it activates the release of the neurotransmitter serotonin, which regulates mood, has an antidepressant effect on emotional balance and is one of the key regulators of sleep. Laughter stimulates multiple physiological systems that decrease levels of stress hormones such as cortisol and epinephrine and stimulates the release of the neurotransmitter dopamine, which elevates mood. Laughter strengthens our immune system, activating natural killer cells and helping to fight off infection. It alleviates anxiety and depression, and helps people judge their problems more objectively.

Humour is one of our greatest defences against stressful or threatening experiences. It completely detaches us from the feelings of threat and immediately provides other perspectives. We could view humour as the mind's creative revenge on the world, transforming painful emotions into something that instantly connects us to others.

Let us pull all of this together

If we are to be at our best – feeling energised, with positive stable mood, feeling good about life, effective in our work lives, engaged in what we are doing at home with spare mental capacity to handle what life randomly throws at us – we need to have key physiological systems in equilibrium, in particular the adrenal-cortisol system and our neurotransmitter system. If they drift away from equilibrium, we feel the effects on our energy, mood, our concentration, anxiety and ultimately on our overall mental health.

We have looked at the key factors that have a stabilising effect on that physiology. The evidence to support each of these variables is impressive. We have looked at the effects of exercise, what we do to unwind, our sleep, the impact of diet on energy and mental functioning, the disruptive effects of alcohol, how friends impact on resilience and mental health and the power of connected, happy relationships on our health, physically and mentally, on our work effectiveness and on our psychological resilience. All of these elements make up a finely balanced system – an ecosystem, interconnecting work, home, energy, mood and ultimately happiness. Disruption in one area can affect all the others to some extent. Which is why, if we are unable to exercise, for example, we might drift away from good sleep routines, our diet might change and we might drink more, as well as affecting how we behave at home, our sense of humour and our levels of irritability. Ultimately, the thing to remember is that distinctions between work, home, physiology, mind and emotions are purely linguistic. It is all one flow.

The challenge, of course, is not letting these things drift away when life becomes more demanding than usual. Having some of them as non-negotiables definitely helps: the idea that one or more are anchored week by week, regardless of how busy you are, because you know that if you stop doing them you will be less effective and more likely to get tired, irritable and moody. Sadly, some people have lost not only the balance that protects their physiological equilibrium but also the balance that their emotional lives need. They have drifted away from real emotional connection.

Home late, rushed, often eating separately, conscious of a list of things they have to do before bed, collapsed on a sofa with the television on and a laptop on their knee, too distracted to have a conversation with the person sitting next to them. Out for a drink with friends or sitting in a meeting with colleagues, superficially connected but doubtful of who they can trust to allow them to be really open about what keeps them awake at night.

To maintain any balance in a life where we are constantly busy needs us to look at what we can take control of to safeguard time for what we value outside of work. We need to discover where the flexibility is. We need to be conscious of habits we have developed that could be undermining flexibility and we need to look critically at the assumptions and habits that define how we are working.

5

Taking control of your life

Cath is an engaging, enthusiastic manager in marketing in an international company. She has worked there for eight years and she was promoted nine months ago into a much more demanding role. She is now responsible for international projects, she travels most weeks, often for no more than a day, but occasionally for three or four days.

She is married to Rick; they have been together for 10 years. They are committed to one another, but she recognises they are not as close as they used to be. Physical intimacy has dwindled and they no longer have much to talk about other than day-to-day practicalities. Rick was made redundant a few years ago and he now looks after their two children, a boy aged seven and a girl who is five. The arrangement works for Cath in that she no longer feels guilty if she is working late or away on a business trip. However, she is very conscious of the financial pressure and the consequences of her losing her job.

Cath rarely works fewer than 11 hours a day, and often goes beyond midnight. She sees her children most mornings unless she is travelling, and tries to see them before they go to bed at least three times a week. Her balance to life has gone. Exercise, yoga, occasionally seeing friends, reading, listening to music – all have been pushed out by work and family demands.

Her days are taken up mostly by back-to-back meetings and short breaks when she responds to emails. She feels constantly under pressure. If she is not in a meeting, there is somebody wanting her view on something. She works most evenings after she gets home and is constantly available and responsive to emails.

She knows she is struggling and often feels overwhelmed; she goes to bed exhausted, but often struggles to get to sleep. On a good night, she might get six hours' sleep. She worries about being less effective and decisive than she used to be. She has been putting off decisions about things that just feel too tough and she rarely finds the time to work through difficult issues on her own.

Over the past six months she has been aware of feeling anxious about something going wrong, dropping a ball, missing a deadline. She has a good team, but they are inexperienced. She meets with them regularly, she coaches them and is as available as she can be for them.

Recently she has had times when she has felt light-headed and had difficulties focusing and concentrating for more than a few minutes. She gets home agitated and exhausted. She has been drinking more – over half a bottle of wine in the evenings to relax. She feels guilty for not seeing more of her children and she is anxious about letting people down and about failing.

Cath knows she is a perfectionist and she finds it very difficult not to take something on if she sees that someone is struggling. She went to a tough inner-city school and was determined to do well; she was the first in her family to go to university. She has gone much further in life than she imagined she would do. She attributes her achievements to hard work rather than to ability and she has always been anxious about 'being found out'. But now she feels closer to that than ever before. She is in a self-perpetuating circle.

Cath needs to make relatively small changes to each part of the circle, starting with an understanding that how she feels is a natural consequence of a physiological shift brought about by a total loss of balance in her life. 'Just doing more' is failing. The focus now needs to be on balance. Cath needs to bring back some of the physiological stabilisers and treat them as non-negotiable, regardless of how busy

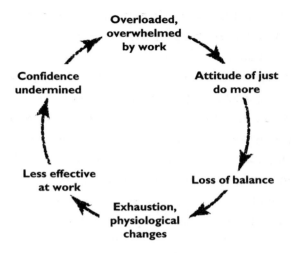

her life is. That means committing to exercising a couple of times a week, maybe the yoga that she used to do, seven hours' sleep, and some routines to protect sleep. This would help stabilise her physiology, bring her anxiety down, and reduce the feeling of exhaustion. It would also help make her more effective at work.

To do this, she has to create definition to her day. Like many people I see in my clinic, Cath's day has lost definition; it has become elastic, expanding to unreasonable hours as demands increase. At the end of her 11-hour day, Cath is leaving with a lot more that she could do, even if she stayed another couple of hours. But even after a 24-hour day, she would not have got everything done. So regardless of the hours she works, there will always be more she feels she needs to do. Therefore, if you are working an 11- or 12-hour day, and it could be a 24-hour day, and you would still have more to do, then you might as well work a 10-hour or even a nine-hour day. Cath got that point and put in place some firm rules for when she would go home and how many hours she would work at home (if any), and the nine-hour day allowed her to build in time for better sleep; some exercise and yoga once a week became part of this package of changes. She also cut out alcohol midweek, and kept it low at the weekends.

This got Cath to a minimum balance to help stabilise her physiology for energy and better control over her mood and anxiety levels. But balance has to be about more than sleep, exercise and yoga. Balance has to be about everything you value in your life. Most people I see talk to me about difficulties balancing life, regardless of the type of work they do. All of the stories we have looked at, including Hannah, Keith and Tom, have lost the balance to their lives as work took more and more of the space, without realising that it is this balance that is crucial for energy and for being effective in our work lives.

Getting to balance involves asking yourself what you value in your life. Or to put it another way: what do you *not* want to lose?

'I don't want to lose my job', you might say. Fair enough, but go further.

'I don't want to lose this really good relationship I'm in.'

'I don't want to lose my connection to my children.'

'I don't want to lose my fitness.'

'I don't want to lose my friends.'

'I don't want to lose being an interesting person.'

So then we need to find flexibility to create time for these important things by shaking up the habits we have developed. So where is the flexibility? Many companies allow more flexibility than lots of people use. They have a zone of flexibility at the start of the day that is quite wide. There's a zone of flexibility around the middle of the day, and of course a flexibility zone at the end of the day; for some organisations there is a two- to three-hour flexibility window at the start of the day. Many organisations are flexible about working from home.

If you wanted to slot in exercise midweek, trying to do it at the end of the day might not be the best choice; it could get pushed out by late meetings or family commitments. Before work might be a better choice, using the flexibility to get in later a couple of days a week. For some, the best time for exercise is during the working day, around midday or lunchtime.

Cath made a commitment to go to the gym before work two mornings a week. She started working from home one day a week. This gave her time to focus on more complex work tasks that needed uninterrupted time, and obviously there was no commuting time. She used some of that time to go to a yoga class in the early evening before getting involved with her children's baths and stories routine.

Cath also broke out of the habit of working after the children were in bed. Many people do this. It is like a second shift that can be for between one and three hours before they go to bed late. It becomes a habit. But you could make it a decision rather than a habit. Ask yourself, is there anything here that if I didn't do it tonight there would be some bad consequence tomorrow morning? If the answer is No, then you're free. Enjoy your evening and have a bath, read a book, snuggle up with your partner on the sofa.

Setting boundaries at work . . .

And what about an email boundary – a time beyond which you don't look at them? Again, it could be a day-to-day decision, and it would give you a work-free couple of hours before bed.

As part of the path to a healthier, more balanced life, everyone we have met in the course of the book so far worked with me to create boundaries, seeing where the flexibility existed to make that possible. Sally started exercising before she got to work. Tom, who admitted that he had come to view almost everything outside work as a chore, something to get through as fast as he could, including time with his children, started having breakfast with his children and taking them to school two mornings a week. Then he realised he was responding to emails as they were having breakfast, so he created an email boundary – not looking at them until he was on the train. Hannah allocated two slots of time to go to the gym around the middle of the day. They all changed the habit of working most evenings after their children went to bed. They created tighter boundaries to protect their weekends. Sally had got into the habit of flying to European offices on a Sunday for Monday morning meetings. She started flying on a Monday morning and arranged later start times for her meetings.

Balance is about creating slots of time for what you enjoy doing – time for yourself, for you and your partner, for children, friends, for those things you would miss if you stopped doing them. Balance is not about working a nine-to-five day, it's about figuring out where the slots could be midweek, not just at the weekend, and creating boundaries to protect them. Many people I see, when I talk to them about balance, only tell me about what they did at the weekend; it is as if they have written off having any time to themselves between Monday and Friday. But you can find time for the things you enjoy doing midweek if you are more flexible in your use of time. What I have found is that people who create midweek balance have much more energy over the week than those who write off the midweek and try to slot everything they enjoy doing into the weekends.

Keith, who we met earlier, was struggling conscientiously with the problems he had inherited when he took over his management job in his IT role. He also adopted the 'just do more' attitude. He too had become overwhelmed by the demands, his balance to life had gone, he had become ineffective in how he was working, and had developed a host of red flags, including disturbed sleep, low mood and anxiety, which ultimately culminated in a panic attack at work and being advised by his GP to take time off.

Keith didn't work in a company where there was flexibility about when he could start work, but he recognised that he needed to create definition to his day, and to create slots of time for his family, his sport, and some time for himself. He could see that as he increased his work hours to try to get on top of an overly busy job, he had drifted away from exercise, social life and interests, and he felt worse – more tired, less effective. The lack of balance certainly had not made him feel more on top of the demands. Keith cut back his hours, leaving work by six, and he created a clearer boundary – not working after he got home, he stopped looking at emails in the evenings, which was difficult for him, and he kept his weekends free from work.

. . . and at home

Not all demands come from work. Some people become overwhelmed by home demands and changes coming on top of their work life. Nadia, who had got so exhausted that she had broken down in tears following a call from a critical customer, realised she had to make some changes to rebalance her life, a job that had become more demanding, two young children, and a mother who lived close by and had developed a heart condition. She was getting by on five hours' sleep, with no time for herself, and she recognised that if she continued like this she would undermine her health. After a very helpful conversation with her supervisor, Nadia started leaving on time and taking a short lunch break again. She realised that not everything had to be done by the end of the work day, and she started to take short periods of time offline to get some of the admin tasks done. In the past, she had felt too guilty to do that, even though the others in her team took time offline and encouraged her to do it.

Nadia also had a chat with her husband and her mother about how she had been feeling. Her mother told Nadia that she didn't need to visit every night, that she was doing all right physically, and if Nadia came around a couple of times a week that would be fine. Her husband, who recognised that Nadia tried to do too much for everyone, took over the bedtime routine on the evenings Nadia visited her mother, allowing her to get to bed earlier. They also reorganised their Saturday morning routine so that Nadia could go back to her Pilates class. Those small changes were enough for Nadia to feel more in control of her life, less pressured, and her sleep and her mood improved. She still had times when she felt guilty about not doing more – at work, for her mother, for her children – but she recognised that the old way of trying to do everything for everyone was not sustainable.

Steve and Sheila

Some people's lives slip out of balance as a result of demands they put on themselves that have nothing to do with work. Steve and Sheila are in their late twenties and both in good jobs – Sheila a nurse in a local hospital, Steve an engineer. They met at university, moved to London and rented a flat together in south London. They had a good life, a relatively short commute to work, lots of friends. Steve played football on Saturdays and trained a few times a week. Sheila did local voluntary work. They enjoyed the cinema, went to concerts and enjoyed eating in local restaurants. After a few years, with some financial help from their parents, they decided to buy a house together. They raised as big a mortgage as they could on their joint salary, and settled on moving to Kent, where houses were more affordable. They found a house and fell in love with the area and with the potential of what they could do with the house. It had been owned by a lady in her late seventies who had done nothing to it for over 30 years. They had no money left over to hire contractors, but they were both resourceful and practically minded, so they committed to renovating the house and decorating it themselves.

Life almost immediately fell out of balance. The commute to work now took close to one and a half hours. They rarely saw their friends. Steve gave up his football and exercise and Sheila gave up her voluntary work and other interests, although she continued to see her friends and family most weeks. Their approach to the project differed, and this led to arguments. Steve wanted to devote all his time outside work to the renovation project, working on it every evening often past midnight, and all weekend. Sheila wanted to pace it with some time for one another, and time to do fun things. They had a big argument over holidays. Steve wanted to use the spare time and money to work on the house,

Sheila wanted to go on holiday and get some sun. They came to what was a strained compromise of a week on a beach holiday. Over time, the project started to affect Steve's mood; he became irritable and impatient and he was annoyed at Sheila for taking the time to visit her friends rather than helping with the work at home. Their relationship started to disconnect and they became more argumentative; the fun had gone out of their relationship. Steve's sleep started to become a problem – going to bed late and often waking up early, he was tired and run down. His work was affected; he became withdrawn and less motivated, often missing a deadline, and his manager had a chat with him about what he had seen as a change in his attitude. None of this led to Steve easing back on the home project or pacing himself differently.

Then, over winter, he came down with a cold, which developed into a chest infection. At first he thought it was because of dust inhalation, but it got worse. His doctor prescribed antibiotics but the infection continued for months, with short periods of recovery before getting ill again. He felt so exhausted he couldn't get out of bed. Eventually, as the symptoms lessened, he got back to work, but he was too tired to do anything in the evenings or for more than a few hours at the weekend. His parents persuaded him that he and Sheila should go on holiday for a couple of weeks, somewhere warm, where he could properly recover. The holiday helped and he slept for over eight hours a day for the first week. He and Sheila had long talks about how he had lost himself and how they needed to rebalance their lives, have more time together, see their friends regularly, get back to their interests and sport. So what if the home project took an extra six months? They decided to get some contractors in to help them finish it. Looking back, Steve recognised that the chest infection had probably prevented him from completely burning out and perhaps irreparably undermining his marriage.

Embracing the alternative approach

All of the people we have looked at here have eventually been forced to come to the conclusion that the approach of 'just do more' and sacrificing balance simply wasn't working. In reality it was making them feel awful, and they felt even less on top of things at work. They learned that the alternative approach, to do less and keep balance, had made them feel better: improved sleep, better mood, less anxious, feeling more energised and more effective at work. But for this to work, we need simultaneous changes in how we are working; we need to become more effective in fewer hours. How do we do that?

First, we need to look critically and objectively at what our day at work looks like. Cath described her working day: up early responding to emails before she gets the children out of bed, a breakfast of coffee and toast, emails on the train, then back-to-back meetings, often running late, apologising for arriving late, distracted by things she hasn't had time to do, dealing with questions from her team whenever she comes out of a meeting, people waiting for decisions, client calls or problems taking priority, meetings cancelled at short notice, her PA getting her a sandwich and a coffee. Recently she had started looking at emails in meetings and she knows this is a bad habit and inconsiderate to others in the room. There's no time now to think through issues on her own, although she recognises that she is more effective and creative if she gets some uninterrupted time. The last few hours before she goes home are a mixture of quick conversations with whoever is still around, phone calls and emails. Home to see the children before bed, often preoccupied by unresolved problems, then replying to emails while she sits in front of the television after her evening meal with her husband, usually too tired to say much.

This is a day that's out of control. There's also an arbitrariness to it. Some meetings will be declined because she is already committed. The work she does at home is catching up on some things she didn't do in the day. There is no contingency time or time to plan.

Cath could limit the number of meetings she goes to in a day; she could create some blocks of time – maybe two hours – when she could focus uninterrupted on her projects for the day. Her PA could scan emails, reducing the number she has to respond to. She could make herself available to her team at set times rather than constantly. She could limit the length of meetings she runs to 30 or even 20 minutes. By really tough prioritising, she could reduce the work she does after she gets home. That has become a habit rather than being priority driven.

As part of his approach to regaining control of his life, Keith made a number of changes in how he was working. After a very constructive conversation with his manager, who recognised Keith's conscientiousness and commitment to the job, Keith came up with a plan to tackle the legacy problems over a year with the help of some external contract workers. He recognised he needed to be more focused on what he gave his time to and started blocking time for key priorities over the week. He developed a tougher approach with internal clients, negotiating with them over demands and deadlines. Crucially, he began to realise that although he had become a manager, he wasn't thinking like one. He was essentially still doing the job he had been doing, but adding his management tasks to the list of things he had to do. With this in mind, he delegated more, stopped picking up work when others were struggling, but gave more time to developing his team and discussing sensible time scales for the various projects they were delivering. None of this came easily to him – his commitment and his fear of disappointing others constantly nagged at him – but the determination not to have another panic attack or to end up on antidepressants gave him a different perspective.

Keith and Cath came to the realisation that if they were to get proper balance in their lives, they needed to become much more decisive in how they ran their work day. In a job that never ends, where every day there is more that could be done, it is easy to get into the habit of working longer days. They had all lost control of their work day. Taking back control needs a much more focused approach and focus involves two things:

1. What is the best use of my time out of everything I could be doing?
2. What is stopping me getting it done? How could I reduce distractions?

Managing distractions

Distractions are a major problem for those who work in office-based jobs. By taking control of distractions you take control of your effectiveness, but you also reduce the degree of stress you experience in the job and increase your job satisfaction and happiness at work.

Email and other messaging systems constantly distract us. A technology research firm estimated that more than 128 billion business emails would be sent and received daily in 2019, with the average business user dealing with 126 messages a day. Many people I see tell me they receive between 200 and 300 emails a day. Various surveys show that we only spend around 11.5 minutes on a single task before being interrupted. Other surveys show that users check emails and messaging systems around every six minutes. Employees check their inboxes on average 77 times a day.

It has been estimated that 28 per cent of a professional or manager's day is taken up by interruptions. After the interruptions we lose time getting back to what we were doing before the interruption. It can take 20 minutes on average to regain momentum. That's assuming you get back to what you had been doing. A third of the time we do not return to the disrupted task.

An observational study of 14 office workers, recording their behaviour as it happened, showed just how fragmented people's work lives are. They found that people only spend about three minutes on a task before switching tasks; they spend on average less than two and a half minutes reading emails before switching to another task or are interrupted. Interruptions cause more mistakes, increase levels of frustration and annoyance and reduce effectiveness. In a controlled experiment with 50 subjects looking at the impact of interruptions, Brian Bailey and Joseph Konstan from the University of Minnesota report how disruptive interruptions are. Specifically, they found that subjects required up to 27 per cent more time to complete a task, made twice as many mistakes and experienced significantly greater levels of annoyance and anxiety when peripheral tasks were introduced in the middle of a task the subject was trying to focus on in comparison to the interruptions occurring at the boundary point between tasks.

Gloria Mark from the University of California and her colleagues Daniela Gudith and Ulrich Klocke created a simulation of an office environment in their lab with designated tasks and interruptions. They found that their subjects worked faster in conditions where they were interrupted in comparison to a phase where they were able to focus without interruptions, but it came at a cost. It appeared that they were working faster to compensate for the time lost to the interruptions, but they experienced more stress, higher levels of frustration and more time pressure as a consequence.

Multitasking does not appear to be the answer. Some researchers have assumed that employees who appear to function through multitasking – or rapid task switching, as it is called – must have some superior cognitive skills. Researchers at Stanford University set out to investigate what gives multitaskers their edge, but they found that heavy multitaskers were actually less productive than those doing a single task at a time. People who are regularly bombarded with several streams of electronic information cannot pay attention, recall information or switch from one task to another as well as those who perform one task at a time. In fact, it is clear that high multitaskers appear to have more trouble filtering out irrelevant information and organising the information they take in.

Constant distractions could also be rewiring your brain to *expect* more distractions, ultimately making you less able to work in a focused way. Researchers at the University of Sussex used functional magnetic resonance imaging to look at the brain structures of 75 adults who had completed a questionnaire regarding their use of media devices including mobile phones and computers, as well as television and print media. They found that those who are constantly distracted by their devices had less brain density in an area of the brain that is associated with cognitive and emotional processing, the anterior cingulate cortex. The research helps to explain why heavy media multitaskers show poor attention in the face of distractions and also report higher levels of emotional difficulties such as anxiety and depression. This is important stuff – how you manage your work in an environment geared to high levels of interruption could be rewiring your neural circuitry, with potential implications for your work effectiveness as well as your emotional life. Almost anything you can take control of to reduce email and messaging distractions will make you more effective in less time, and potentially could lead to a better balance to life.

Let's find out what your baseline is:

1. Roughly determine how frequently you look at your inbox or other messaging inputs. Is it whatever signals a new message? Is it every six to 10 minutes?

    This is of course assuming that your job is not just about answering emails, but about delivering something like a sales target, or creating campaigns or producing technical documents or negotiating a deal or managing a team, and dealing with emails and other interruptions comes on top of those primary tasks.

2. Roughly determine how long you focus on any single task before you break off to do something else. What is the cause of the interruption? Is it a person breaking in on what you are doing, an email, or is it you feeling you need a break?

Tips for a more effective, less stressed working day

1. Set your goals

Be clear about what the primary tasks are that you want to get done today – three at most. Sounds obvious, but most people walk in and just let the day slap them in the face as soon as they arrive – emails, problems, meetings, and people wanting a few minutes of their time before they have even taken their coat off. Give yourself 20 or 30 minutes to clarify what three things you want to get done today and ideally block out some time to get them done.

2. Adopt a proactive attitude to messages

Bearing in mind the research that suggests that people spend no more than around 11 minutes on a focused task, try to give yourself 20 to 30 minutes on a focused task without looking at a message.

If not looking at messages and emails makes you feel uneasy, you could scan them but only respond if it is really urgent or a very high priority source, like your boss or a client. Some interruptions could be helpful if they are aligned with the primary task you are working on.

In a recent article in *The New Yorker* magazine, Cal Newport, a Professor of Computer Science at Georgetown University, makes the distinction between synchronised and asynchronised messages. Synchronised communication happens in a meeting where a group of people focus on an issue that needs developing and most of the communication around the table is synchronised to that topic. It also happens on the phone when two people arrange a meeting.

An asynchronised meeting would be where a large number of people wander in and out of a room and throw in comments about any number of topics without them being focused on any agreed issue. Imagine the chaos and the jumbled head space of anyone trying to make sense of the meeting, but that is essentially what a day's worth of emails is like. Regardless of the importance of what you are working on, you can receive at frequent random intervals messages about any number of topics with an expectation that you respond to them – and you wonder why at the end of a 10-hour day you feel like your head is scrambled.

The tip here is: scan for synchronised messages, where someone is making a contribution to the project you are working on, and leave asynchronised messages until after you have completed the task.

3. Resist interrupting yourself

About half of interruptions noted in observational studies of people at work are self-created, as we go from one unfinished task to another, randomly looking at a newsfeed, social media or whatever. Just stick with the task in hand, and work through the urge to interrupt yourself, keeping going for another 20 minutes or so until you have completed it. There is a big pay-off for taking this more self-disciplined approach. A study by Wilhelm Hofmann and colleagues from the University of Chicago in 2013 shows how avoiding distractions makes you happier and more satisfied with life. They looked at the relationship between self-control and satisfaction with life. Self-control is about resisting the urge of distractions that allow you to avoid the task you don't want to do. They found that subjects who are high in self-control report higher levels of happiness and higher levels of satisfaction with their lives as a whole.

Procrastination, of course, can interfere with this focused approach to work. Faffing about on low-priority tasks as a way of avoiding getting started on some bigger or more 'difficult' task wastes time and can lead to longer days doing the now urgent task right up against the deadline. The tip here is – set yourself a deadline to begin the task and spend around 30 to 45 minutes on it without interruptions. You may need to close your emails and take yourself away from other interruptions for this. Then sketch out your ideas as if you were talking it through with somebody. It is amazing how much you can get done in 30 to 45 minutes focusing on one topic with no distractions. Then leave it until closer to the deadline, schedule another block of uninterrupted time, and it will be much easier to start on it and get it finished. Essentially, our brains continue to work on the topic, often in creative ways, after the initial 'breaking in' session.

4. Be sure you are focusing on the right tasks

Focusing is about getting on with something without being distracted but it is also about clarity about the *best use of your time*. We all have a list of things we would like to do in our work lives. It could be written down – on a to-do list – or it could be in our head. And there could be a very large number of items on this list.

There are two approaches to this: the first is to be determined to get to the bottom of the list. The second is to accept that you will never get to the bottom of the list and instead become a really tough prioritiser.

Those taking the first approach will have a miserable life. They will work very long days, often past midnight; they will try to kill off items on the list at weekends; they might wake early and spend time before they get to work trying to get more tasks done. They will constantly feel harassed, stressed and probably guilty about never getting to the bottom of the list.

The second approach is much more rational – accepting you will never get everything done, you adopt tough prioritising. This means scanning the list to see if there is anything where something will go wrong if you do not do it today and, if there is, blocking time uninterrupted to get it done. Otherwise, identify the key tasks – say two or three –you want to get done today and focus on these.

5. Keep a flexible attitude to your priorities

If some new priority hits your day, pull out of meetings and reprioritise the other things you wanted to do so that you can focus on what is now the most important thing. Prioritise by the consequences of *not* doing something. Fixing a client problem has a bigger consequence than pulling out of an internal meeting. Flexible reprioritising is the alternative to working later and trying to get it all done.

From the overall list, create two priority lists. List A is the key tasks you want to get done today and tasks that will have a bad consequence if you don't do them today. List B is tasks that would put you ahead of your agenda. These are optional and good to do, but List A takes the priority.

This approach can allow you to stay on top of a really busy job without getting overwhelmed by it. It can allow you to define what a working day is with reasonable boundaries so that your balance to life is not sacrificed.

6. Delegate what you can

Some people don't delegate because their teams are already busy, but if you help them prioritise they could take on what you need them to do. Let your assistant, if you have one, scan and respond to routine emails. Arrange times you are available to your team rather than letting them interrupt you at any time. As one example, I see many people in my clinical work who use headphones when working to signal they are focused on a piece of work and are not available. Sometimes going around the team at the start of the day clarifies priorities and is an opportunity to give advice and can lead to fewer interruptions later. Arrange deadlines that are comfortable for you to have time to review work. Encourage and support your team, be available if they are out of their depth, help them prioritise, but don't over-manage them.

7. Be really tough on what meetings you accept

Do you know why you've been invited to this meeting or what the agenda is? What would be the consequences of turning it down? Some people only turn down a meeting because they have another meeting in that time slot, but think about what you could get done if you turned it down. If it's your meeting, how long does it need to be? Would 20 minutes do, maximum 45 minutes, allowing time to catch up before the next meeting, rather than attending back-to-back meetings? This is kinder to your bladder as well as your effectiveness.

8. Negotiate

If you are getting overloaded, consider negotiating deadlines, priorities and how much detail is needed. If need be, push back.

A partner in a law firm told me this story: he approached an associate one day and asked for her timesheets, pointing out she hadn't completed them for a while. He told me the associate looked at him as if she was caught in the headlights, broke down in tears and ran off, leaving him completely perplexed. It was only later that he realised that what she might have thought he meant was 'I need your timesheets now' and she already had too much to do. If she had said, 'I know, but I've got two tight deadlines for Friday lunchtime. By Friday afternoon you'll have the timesheets', he would have been fine, and she would not have got overwhelmed. Negotiate deadlines rather than getting overwhelmed or pushing your day later and later. Negotiating can protect your balance to life, your evenings, and your weekends. Sometimes it doesn't work, but at least you have tried.

Negotiate with yourself. How good does this need to be? Sometimes, dial down the standards to be more pragmatic and get it done in less time. What does the person really need in this email? Three points? Then give them three points, not three pages.

9. Have a positive mindset

Adopt a mindset that you are in control, that this is a challenge, and that by making the right choices you will stay on top of it.

Some people with too much to do are waiting for their manager to give them less. They have turned themselves into victims; they feel helpless in the face of all the things they have been given to do. Don't wait for your manager to give you less – take control of the problem, and take control of the conversation.

Alex

Alex is staying on top of a seriously overloaded job by doing all of this. She is in a senior role in a manufacturing company. It is a very busy job in its own right with several projects, as well as accommodating recent regulatory changes. Then her head of HR went off sick, leaving several very sensitive issues unresolved, including some senior recruitment decisions. Alex took on the HR role on top of her normal job. She has a son who is coming up to key exams. She has a sympathetic husband and they tend to share responsibilities, but her husband has a busy job in an architectural firm with some overseas clients. Nevertheless, they have a good relationship. Alex tries to get home to have some time with her son most evenings, and she tries to have time with her husband for a light-hearted chat before bed.

She is constantly aware of an endless list of things to do at work. Her email volume is huge; her PA scans them, and Alex deals with the ones that matter, as briefly as possible, but accepts that there are some she hasn't even looked at – 'If it's really important, they'll call me.' She is clear about her top priorities; with her PA's help, she blocks time in the calendar for key tasks, anything that can be delegated is delegated. She is ruthless in how she runs meetings and pulls out of meetings if other matters arise. She keeps her boss completely updated on what her priorities are and negotiates with him over some of the issues he needs.

She knows she is disappointing some people by not getting involved in things they think are important, and she knows she has had to ignore some things she would normally have focused on. But she is on top of the key priorities, she has not sacrificed her balance to life, she sees her son and husband most days, she cycles to work, she prioritises seven hours' sleep, she takes a break at lunchtime to have something nutritious to eat.

She occasionally uses Saturday as contingency time, getting up early and killing off some work that has to be done for Monday, but closes it off by lunchtime and her weekend starts there. She finds this works better than having a list of tasks hanging over her until Sunday night. She is holding it together by making good choices about her use of time, boundaries, maintaining some balance to life, not neglecting herself and her energy – all by ruthlessly prioritising.

Many people, however, even if they see the logic, find those changes in their behaviours too difficult to do. Some of them just appear to be too risky. Do emails in blocks? Risky – my clients/managers need to get my view on something, and it looks like I don't care if I don't respond immediately. Have an email boundary in the evening? Risky – someone might want to contact me and it looks like I'm not committed. Exercise at lunchtime? Well, I could – we even have a gym in the building – but it looks like I'm not one of the team. Negotiate a deadline, push back on some expectations? Risky – it looks like I'm not coping. Pull out of a meeting for an unexpected demand? Looks disorganised and as if I don't care about that issue or those people.

Any changes require two things: first, a realisation that our existing range of behaviours isn't working and we need to do something differently, and second, a change in mindset. Our attitude needs to change to unlock the flexibility to allow that change in our behaviour to happen. For example, the overloaded associate at the point of being overwhelmed should consider going to her boss and asking for advice or negotiating the deadline, but if her mindset is that asking for help indicates she is not up to the job and her boss will lose respect for her, she is blocked. Many of the attitudes that block us come from the personality pressures we have already looked at: conscientiousness, over-responsibility, fear of letting ourselves down. Sometimes we have to get close to a crisis to challenge those attitudes. It is just easier to work longer hours. Sometimes the attitude is so locked in that it makes us believe change is impossible.

Stefano

Stefano is a young analyst in a trading company. He is in one of the global teams, and his demands are constant. He is working for an overloaded manager who has given him good feedback on how he is working. He is bright, keen to learn, very committed, afraid of letting himself down. He works long hours and is exhausted by the end of the day. His balance to life has gone and he no longer gets the enjoyment from the work that he used to. He talks about the impossibility of getting everything done, despite working as hard as he can and taking very few breaks. He never gets to the bottom of the list that he has to do. Some days there are more items on the list at the end of the day than there were at the beginning. He feels he is failing, that he doesn't have the capability for the job.

Stefano is essentially working with a mindset that has him locked into a way of working that is making him feel he is failing in his job. First, he believes that if he were more experienced, faster, brighter, he would be more on top of his job. Essentially, as he sees it, because there is always more to do, this is proof that he is failing. That attitude could have many consequences, including working longer, often close to exhaustion, and feeling frustrated with himself. That attitude needs to shift to one of acceptance – there will *always* be too much to do; it's *just the way it is*. So long as I'm prioritising what really matters, I'm on top of it. The consequences of that could be a shorter day, better balance and feeling good about managing a challenging job.

The second attitude that has him locked in has to do with his perception of control. This attitude is basically expressed as 'it is up to my manager to control the flow of my work; if she wanted me to work fewer hours, she would give me less to do'. This is a helpless mindset. Stefano needs to find a more empowered way of thinking: 'It is up to me to take control of the demands, negotiate and discuss the priorities and push back. I need to take control rather than waiting for my manager to do something.'

The Big Wheel

One consequence of making better decisions about how we prioritise and how we deal with distractions could be that it gives us more flexibility to think about how we would like our future to look.

What goals do you have for your future? In a sense, what goals do you have that will shape your future? In future years, looking back on your life, what are the things you might regret not making time for? This gets to the Big Wheel. The Little Wheel is the day-to-day, week by week, never-ending list of priorities, tasks, projects, emails, admin things we do to keep others off our backs – a mixture of what matters and stuff that we can't really avoid doing. This can take the week, this can take your life.

But what would you like to bring into your life at some point in the future? What do people say when I ask them those questions?

- I'd like to work in another country for a while.
- I'd like to do an MBA.
- I'd like to play a musical instrument.
- I'd like to take six months off and work for a charity in Africa.
- I'd like to renovate a cottage in the mountains.
- I'd like to learn another language.
- I'd like to have children.

These are the decisions that could shape your future. These are the things you could regret not doing. None of these things are a priority for this week or this month. They can all be pushed out. But we can get to a point where we can no longer do them. They belong to a future that is now in the past.

So how could we bring these goals closer to the present? First, are you expressing the goal positively or negatively? When some people talk about longer-term goals, they say things like:

'I want to get out of London' or 'I need to get out of this job'. Put bluntly, these could be achieved by dying. And they give you no reference point for what a good decision is. You could move out of London to another location and still be unhappy. Positively phrased goals would be: 'I want to move somewhere where I could have access to the countryside' or 'I want to move to a job that would give me more opportunities to learn new skills and work with bigger clients.'

It helps if we share the goal with someone – a friend, a partner, a good colleague. Create a space among all the priorities, maybe once a month, to discuss it, to keep the goal alive. Research what you need to do, break it down into easier steps, build your enthusiasm, build the imagery of doing it. Now, how could you make it happen? Confront the risks, the fears, the costs. Balance the risks with how it would feel never to have done this. Now decide when you are going to create space for the Big Wheel.

Cath had become so overwhelmed and exhausted by work demands that she had no mental space to look at any of these longer-term questions. It was often too much of an effort even to make plans for the weekend.

Making better decisions about priorities, cutting back distractions, creating better boundaries, rebuilding midweek balance to life, making her energy and well-being a priority were all central to taking back control of her life. But less obvious were the subtle changes in how Cath was thinking about her life and work. Her mindset changed from a guilty, self-critical 'just do more' attitude to a mindset that balanced work with other priorities that were essential for her energy and good mental effectiveness. Without this attitude of flexibility and permission, none of the other changes would have occurred.

We have choices over how we think and consciously taking control of our attitudes can allow us much greater flexibility in our behaviour, having a direct effect on our emotions. Our mindset, our attitudes, directly affect the flexibility of our choices, our emotional stability and our health, physically and mentally. Our mindset affects every aspect of how we work, our relationships – ultimately our happiness.

6

Glimpses of reality

Imagine being inside Cath's head, listening to her inner dialogue and the emotions that go with it. As she has gradually slipped down the pathway that has taken her closer to exhaustion, her inner dialogue has become more self-critical and relentlessly pressurising, fearful of making a mistake or making the wrong decision, or of failing in some way; she is more aware of her inadequacies than of what she is achieving in difficult circumstances, guilty about letting people down. Her mindset is one of threat, of failure. You may recognise this in your own attitude to work.

Imagine being in Stefano's head as he struggles to stay on top of a constantly overloaded job, despite the long hours he is working. He too is in a mindset of failure and self-criticism, with every day a confirmation of his inability to live up to his expectations through the amount of work he has to do, and a perception that he is failing his boss by not getting everything done.

Imagine being in Nadia's head as she struggles to get everything done at work, fearful of being criticised and possibly losing her job, rushing home to make supper and get her children to bed before darting over to see her mother, feeling guilty about not having more time for them all, despite everything she is doing for them. Imagine her sitting with her mother, checking on her health, worrying about her, and making sure she has all she needs, vaguely apprehensive about how she will cope with everything tomorrow.

Now imagine being in Alex's head, listening to her inner dialogue. She is also in an overloaded job, doing essentially the work of two senior people, but she is much more accepting of the reality. Realistically, she knows she is letting some people down, but she does not feel guilty about it. She knows she is on top of what really matters, she perceives that her boss thinks she is doing an effective job in very difficult circumstances, she feels confident about her decisions and knows she is doing a good job as a mother as well as at work. Essentially, she is in a mindset of challenge – this is tough, but I'm making good decisions and I'm on top of it.

Those two mindsets – challenge or threat – will drive different emotions, but they also drive very different physiological reactions that ultimately impact on our physical and mental well-being.

There is an increasing body of fascinating research on how our mindset affects our health, our psychological well-being, our emotions, how we respond to stressful circumstances, and how effective and engaged we are at work. People who have positive attitudes about ageing live longer: they have a 7.5-year advantage. Researchers from Yale University note that as much as 75 per cent of longevity may be due to non-genetic factors. They looked at the impact of attitudes to ageing on longevity in a sample of 660 participants aged over 50, who responded to questions and statements such as 'As you get older, are you less useful?', 'Do I have as much pep as I did last year?', 'I am as happy now as I was when I was younger'. Controlling for other factors such as health, gender and socio-economic status, they found remarkably that those with positive attitudes about ageing lived on average 22.6 years past the baseline measure point, whereas those with more negative attitudes lived on average 15 years beyond the baseline. They essentially found that the effect of positive attitudes about ageing are greater than the effects on longevity of blood pressure, cholesterol, lower body mass index, no history of smoking and exercise.

I found it hard to believe this study when I first read it. How could the way you think have such an impact on how long people lived? But dig deeper. In a later study from Yale University, the researchers looked at the impact of positive perceptions of ageing and engagement with healthy behaviours. They found that those with more positive perceptions of ageing were more likely to have good diets, visit their physicians more regularly and maintain good exercise patterns in comparison to others who viewed ageing more negatively. It is as if those who view ageing more negatively were essentially saying, 'It's all downhill from here, so why bother?' So the mindset influences the choices that give rise to the outcomes.

Even the point where you see old age beginning has an effect on health. A UK study of over 7000 civil servants aged between 40 and 60 asked at what point they saw middle age ending and old age beginning. Over a seven-year follow-up period, those who believed old age begins at 60 were more likely to have suffered heart diseases and to be in poorer physical and mental health than those who believed old age began at 70 or later, when a host of other variables were controlled for.

A study by researchers in Ireland reports that having a positive attitude about ageing may help prevent older adults from becoming frail, and may help keep their minds sharp. On the other hand, having negative attitudes about ageing affects both physical and cognitive health in later years. This study assessed over 4000 men and women as part of the Irish longitudinal study of ageing on cognitive tests and assessments of physical frailty. Older adults with negative attitudes about ageing had slower walking speeds, and worse cognitive performance at a two-year follow-up compared to subjects with more positive attitudes, after controlling for other health factors.

You might think that the effects of exercise would be dependent on the type of exercise you do, or its intensity and frequency. But it's not that simple. Your attitude towards exercise has a major effect on what exercise does for you. In one study of 61,000 adults, researchers at Stanford University looked at mortality data over 21 years, and how much exercise the group did and how much exercise they thought they did compared with others of their age. What they found is fascinating. People who thought they weren't doing as much exercise as their peers died younger than those who thought they did more, even when the actual amount of exercise they did was the same. The mortality rate was 71 per cent higher in the group that saw themselves as less active than their peers, even when other health variables were controlled for.

Many people, through the type of work they are doing, are exercising more than they realise, and it is only when they are made aware of this that the effect of exercise becomes apparent. Researchers at Harvard University looked at the activity levels of 84 hotel housekeepers over seven different hotels. In their daily work, cleaning approximately 15 rooms, they get lots of exercise climbing stairs, pushing trolleys, lifting, vacuuming, changing sheets. The researchers simply made the housekeepers aware of how much exercise they were doing and how many calories they were burning. For example, changing linen for 15 minutes burns 40 calories, vaccuming for 15 minutes burns 50 calories, cleaning bathrooms for 15 minutes burns 60 calories (based on results for a 63kg/140lb woman). They were told that as a consequence of this activity, they were easily meeting recommended criteria for a healthy lifestyle.

The researchers divided the housekeepers into two groups. One group acted as a control, and the others were informed about how much exercise they were doing. Four weeks later, the women in the informed group perceived themselves to be getting much more exercise than before. As a result, they had lost weight, had lower blood pressure, lower body fat, and lower waist-to-hip ratios, and this despite *no change to their actual behaviours*. The subjects were not exercising more outside work, and they had apparently not changed their diets. The change in mindset alone seems to have created the physical changes.

Similarly, you might think that the number of calories you consume would have a direct effect on how your body registers that you have had enough to eat. Our satiation point is signalled by changes in the level of the gut peptide ghrelin. Yet in a study reported by Alia Crum, a professor of Psychology at Stanford University, we see that the production of this peptide is not only influenced by our calorie intake, it is also significantly influenced by our mindset. In this ingenious experiment, a group of 46 participants consumed a 380-calorie milkshake under the pretence that it was either a 620-calorie 'indulgent' drink or a 140-calorie 'sensible' drink. Their ghrelin levels were measured via blood samples before and after consumption of the drinks. Those who believed they had drunk an indulgent high-calorie milkshake showed a dramatically steeper change in ghrelin levels in comparison to those who thought they had drunk a low-calorie sensible shake. So our attitude towards what we have consumed has a bigger impact on physiological response than what we have actually ingested.

People who have a generally optimistic mindset tend to be healthier. Higher levels of optimism are associated with stronger immune function, lower levels of inflammatory markers, a healthier lipid profile, and healthier telomeres protecting us from age-related diseases. A recent study in the *American Journal of Epidemiology* following up a group of over 70,000 women found that higher levels of optimism were associated with a reduced mortality rate from a host of causes including cancers, heart disease and stroke. They are less likely to become depressed and have a higher quality of life after major surgery in comparison to those with more pessimistic attitudes.

People with an optimistic mindset cope with adversity differently from pessimists. They tend to face up to the problems rather than avoid or deny them. They are more likely to see the good in difficult life circumstances and even see how the experience has been of benefit to them. They are more likely to adopt direct problem-solving approaches, accepting the situation as it is rather than ignoring it, or going to self-blame, all of which is protective of their mental health.

Some of the research on optimism looks at specific ways in which optimistic attitudes have an impact on physiological measures. In one study, 200 healthy middle-aged women were given artery scans up to 14 years after they completed a measure of optimism. The study authors, Karen Matthews and colleagues from the University of Pittsburgh, report that the higher the optimism score, the healthier was the state of the women's arteries.

Your mindset about stress can affect your physiological response to being exposed to some realistically stressful situation. Being asked to give a speech while being evaluated by a group of experienced judges and being videoed at the same time is a standard technique for inducing stress in subjects, but Alia Crum at Stanford University found that our mindset about stress – whether you see stress as potentially enhancing your performance or as potentially undermining – influences how your physiology responds to the task. Subjects whose mindset about stress was that it was inherently performance-enhancing showed a much more moderated physiological response to the stressful task than did those who saw stress as potentially debilitating. The mindset acted as a buffer, helping to stabilise cortisol under stressful circumstances. Those who see stress as inherently harmful showed a more marked cortisol response to the stressful situation. The increased cortisol reaction of course would have an effect on breathing, heart rate and attentiveness, reinforcing their belief that stress was destructive to their performance.

Seeing stress as something that helps you to get to your best moderates your cortisol response, but also leads to higher levels of another adrenal hormone, Dehydroepiandrosterone (DHEA), a growth hormone that has a protective and regenerative role and is associated with physiological thriving.

While it is undoubtedly the case that many people standing up to give a speech while being filmed and assessed would feel threatened, others would not; they might feel challenged by the opportunity to do well, to make an impact, they might feel a competitive need to achieve. The situation would excite them. Threat or challenge are two opposed mindsets, which have dramatically different effects not only on how we behave, but also on how our physiology responds.

If you perceive some situation to be threatening, you switch on a cascade of physiological changes, including increased cortisol release, reduced cardiac efficiency, poorer cognitive performance, lower mood and increased anxiety; it can lead to avoidance and a sense of defeat. However, if you perceive the situation to be challenging, you trigger the adrenal motivational system that makes us mentally sharper and increases our energy and effectiveness. Essentially, it is the same situation; your body is responding to whether you see it as challenging or threatening.

Traditionally, it has been thought that people go to a mindset of threat when they face some situation without having the resources to master it. This is a logical way of seeing it, but I know many people who go to a perception of threat when they undoubtedly have the resources to deal with it. It is as if *threat has become a mental habit.*

The idea that we have mental habits, not just physical habits, can take us closer to the mental flexibility we need to manage the complex ambiguities of our pressurised lives. Generally, we assume that our perception of threat in some situation and the reality of threat are aligned, and most of the time they are. If you are walking back to your hotel through an underpass in an unfamiliar city late at night, the perception of threat could well be telling you something about the actual threat of being mugged. If you are skiing badly down a black slope and you suddenly remember you haven't bought insurance, then the perception of threat and the actual threat are aligned. But sometimes they are not aligned, and this can lead to lengthy periods of needless anxiety.

Sheena

Sheena, a young associate in a professional firm, discovers a mistake in a document she has sent to a client. Instantly, her head goes to an unforgiving catastrophe, imagining the client's angry reaction, complaints to the firm, an unrectifiable mess with her to blame, even the loss of her job. This can lead to sleepless nights, real physiological anxiety, a feeling of dread when she wakes. Eventually, she forces herself to confront the issue and talk to her boss. Then she faces reality, and reality is an experienced person who has seen this many times and calmly tells her how to deal with it. She hasn't lost her job; she doesn't appear to have lost credibility; life goes on, no disaster.

Will this experience change the habit of going to the worst outcome if anything goes wrong? Well, it might, but more often it doesn't. There is a temporary feeling of relief, but the mental habit remains as strong, waiting for the next mistake to trigger it again. In some cases there doesn't have to be a mistake to set off the sense of dread and imminent disaster. An experienced lawyer I know, having been informed that documents he had written years ago were being looked at by another firm of lawyers as part of a due-diligence exercise, immediately assumed they would find some error he had made and that there would be catastrophic consequences for his career. This feeling lingered on for some months until he eventually came to the conclusion that he would have probably been informed if anything had come to light. In both cases, the attitude of threat and reality were nowhere near aligned.

The task here is to find reality despite where your head may have taken you. Reality is not a catastrophe. Reality might involve an awkward conversation, as it did for Sheena, but the problem is solvable.

Unchallenged mental habits can create a wide variety of misplaced emotions: anxiety, depressed mood, guilt, unhappiness. They can unbalance the physiology of mental well-being, they can mess up our work effectiveness and our confidence, they can lead to avoidances, with us restricting our choices and our lives. Unchallenged mental habits can come to define us in negative restricted ways. But they are habits, and like all habits we can change them, resulting in far greater mental flexibility.

Mental habits we can learn to change

The first step in changing any habit is to develop a greater awareness of its impact. In the case of mental habits, we are dealing with attitudes and assumptions that lie just below the level of our awareness. We need to draw them into our consciousness and observe how they affect our emotions and our behaviours. Then we need to try to align what we are anticipating with the reality of what actually happens.

Look at the pairs of statements below and think about which one is more like you. This could give you a start in anticipating some of the mental habits that could be interfering with your emotional equilibrium and creating needless anxiety or undermining your mood and self-confidence.

1a. If I am anticipating some task I haven't done before, something a bit daunting, my head is likely to see how it could go wrong, how I could mess it up.
OR
1b. If I am facing something new, I tend to see it as an opportunity to develop and learn new skills.

2a. If I make a mistake, I typically see it as a personal failure. I have let myself down.
OR
2b. I view mistakes as inevitable and an opportunity to do something better.

3a. If something I am responsible for goes wrong, I tend to imagine really bad consequences.

OR

3b. Even if something goes wrong, I tend to believe that things will work out.

4a. If someone is annoyed at me, I tend to blame myself and see it as my having failed them.

OR

4b. If someone is upset with me, I tend to look at all the reasons they might be feeling that way.

5a. If I ask for help, people will see it as a sign that I am not coping and lose respect for me.

OR

5b. I tend to view people as approachable and understanding if I need help or if something goes wrong.

The statements reflect five mental habits that can adversely affect your mood and your confidence, make you feel more anxious and interfere with how effective you are at work.

1) The tendency to anticipate threat in some situation that is out of the ordinary. This could be taking on a new role at work, having to make a presentation to a large group, taking on a management position, but it could equally be something outside of work, like giving a speech at a friend's wedding, organising a family party, becoming a trustee of a charity or whatever.

2) The tendency to turn something going wrong into a critical generalisation or a judgement about yourself. For example, you can't get your new software to work, and instead of seeing it as a problem that you may need some help to resolve, you immediately go to how hopeless you are with technology.

3) The tendency to see unrealistic disastrous consequences of some mistake you have made. This is part of a perfectionist approach to life: if something goes wrong with you responsible for it, the result will be catastrophic for your career, reputation, future opportunities – the game is up.

4) The tendency to internalise, to see someone else's mood, particularly irritation or a bad mood, as being caused by something we have done.

5) The tendency to see other people as being too busy to help, or to feel that you will lose credibility if you ask for help.

Now, take a few weeks and, as objectively as you can, observe any examples of those mental habits, the emotions they created, and what the actual outcome turned out to be. For example, you are anticipating a meeting you have to run with a sense of threat, but when you are in the meeting, you can see that you are running it really efficiently. The anticipation of threat and reality are not aligned. The goal here is to get a more *objective* picture of reality, despite the mental habit.

Here are five mental habits you can change.

1. Going from threat to challenge

You are facing something new, something outside your experience; it feels daunting, where has your head gone?

Some people instantly go to threat: how I could fail. We have already looked at the physiological implications of perceiving something as a threat. If we see the event as a challenge rather than a threat, we switch on a more energising physiology, still linked to adrenaline, but driving competitiveness, taking us closer to our best.

So how can we take our head from threat to challenge?

Examine the threat. What is the worst that could happen? Often, if you examine the threat, it begins to dissolve. Don't let the threat lead to you avoiding it – avoidance is very damaging to confidence. Some

people perceive threat even in situations that are not novel, situations they have dealt with many times before. Talking in public often creates that perception of threat, an anxious anticipation that something will go wrong or of embarrassing yourself.

See what you are really good at, see what skills and qualities you have and how they could be applied to this task. Who could help you? Who could you talk it through with? Who has resources you could use? Visualise the opportunity here. What could success look like?

Think about your experience: other situations appeared to be threatening, but you took them on and succeeded. Play through the memory. Remember how you felt when you tackled it, the feeling of success afterwards, what the example led to. Taking the time to visualise how you will approach the task, replaying past experiences and connecting with the confidence that those experiences gave you can get you to the challenge mindset and help you mentally prepare for it.

Deliberately setting aside time for mental preparation after you have prepared the material greatly helps. Visualising presentations that have gone well and mentally rehearsing the presentation you are about to give, imagining the presentation going well with you engaging the group, can all take you to the challenge mindset, switching on the adrenalisation energised physiology.

2. Externalise the threat

Does your head go in or out?

- You are giving a talk and someone yawns. Does your head go to: 'She's bored, they're all bored, I'm boring', and you can feel your confidence dropping?
- You have someone on the phone giving you a hard time. Does your head go to: 'I've let them down – I'm just not up to this.'
- Your boss is in a bad mood. Do you see it as 'I've upset her' or do you see it as 'She's moody'?

Internalising is where you attribute circumstances that could be disappointing or threatening somehow to you – you have personalised the circumstances. This can create a feeling of apprehension, knock your confidence, or affect your mood adversely. It can take away the sense of achievement you could get in some situation.

Bear in mind that what we are aware of is simply our subjective reality and that can be driven by our mental habits. This is particularly evident in ambiguous situations. The task here is to find a possible alternative, more objective reality.

The meaning of a yawn:

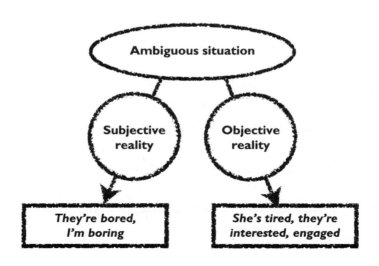

The objective reality focuses out, it externalises it. That yawning person might be tired, but the others in the meeting or presentation look interested, engaged.

Similarly, that person giving you a hard time on the phone might be really stressed. Take it slowly, explain the circumstances in more detail. Don't just assume you are failing. This is about finding two possible causes rather than attributing anything going wrong to your inadequacies.

By constructing another way of seeing the situation based on some external evidence, you allow a second perception to compete with the mental habit. If possible, validate your perceptions against the actual outcome.

Jason

Jason is an example of this. He is experienced in his job, ordinarily optimistic, determined, hard-working, someone who enjoys what he does, but one long-term client assignment threatened to completely undermine him. This client was a nightmare; nothing Jason did was good enough. Constantly demanding, he would call late at night, at weekends; he was emotionally volatile, would occasionally shout and rant on calls to Jason. It got to the point where Jason would feel panicky just seeing this client's number coming up on his phone. He was even occasionally dreaming about him. Jason realised he could not change the client or his behaviour. Could he change the way he saw him?

Jason tried putting himself in the client's shoes. What was it like being this person? Then he saw the awful reality of this person's life. Working for a company that was in a vulnerable state, trying to do something he had never done before, reporting to a volatile aggressive boss – Jason suddenly saw that this person's unpredictable rants were basically a very dysfunctional way of saying, 'Jason, I'm in trouble, I need your help.' When Jason saw this, his approach to his client changed – he became calmer and he felt less intimidated, more understanding. Interestingly, over time, the client's behaviour also changed in a more cooperative, less demanding way as the subtle dynamic of their relationship changed. Essentially, Jason had gone from a mindset of threat to one of challenge – how can I make this relationship with an unpredictable client work?

These mental habits are very common – they underlie many of the day-to-day anxieties that we experience. But think about their implications: an announcement about strategic changes, a new boss, regulatory changes, a company merger, automatically giving rise to a perception of threat. We would be living in a state of constantly raised anxiety.

3. Going from a catastrophe to a platform

Sheena's head immediately conjured up a catastrophe when she discovered the mistake she had made at work. After forcing herself to face up to a conversation with her boss, the expectation that she was facing some terrible unresolvable mess was disconfirmed as he calmly told her how to deal with it.

If you identify with this tendency to go to some mental disaster if something goes wrong, you will know that this is not a once-in-a-lifetime experience – it will have happened many times. But if you examine the actual outcome, it is highly probable that you are looking at events that were resolved or did not come to anything.

The expectation is that you are about to launch off a cliff edge and are facing some type of disaster, but reality is in fact a platform – maybe an awkward conversation, but it gets resolved.

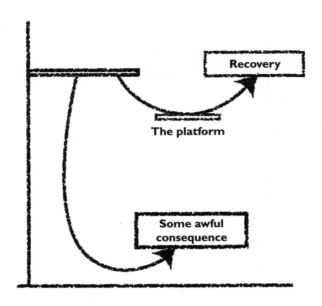

The first thing is to accept that your head goes to the disaster. This is the mental habit, but don't believe this will be the outcome. Construct a more likely outcome – the platform – in your head, and check what the outcome is over time.

If you think of all the times your head went to an anticipated disaster as a result of some mistake you made, and think about what the outcome actually was, what conclusions might you come to? Possibly that mistakes are fixable, or in some cases that nothing happens. Your head has taken you to an anxiety-producing black hole where all is lost, but reality is a platform – perhaps a conversation with someone – and we fix it.

4. Going from a judgement to a fact of life

Life is a series of facts, not disasters. Seeing them as facts will get us closer to dealing with them in a planned, effective way. But suppose you don't see the events as facts; suppose you see them as judgements.

Imagine you are a student looking forward to going on holiday after getting your exam results. The results come out and you discover you have failed one of them. Where does your head go? You give yourself a hard time, which is fair enough – that shouldn't have happened. You cancel the holiday, put together a study plan, and pass on the resit. Essentially, you are treating life as a fact: this has gone wrong, I need a plan. But suppose you don't treat it as a fact; suppose you treat it as a judgement. Then your head would go to: 'I failed the exam – I'm a failure.' That mindset of failure will undermine your mood and your motivation to study; it may make it very difficult for you to rescue your confidence enough to put a plan together.

Take some other examples. Imagine . . .

You work in sales; you have just done your third pitch, which has not succeeded.

- Life as a judgement: 'I haven't got what it takes, I'll never succeed.' With this mindset, you could give up, or have real difficulty reassuring yourself that this job will work out.
- Life as a fact: 'The economy is tough right now – keep going, the next one might succeed.' Or: 'I should consider some coaching to improve my presentation style in pitches.'

Your daughter has failed an important exam.

- Life as a judgment: 'I've let her down. I should have done more homework with her – this is my fault.'
- Life as a fact: 'OK, this has happened – let's put a plan together. I'll discuss it with the school and set aside some regular time to help her.'

This is about building the mental flexibility to deal with the circumstances more coolly and more effectively, without the emotion interfering with how you handle it. Essentially, this is about hearing the mental habit, the judgemental voice, and trying to set it aside. Then articulating the plan to deal with the actual circumstances – trying to separate the circumstances from the judgement. Now you have two dialogues: the judgemental voice, and the plan that deals with the reality. Two dialogues are better than one unchallenged judgement about yourself.

5. Going from over self-reliance to building support

Why don't some of us talk about what we are struggling with? Life would be easier for us if we did. In all likelihood, people around us would be helpful: they might give practical help, or help us see the circumstances in a less pressuring way; they might give us some ideas about how we could change the circumstances we are in.

As a minimum, they might help us feel less alone with the pressure we are under. It was only when Nadia had broken down in tears at work that she told her manager she was struggling to cope with the work pressures following the loss of the administrative supports. But the conversation was instantly helpful. Her manager pointed out that many people in the team were struggling with the demands, and encouraged her to be more flexible in how she worked, pointing out that she could take herself offline to get through some of the admin work if she wanted to. She also asserted that she was a really good team member, and that she should take a lunch break rather than work through the day with no breaks. She encouraged Nadia to talk to her if she was struggling, and she would help her prioritise what mattered.

It was only when Keith had had a panic attack in the office and seen his GP, who urged him to take time off, that he talked to his manager about how he had been struggling at work. Again, the conversation was immediately helpful. His manager told him about a time when she had sought help because of a combination of work and home pressures, and together they worked on a plan to prioritise what mattered, and what Keith could let go of. She urged Keith to delegate more and discussed how to push back with over-demanding internal clients.

But why wait until you are at breaking point before having the conversation? Many people feel that asking for help equates with saying that they can't cope; they fear others will lose respect for them, or there may be other consequences, like not being promoted or not trusted with other opportunities. Many fear that others will see them as having failed.

In some cases, the root of their excessive self-reliance can be seen in their childhood. Nadia grew up as the oldest girl in a family of four children; her mother suffered on and off with depression, her father was emotionally distant. Nadia took responsibility for bringing up her younger siblings; she learned to suppress her worries and get on with it. Keith was bullied at school and learned not to trust others, to keep his thoughts to himself and hide his feelings. It was only when he met his wife that he learned to be more open about his feelings, but only cautiously, unless what he said might be used against him.

Keith and Nadia both show a combination of four circumstances that have eventually destabilised them, and are evident in many of the people I see in my clinical work. You may see yourself in all or some of these.

1) An overly busy job has become overwhelming.
2) You feel alone with the demands.
3) You feel trapped.
4) Your balance to life has gone as the demands have taken over, leaving nothing to protect your energy.

Out of these four things, the one you can do something about with very little effort is that you do not need to feel alone. Opening up a conversation with a colleague or with your manager, even tentatively, could open a doorway that could change your circumstances well before it gets to a crisis point.

It could start by looking at people who you respect who are open with you about what they might be having difficulty with. Do you feel they are somehow diminished in your eyes because they asked you for help, or do you feel good about having helped them?

7

Our mental foundations: three powerful mindsets

One does not have to scratch far below the surface of some of the characters we have met to find a rich vein of perfectionism – standards so high that mistakes or setbacks trigger catastrophising thoughts and feelings of guilt or inadequacy if they are falling short of their expectations of themselves. You may now be identifying with some of these characteristics yourself.

Perfectionism is a mindset, a learned way of thinking that links directly to our behavioural choices and to our emotions. Some mindsets are particularly powerful for mental health, the stability of our emotions, our happiness, how we balance our lives and how we relate to our work. Some mindsets work for us and some undermine our emotional well-being. There are three mindsets in particular that we should be conscious of and try to shape so that they can work for us – perfectionism, our perception of control over life circumstances, and the purpose we see in what we do.

Some people see perfectionism as a virtue – indeed, some professional firms hold it up as what they expect of their employees – but perfectionism can become a mental tyrant. The perfectionist has a binary perception of their achievements. Something is either utterly flawless or a personal failure. There is nothing in-between, but of course most of life is in-between. Perfectionism can extend to all areas of life: work, being a parent, their social lives, the state of their home. There is a constant striving by the perfectionist and always the spectre of failure.

It is difficult for the perfectionist to feel a real sense of achievement or joy in what they have done. The best they get is relief that they have not disappointed themselves. It is difficult for the perfectionist to be happy.

So how do we get to grips with perfectionism? Perfectionism is a well-protected mindset. The idea of dialling it down equates negatively with lowering standards and embracing mediocrity. Perfectionism can be turned into a virtue and then you're in trouble. Perfectionism is no virtue. It is a real handicap to a good life, to a successful life, to a healthy, happy life.

Ellie

Ellie, in her mid-30s, was brought up in a commuter town outside London, and is now a mother with two young children alongside a demanding job in regulatory compliance. She now recognises how her perfectionistic mindset is working against her. She had always seen her very high standards as a good thing. She was encouraged by her parents to excel, both academically and in her sports interests: 'My parents always wanted to know where I had lost marks in exams.' She did well at school but didn't get into Oxford: 'It took me a long time to get over that rejection. It felt like a terrible failure. My parents were so disappointed.' She studied Economics, got a First degree, but it gave her little pleasure: 'To be honest, I just felt relief – I had been working so hard for a First, anything less would have felt like a fail.'

She gives everything to this job and to being a mother. She takes her children to school when she can and works an 11-hour day without breaks, constantly aware of the relentless pressures of the job. Her husband, Dave, usually gets home before her and does the homework routine – but not as well as Ellie would like: 'Dave doesn't push the girls so I go over their homework with them at the weekends.'

There is no balance to her life now: 'I used to have interests and I used to enjoy playing sports, but I don't have the time now. It would be selfish to take time for those things when there is so much more to do at work. And the weekends are dedicated to the children because I don't see as much of them as I would like midweek.'

Her standards are uncompromising. 'There is so much to do. Last Friday I didn't get to bed before two in the morning because I was decorating a cake for my daughter's birthday.' She is sleeping badly, and she is struggling with energy: 'I just feel tired all the time.' She is frequently in tears when faced with an unexpected demand. Her mood is low, she has lost her enjoyment in life, she is irritable with her children and then feels guilty and angry at herself: 'I'm just not fun to be around any more.'

Her relationship with Dave is strong but they get very little time together. They both work after the girls have gone to bed. They often go to bed at different times. Dave gets up early on a Saturday and gives the girls their breakfast, allowing Ellie a lie-in, and he plays squash on a Sunday morning. They are good friends, but no longer sexually close. 'I can't remember when we last made love – I just feel so tired,' she says.

Ten reasons *not* to be a perfectionist

There are 10 good reasons not to be a perfectionist, and Ellie exemplifies them:

1) Ellie's life has lost all balance. Working late, neglecting sleep, and with nothing to maintain her energy, she is becoming exhausted and heading towards burnout. Time for herself makes her feel guilty. Most perfectionists struggle to get any balance in life. They do not give themselves the permission to put themselves first.

2) Perfectionism is linked to depression, which is hardly surprising if you consider how high Ellie's standards are. Anything less than a First

equated with failure. There is very little scope for feeling good, for celebrating a success. If something doesn't work out it is attributed to not working hard enough or not having the ability. Ellie frequently compares herself negatively to others – at work with those who appear to handle work demands with less stress, and at home feeling guilty when she sees what other mothers are doing for their children.

3) Perfectionism is one of the main reasons people suffer from low self-esteem, which is also linked to depression. Ellie learned early on that to gain her parents' approval she had to excel at whatever she did. She compared herself to her older brother, who appeared to do well effortlessly at school, had lots of friends, and played rugby for his university before sailing into a well-paid job in a law firm.

4) The perfectionist lives in a constant state of agitation and busyness – they cannot relax. They might take up yoga or mindfulness but then they have to do that perfectly, which undermines the point. The agitation undermines their relationships and frequently the intimacy within it, which requires the ability to let go of demands and mentally and physically relax with your partner.

5) They can be over-pressurising as parents. Ellie recognises how anxious she gets about how her daughters are doing at school. She spends hours at weekends doing homework with them. She has organised tennis, drama and dance classes for them. If they go swimming she tends to coach them, correcting their swimming style, rather than just having fun with them.

6) The perfectionist makes a poor manager of others. They find it hard to delegate – in their view, nobody does it as well as they do. As Ellie put it, 'I don't trust anyone to be really on top of the detail. I do delegate but I check everything.' They tend to over-manage others to make sure their team members don't make mistakes. Ellie hates seeing typos in a document that one of her team has written: 'It has to be perfect,' she says. 'Typos are sloppy, they show you don't care about your work.' Ellie recognises that she overreacts to problems.

A problem will reflect on her not being on top of the job. For Ellie, it can be hard to suppress frustration and not get annoyed when others make mistakes or don't think issues through properly.

7) Someone with a perfectionistic mindset can be less productive because perfectionism can lead to procrastination. The anxiety about not doing something *really* well can lead to them putting off a difficult task in case they do not give it their best. Even replying to an email can take several drafts before they press send.

8) Change tends to lead to anxiety for the perfectionist. Change requires new behaviours, adapting to new circumstances, dealing with people with whom they are not familiar – greater scope for mistakes or making a poor impression. Change carries too much ambiguity for the perfectionist.

9) The perfectionist makes a poor leader. Leadership calls for fast decision-making, usually with imperfect information, and the ability to move on. The perfectionist is handicapped by the fear of making the wrong decision. They can become paralysed and bogged down in detail, and can become a bottleneck in decision-making, frustrating their team.

10) At the end of the day, perfectionism takes time away from other things that could be more worthwhile or rewarding; it has an opportunity cost. Some things need a lot of attention to detail, real care not to get something wrong, but other things don't. Yet to the perfectionist, everything is equal; there is no hierarchy of importance. Focusing – in the sense of being clear about what needs your time and what doesn't – does not come easily to a perfectionist. While some meetings need a lot of preparation, most don't; you can get by on your experience and knowledge. But not for Ellie: 'You have to be 100 per cent prepared for every meeting in case you are asked something you weren't expecting.' Time is finite, but the task list is infinite; you have to be very focused to cope with that. Anything you are choosing to spend time on is time away from something else – and that something else could be developing a new opportunity, or

making a decision about your balance to life so that your job doesn't end up burning you out.

Loosening the grip of perfectionism

Perfectionism is becoming more prevalent. A recent article in *Psychological Bulletin* reports the results of 164 samples, taken over a 27-year period, of over 41,000 college students in the US, Canada and the UK who had completed a perfectionism questionnaire. The average age of the participants at the time of completing the questionnaire was 20. The authors report that perfectionism measures have increased linearly over that time. They note that recent generations of young people perceive that others are more demanding of them, and they are more demanding of others and of themselves.

So how can we loosen ourselves from the grip of perfectionism, without running up against the fear of mediocrity? Telling yourself not to be perfectionistic won't work. Our brain is more adept at learning a new behaviour or a new way of seeing something, rather than trying to unlearn a well-practised mental habit. However, recognising which of the handicaps of perfectionism is affecting you could act as a strong motivator to change. You could try opening the zone that exists between something being flawless and it being a personal failure.

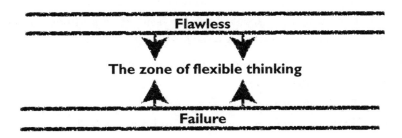

Seeing the zone of flexibility could allow you to recognise that this is the learning zone.

If you are in a new job, a trainee, newly promoted, doing a course, or a parent, you are going to make mistakes. It's through mistakes that you learn. If you are not making mistakes, you are being too cautious. The easiest way not to make a fool of yourself when you're learning to ski is by sticking to the green runs, but there is no fun in that.

It doesn't matter how experienced you are, life is changing fast. You will inevitably encounter circumstances that you haven't had to deal with before. At first you muddle through, but really it is an opportunity to learn and enjoy the discovery. This is the zone of self-deprecating humour, funny stories about skiing off-piste, cooking disasters, hours spent putting together a chest of drawers that falls apart after a week. Shared stories around the dinner table, told with warmth and humour, all coming out of being a long way from perfect.

The joy of pragmatism

This is the zone of pragmatism, of focused use of time. Let's consider Alex – she is doing two full-time jobs after her head of HR went off sick. She is a model of pragmatism. A perfectionist would have collapsed in her place, unable to let go of what doesn't matter, fearful of the consequences of letting people down; she would have ended up working impossible hours, neglecting sleep and in all probability getting ill.

This is the zone of experimentation and flexibility. Enjoy adapting how you run your life – always look for how you could make it work better. Many of the practical ideas we have looked at will be difficult for the perfectionist at first – more conscious of how they could fail than conscious of the opportunity they might be creating.

Exercising at lunchtime, doing emails in blocks, discussing priorities and deadlines with your manager, not looking at emails after you get home, turning down meetings in favour of other priorities, cutting an email to three points that the person needs to read rather than three pages of detail – these are all risky to the perfectionist. The pragmatist would embrace all of them with an open attitude of experimentation, and 'let's see what happens'.

Pragmatists are more focused on what really matters, they know what doesn't need their time, they get more done, they make faster decisions, they are more agile in the face of an unexpected demand, and they are better adapted to the fast-moving culture of life today. 'Be open – life is changing, I need to experiment' is the alternative to perfectionism.

It boils down to being kinder to ourselves. Realising that no matter how much we would like to do everything perfectly – at work, as parents – we just can't. Some things will go wrong, but life goes on. We might learn something from it, and while sometimes we don't, we are no less a person for this having happened. The core of who we are – hard-working, caring, reliable, likeable, bright – is still there. The discomfort, disappointment and embarrassment we might be feeling as a result of something going wrong will quickly fade if we let it. But if we hold on to it, over-examine it, ruminate on it, it will linger longer. It helps if you see this feeling of disappointment – from having made a mistake or not being judged as well as we would have liked – as part of what it is to be human; everyone around you at work or at the school gate will have felt this sense of letting themselves down at some point. It may have happened this morning after snapping at the children, who ended up crying on the way to school, or yesterday when you were reminded about an email you hadn't responded to by an irritated manager. Accept what has happened, try to be kind to yourself, and let it go.

Self-compassion

This touches on an area that is getting increasing attention in psychological research – self-compassion. This is about finding an inner voice of kindness to oneself when we have done something that falls short of our standards. Essentially, it is a healthy way of relating to ourselves. Many people I see in my clinic make the observation that they are often kinder to others than they are to themselves. But could you apply that compassionate voice to yourself, rather than being self-critical or judgemental? Self-criticism is a particularly destructive mental habit that can trigger feelings of low self-worth, anxiety and depression.

Self-compassion involves a recognition that *everyone* is imperfect; we all make mistakes and fail in some ways, and that realisation can make us feel that we are part of a 'shared human condition' rather than being alone in this experience. These realisations can allow us to reduce feelings of disappointment, shame or self-reproach, rather than agonise over them. Individuals who are high in self-compassion have better psychological health than individuals who tend to be more self-critical and judgemental.

Self-compassion is associated with higher ratings of happiness, optimism and curiosity. People who are high in self-compassion are more likely to persist in the face of setbacks and, as you might expect, they are less afraid of failure. Practising self-compassion has been shown to lower cortisol levels and heart rate variability. One study in 2018, conducted by Madeleine Ferrari and colleagues from Australian Catholic University, showed that self-compassion reduced the link between perfectionism and depression in groups of both teenagers and adults.

Serena Chen from the University of California, Berkeley, brings a business perspective to the topic of self-compassion. She found that people who can take a kinder perspective on their weaknesses and limitations are more motivated towards self-improvement and are more likely to see the potential for growth in difficult situations and work harder to improve their performance after feedback that they had performed poorly on an experimental task. She makes the point that self-compassion can be encouraged like any other skill, by thinking about shortcomings as something we all have and learning to keep them in perspective.

So how do you get closer to feelings of self-compassion? One way is to acknowledge to yourself how you are feeling about a mistake or disappointment. Detach by putting yourself in the role of a good friend hearing what has happened, and then writing out what that person is likely to say to you in a non-judgemental way. For example, if you're feeling guilty for being tied up at work and missing your children's swimming competition, and you are blaming yourself, what might a good friend say? Perhaps something like: 'Be kinder to yourself – you've been to every game this year so far, you would have had to cancel an important client meeting for this event, your kids know you try your best, you're encouraging of their sports, and sometimes life gets in the way.'

Researchers at York University in Toronto conducted a study in 2010 whereby they asked adults to write a compassionate letter to themselves once a day for a week, about any upsetting events they were experiencing. They found that their subjects showed a significant reduction in depression ratings and increases in happiness up to six months after the intervention, compared to a control group who were asked to write about early memories.

Our perception of control

Perfectionism can be seen as a struggle to keep life in control, but for a perfectionist the standards are set so high that there is the constant danger of feeling out of control. When life slips out of control, we start to feel overwhelmed and that perception gradually takes us down the pathway that can lead to ill health, physically or mentally – the pathway that can lead to depression, heightened anxiety and burnout. Retaining a sense of control over our life circumstances is a powerful mindset for health, energy, effectiveness in our work lives, and ultimately our happiness. But control-seeking needs to be held in balance. Excessive control seeking can work against our psychological coping and this is particularly the case for those who have perfectionistic qualities.

Imagine a dimension that goes from 'I feel empowered to exercise choices to make life work for me' all the way to 'I feel helpless, I do not feel in control of my life'. The closer you are to the helplessness end, the more likely it will open a doorway to ill health and depression. Many of the people whose stories we have looked at ended up at the helplessness end of the dimension, but they all then took a few steps to regain their sense of control.

Cath took control of the length of her work day, her diary, and how she dealt with emails. She created blocks of time for work tasks she prioritised, and delegated more to her team. Keith took control of boundaries to separate his work and home life, and negotiated an orderly approach to work so that he could prioritise exercise and time with his children. Hannah took control of her diary meetings, her availability to her team, and how she prioritised.

The very interesting thing is that at some point in taking control of those specifics, they all started to feel that they were in control of their lives. This renewed perception of being in control of their lives, rather than just their diaries or their emails, led to a raft of changes in their mood, their confidence and their energy, and they felt less anxious and generally happier about life.

Our perception of the extent to which we feel in control of our lives has a profound effect on our emotional well-being, our resilience and our physical health. Sally Dickerson and Margaret Kemeny at the University of California, in reviewing the findings of 208 laboratory studies of acute psychological stressors in 2004, found that two sets of circumstances could reliably lead to increased cortisol output: one was where subjects were put into a situation where they were evaluated by others, and the other was where the experiment involved uncontrollable outcomes. In real-life situations this would include people being rejected, humiliated or criticised in front of others in circumstances where they feel they have very little control over those circumstances. These are the characteristics that can create a really toxic work environment with the potential to undermine our psychological resilience.

Many of the studies on the effects of uncontrollable stressful events have been carried out on animals in laboratory conditions. Martin Seligman's classic studies in this area exposed dogs to uncontrollable electric shocks. When the dogs were later put into situations where they could learn to terminate the shocks, they failed to do so. Essentially, they had learned to be helpless. Subsequent studies on inescapable punishing circumstances have shown that the experimental animals show behaviours indicative of increased anxiety, immobility and withdrawal, as if the animals had become depressed.

These animal studies were carried out in the 1970s, and since then numerous studies on human subjects in controlled laboratory conditions have shown that when people believe they are in control of potentially stressful circumstances they are less prone to anxiety or depressed mood, they are more optimistic, and they persist for longer in the face of setbacks.

In a recent article, Steven Maier from the University of Colorado reviewed the evidence on the effects of controllable and uncontrollable stressful events on animals' behaviour and the neurological changes these conditions created in the brain. The studies show that the experience of control creates lasting changes in brain structures, which act to reduce the harmful effects of later stressful events, including events that are actually uncontrollable. In other words, the experience of control provides a form of immunisation against future stress.

According to a 2008 study, reported in *Biological Psychiatry*, by James Abelson and colleagues from the University of Michigan, a sense of control can even buffer us against the effects of a drug that directly stimulates cortisol release. The researchers led subjects to believe they had a sense of control over the unpleasant physiological effects caused by the drug, and found that this perception directly reduced their cortisol response, as well as their perceived distress. They gave subjects an injection of Pentagastrin to stimulate cortisol release. While administering the drug, one group of subjects was told that if the light on the table next to them was on, they could use the pump-control to stop or slow the infusion of the drug. They were told not to do so unless it was really necessary, but were assured the option was available to them. They were compared to a group that did not have this control option. Cortisol rose in all subjects in response to the Pentagastrin, but those who were told they had the option to control the release of the drug had a significantly reduced cortisol response – even if that option was not actually used. Such is the power of the perception of control.

How much control would you say you had over your cardiovascular health? Some people would say 'A lot', and back it up by telling you about their exercise habits, their diet, not smoking and so on. Others would say 'Not much', and say cardiac health is down to your genes, giving examples of people they know in their 80s who smoke 20 cigarettes a day and enjoy bacon sandwiches. In a study of over 10,000 people aged between 45 and 69 living in Poland, researchers from the Jagiellonian University Medical College in Krakow investigated the degree to which perceived control over health influences cardiac risk. Subjects completed a perceived control questionnaire and were followed up for five years. They found that those who perceived themselves as having low control over their health were more likely to suffer from cardiac illness over the five-year period. This was significant even after accounting for other factors related to their cardiac health, such as history of cardiovascular disease, hypertension, cholesterol levels, smoking, BMI, physical activity and diabetes. In other words, *perceiving* that you have high control over your health could be significantly protective of your health, irrespective of other variables.

People in senior executive positions, despite having to contend with greater demands as they become more senior, tend to have lower cortisol levels and lower anxiety ratings than people in non-leadership positions. Researchers at Harvard University in 2012, investigating the link between leadership and both physiological and psychological stress responses, compared people in senior positions attending an executive education programme at Harvard with participants recruited from the Boston metropolitan area. They found significantly lower cortisol and anxiety measures in the leadership group. In a second study, they found that those in senior leadership positions had lower cortisol and anxiety measures than other executives who held less senior leadership positions. They concluded that it is the perception of increased control acquired with leadership that has a stress-buffering effect, despite the increased work pressures.

How to build a stronger mindset

So in view of how powerful a perception of control is for our mental and physical well-being, what can we do in practical ways to build a stronger mindset of control over our life circumstances? So-Hyeon Shim, Alia Crum and Adam Galinsky, researchers from the University of Hong Kong, Stanford University and Columbia University respectively, addressed this question in a highly novel way in an article entitled 'The Grace of Control: How A Can-Control Mindset Increases Well-Being, Health, and Performance'. Making the point that most experimental attempts to increase people's sense of control have involved lengthy interventions commonly targeting the chronically sick or underprivileged, they describe it as 'a hodgepodge of different programs, making it difficult to tease out the most active and effective ingredients necessary to increase perceived control'. For two weeks, they encouraged their participants to develop a 'can-control' mindset by reflecting on aspects of their lives that they could control, while others reflected on what they couldn't control. So, for example, they might think about discussing or negotiating deadlines, or pushing back on some demands as things they could control, whereas not having anyone to delegate to would be something they couldn't control.

They found that the 'can-control' mindset group reported increased subjective well-being scores after the two-week intervention, while those who had been reflecting on what they couldn't control in their lives reported reduced scores. Ratings of optimism also increased in the 'can-control' group and dropped in the 'cannot-control' group. They also found that those in the 'can-control' group reported fewer days when they felt physically or mentally unwell in comparison to the 'cannot-control' group at a seven-month follow-up assessment. In a subsequent study, the researchers found that sales assistants, who had been taught how to develop a mindset of control, showed better sales performance over a two-week period, as well as increased measures of well-being and optimism, in comparison to a control group.

So-Hyeon Shim and her colleagues, by encouraging subjects to adopt a mindset of increased control over life circumstances, created changes in their subjects' physiology, emotions, behaviour and work performance. Cath, Keith, Tom and Hannah, by making some changes in how they managed their work lives, boundaries and priorities, arrived at a perception of being in control of their lives and their emotions became more balanced. Their physiology also stabilised, reporting better sleep, lower anxiety and better mood patterns. These factors – mindset, emotions, physiology and behavioural choices – are intimately interconnected: change one and the others change.

Purpose and meaning

To what extent do you feel that what you do in your life is worthwhile? Do you agree or disagree with this statement: 'I live one day at a time, and don't really think about the future?'

This question is getting at your sense of purpose in life – how meaningful you see your life to be. Purpose, the meaning you find in what you do, is a powerful mindset, predicting better health physically and mentally and protecting us from depression, and is linked to longevity. In later years, a strong sense of purpose correlates with better quality of life and has a protective effect on cognitive abilities. Research has shown that people with a stronger sense of purpose in later life walk faster and have greater upper body strength. Seeing purpose and meaning in life is associated with greater resilience and better recovery from traumatic events, whereas a sense of futility raises the risk of depression and overall ill health.

The Austrian neurologist and psychologist Viktor Frankl understood this all too well. In his short and highly inspiring book, *Man's Search for Meaning*, he describes how, by finding meaning in small day-to-day things, he survived his time in Auschwitz. Those who found purpose in even the most awful of circumstances were more resilient to suffering, compared to those who did not.

Frankl provides many examples of how apathy could be overcome and how spiritual freedom and independence of mind could be preserved. He remembers those who comforted others or gave away their last piece of bread. He tells a story of how he taught a friend who worked with him on the building site about the power of humour. According to Frankl, humour is one of our greatest weapons in our battle for individual preservation. He and his friend gave themselves the task of finding one humorous story a day, even in the midst of all the horror of the camps.

Frankl describes two examples where he helped fellow prisoners find meaning again to the extent that they stepped back from taking their own lives. In the first prisoner's case, Frankl did this by encouraging him to live for the day when he could be reunited with his child who was in another country, and in the second prisoner's case by reminding him of a scientific project that he had been working on and that only he could complete.

After the war, Frankl went on to develop his own school of psychotherapy, focusing on how we can find meaning in our lives. The approach is known as Logotherapy, from *logos*, the Greek word for meaning. At its heart is the belief that 'Man's search for meaning is the primary motivation in his life'.

Having a purpose in life reduces mortality risk across the adult years, as Patrick Hill and colleagues from Carleton University found in a 14-year follow-up study in 2014 of over 6000 adults ranging in age from 20 to 75. Participants responded to statements such as: 'Some people wander aimlessly through life but I am not one of them', 'I live one day at a time and don't really think about the future', and 'I sometimes feel as if I have done all there is to do in life.' Over the course of the follow-up period, 569 participants died and a significantly higher proportion of those people had lower scores on the 'purpose in life' questions.

For some people, a sense of purpose in life never dies, no matter how long they live. Robert Marchand holds the record for fastest cycling speed in the over-105 age category. Marchand took up cycling at age 68, broke the record in the over-100s category (at more than 14 miles in an hour), and in 2017 broke his own record in the new over-105s category. He was a bit disappointed by his time, however, and is waiting for a rival to take him on. Commenting on his achievement after the race, he said: 'I did not see the sign warning me I had 10 minutes left. Otherwise I would have gone faster. I would have posted a better time. I'm now waiting for a rival.'

A 2019 study from UCL researchers Andrew Steptoe and Daisy Fancourt extended the findings on the advantages of having purpose in life. Their longitudinal analysis also showed that those who scored more highly on their measures of purpose went on to do better financially than those scoring lower on purpose and meaning. In other words, feeling that you have a purposeful life gives you a better life mentally, physically and economically.

Unfortunately, it is easy to lose sight of this in an overly busy life where you feel constantly pressured to do more and more at work and at home. The purpose can be reduced to just getting through the day, ticking off as many things on the list as possible, not letting the inbox get out of hand, making sure the homework gets done and the children are in bed by a reasonable time. But occasionally, slow the day down and take a few moments to reflect on the purpose of what you are doing, to allow a sense of appreciation. The purpose in reading your son that story before he goes to sleep, the purpose in helping with the homework, is bigger than just getting it done so you can move on to the next thing.

If you are coming into work looking at a list of meetings and your head loses the reason you are going to those meetings, you are moving closer to a sense of futility and that mindset will undermine your motivation, your energy and your potential enjoyment of the day. If you really can't see why you've been asked to go to a meeting, then it might be worth considering if there is something you could do that you would find more purposeful instead.

It is no surprise that in Andrew Steptoe and Daisy Fancourt's article, those who see life as more purposeful were more socially connected and engaged in community activities, and were more likely to be doing voluntary work rather than pursuing passive activities and watching television. Even in a really busy life, doing something for others can increase our sense of purpose and meaning. This could be helping a colleague with a task that is confusing them, phoning a friend for a chat, taking an interest in a colleague's home life, getting some groceries for an elderly neighbour, or making life easier for someone in a practical way. Just being cheerful can add to your sense of purpose when you observe the impact it has. Find the meaning in the small, day-to-day things you do.

'Everything lies in our attitudes. If we can master our attitudes, we can master ourselves and our lives' is a highly empowering quote from the British philosopher A.C. Grayling. Hopefully this has made you more aware of how your attitudes influence your physical and mental health and how old, unchallenged mental habits can create feelings of anxiety and disappointment and undermine your mood and self-confidence, and given you some ideas for creating more flexible ways of thinking. All of this could have a very beneficial effect on every aspect of your life.

Three core attitudes

1. Approaching life with a flexible, pragmatic, self-accepting attitude	vs	Closed, inflexible, perfectionism
2. Seeing how we can take control of some aspects of our lives, however difficult the circumstances	vs	Helplessness
3. Seeing purpose in our lives	vs	Futility; what's the point?

These three core attitudes provide a foundation to our mental health. If these are solid, it is much easier to challenge and change the mental habits we looked at in the last chapter: the tendency to build catastrophes or to attribute any mistakes to our incompetence, and to build critical judgements about ourselves when something goes wrong.

Having those core attitudes grounded in our thinking can allow us to approach challenges in life with greater confidence and resilience. But if they weaken, it can leave us feeling more emotionally vulnerable, more self-doubting, more prone to feeling anxious and threatened by life events turning against us.

The choices we make about our mindset is one more crucial piece in the integrated system of cause and effect relationships that keep us closer to the optimal place in the energy and effectiveness curve. Making good mental choices can take us closer to happiness and overall contentment with our lives. All of this can have a major effect on how we work, how we deal with uncertainty and change, and the chances that we will thrive and succeed in the work we do.

Ten exercises to change your mindset

Now let's look at 10 short exercises that could help you to change how you think for greater mental flexibility and resilience – how talking, rationalising and visualising can make a difference to how you feel.

Depending on what comes up in your day, try doing one or two of these mental exercises. They'll take no more than a few minutes, but the effects could make a real difference to developing healthier, more robust attitudes to life. With practice, they could become your alternative way of seeing what is going on in your life – your new mental default position, rather than self-criticism or threat – and you'll start to rewire your thinking.

1. Develop the challenge mindset

Visualise whatever it is that you are anticipating with some sense of threat. Visualise yourself doing it well, even enjoying doing it. Visualise your surroundings and who you are engaging with. Keep this image in your mind for 20 seconds or so while you are relaxing in some way – going for a walk or sitting somewhere where there are no other demands on you. Do this several times until the image becomes stronger and more convincing. Then write down three qualities or skills you have that could allow you to succeed in that situation.

2. See platforms, not catastrophes

Think about whatever has gone wrong that is propelling your head to a potential catastrophe. Now visualise what a platform would be – a more likely outcome rather than a catastrophe. Talk it through with someone you trust to get another perspective and add their perspective to reinforce the platform. This could be a conversation you need to have with someone who could resolve the problem or visualise some point in the future where in all likelihood this will be behind you. Now visualise a second image: the last time some imagined disaster came to nothing or was resolved after a conversation with someone helpful.

3. Reinforce a mindset of control

Do you sometimes get overwhelmed by too much to do, or anxious about too much uncertainty? Write down two things you could take control of. Step back, make a tentative plan about how these two things could help you get on top of it.

Back up the image – visualise the last time you felt this way and the point where you got on top of it and felt in control. What helped you get there? For example, a teacher I know has become overwhelmed by everything she has to do before the end of term – the exam papers, end-of-term assessments, and preparation for the end-of-term concert she is leading. It all seems too much, she is feeling panicky about all of it, and her sleep is disturbed by anxious dreams about work.

So what can she control? She could make a plan and decide what needs to be done daily. She could cancel some commitments that are in her diary but are not so important. She could also develop an image in her head: she could recognise that she often feels this way towards the end of term, but she always gets everything done. So, in this case, visualise the last day of term, the final performance of the concert, the marking is done and the assessments. This day will come and she will have achieved all of these things, because she always does.

4. Visualise perseverance

A setback has undermined your confidence – you have become self-critical and judgemental of yourself. Visualise what a plan would look like to deal with this event – imagine persevering, making one more attempt. Write down two reasons why you believe you have the capability to do this. Now visualise having overcome this setback and succeeding – hold this image for 15 to 20 seconds.

5. Try to externalise what has upset you

You have attributed someone's behaviour to a weakness you perceive within yourself – psychologists would say you have *internalised* it. For example, you are in a conversation with someone who is irritable and you assume they are annoyed at you. Well, maybe the irritability isn't caused by you. Maybe they are frustrated by something that happened before this conversation. But by assuming you are the cause, their behaviour has made you feel guilty or anxious. Write down two reasons why the person could be behaving this way, and how it has nothing to do with you.

6. Practise letting go of tasks

Having difficulty letting go of something because it's not perfect? Think pragmatically: what is the purpose of this task and what do you need to do to achieve this? Then think of two other things you could be doing with the time if you didn't spend it improving this task. Visualise what you could do with the time and see the purpose you would get from those choices.

7. Replace perfectionism with pragmatism

About to start on something where you would normally be perfectionistic? Ask yourself: 'What would a pragmatic approach look like?', 'In this situation, what would be the advantages of being pragmatic?' The purpose is to help you become aware that there is a choice, even though you would normally see perfectionism as the only way.

8. Use humour
If you have messed something up, rather than get embarrassed or self-critical, turn it into humour and share the story with a good friend.

9. Learn from the setbacks
Think about something that has not gone according to plan – write down anything you have learned from this experience.

10. See the purpose
Take a few moments to visualise something you did today that gave you a real sense of purpose. Hold this image in your mind to really connect with that sense of purpose and meaning.

8

Mindset at work

What about happiness? Happiness is an emotion – and also a mindset. Are some people just more naturally happy and others are not? The technical word for the naturally cheerful, by the way, is euthymia. Does happiness give us an advantage in life – in our work lives and in our personal lives – or does it just follow from good experiences? Can we learn how to enhance happiness, or will it always be a transient feeling, disappearing as soon as the temporary cause of it has gone?

Happiness gives you an edge when it comes to having a good life. But what do we mean by happiness? Historically, happiness was a subject for philosophers and, in their hands, it did not fare that well. The Canadian philosopher Charles Taylor described it as a thin concept. Not as insulting as George Bernard Shaw, however: 'There is nothing so insufferable as happiness, except perhaps unhappiness.' Happiness for him was 'self-centred, transient, sterile, and uncreative'. Or Terry Eagleton, the British philosopher and author of *The Meaning of Life*, who described happiness as 'a feeble holiday-camp sort of world'. And then there is Beckett, who dismisses happiness as something so transient that it disappears as soon as we are aware of it.

Not encouraging stuff. It is as if, to them, happiness is a state of complacent, idle contentment that takes away any drive to do anything meaningful with our lives. But the current research suggests the opposite: that happiness is a driver of success. Today, happiness is a subject of considerable scientific interest, studied by psychologists, neuroscientists and even economists.

We could look at happiness simply as generally feeling good about life more often than not. Researchers Julia Boehm and Sonja Lyubomirsky from the University of California define a happy person as 'someone who frequently experiences positive emotions such as joy, happiness, and contentment'. It is not about experiencing enduring intense feelings of pleasure, but about frequently experiencing positive emotions. And it's not about being happy all the time. Our emotions are reactive to changes in our circumstances, not just over a long time span but day-to-day, hour by hour. Changes in our circumstances could create feelings of sadness, disappointment, frustration, perhaps anger, apprehension or anxiety, as well as feeling great some of the time. Variations in how we feel is a sign of emotional health, just like heart rate variability is a sign of physical health. These emotions are transient; our mood then returns to its baseline and if that baseline is generally positive more often than not, then that reflects a positive mindset about your life.

Happiness brings many rewards. Happy people are less prone to depression, they are less likely to use drugs, they report higher quality of life. Even when they are suffering from illnesses, they report better health; they show a stronger immune response. People who report higher levels of well-being have lower mortality rates. Happiness links to more satisfying relationships and better friendships.

Happiness also creates conditions for greater work success. Employees who are generally happy about life get better job evaluations from their managers, they handle managerial jobs better and show higher work performance and productivity. They are also more likely to earn more. Over 30 years ago Martin Seligman, a Professor of Psychology and one of the founding figures of the positive psychology movement, reported that insurance agents with a more positive approach to life sold more policies than less happy colleagues.

Now, since much of the evidence is correlational, you could say: 'Well, if I had a happy relationship with lots of friends, I was in a good job, rated highly by my managers, and was earning a lot, I'd be happy as well.' But there are many longitudinal studies that lead to the conclusion that happiness precedes those positive outcomes, rather than being the consequence of them. A review of the evidence on the advantage of happiness on our health, relationships and on work success by Sonia Lyubomirsky and colleagues in an article titled 'The benefits of frequent positive affect: does happiness lead to success?' leaves us in little doubt that happiness precedes those positive outcomes. For instance, happiness assessed at the age of 21 predicted marital satisfaction many years later. As far as work outcomes go, college students rated as more cheerful were earning more in their 30s. They were also likely to get more favourable ratings from their managers and were less likely to lose their jobs.

For Gretchen Spreitzer and Christine Porath, professors in US business schools, happiness is about thriving. Others see it as flourishing. They identify those people as having vitality and being constantly interested in learning. They report that across various industries and job types, individuals with a thriving mindset showed 16 per cent better work performance and were 46 per cent more satisfied with their jobs. They were also less prone to burnout and had less sickness absence. Blue-collar workers who scored highly on their measures of thriving had performance measures 27 per cent higher than their lower-thriving colleagues, and were 53 per cent more likely to progress in their careers.

So, it looks as if happiness gives you an edge as far as success in life goes. If you look at some of the other characteristics that happy people tend to show, it goes some way to explaining why they have that edge. It is as if happiness creates the conditions for success.

People rated as happy tend to be more energetic and active, and more engaged in life. They are more likely to be cooperative and less likely to get into conflicts with others. They are more skilled at conflict resolution. They are more likely to be creative, mentally flexible and to persist if they encounter obstacles. They are better able to cope with organisational change and they are more likely to receive support from others as a consequence of how they relate to people and their positive mood.

Now, you might say that happiness is dispositional, that some people are born happy, others are more likely to see the more miserable side of life – glass half-empty, and so on. But it has been estimated that happiness is 40–50 per cent due to heredity, and 10 per cent due to the circumstances we are in – which leaves a large percentage for us to use to develop this positive mindset.

Daniel Sgroi, from the University of Warwick, induced feelings of happiness in subjects in a laboratory setting, either by asking them to watch a 10-minute comedy sketch or by providing drinks and snacks. He then measured their productivity, including accuracy and effort, on numerical tasks lasting 10 minutes. He found that the simple interventions did increase happiness on a rating scale and that increase in happiness resulted in an improvement in productivity of between 10 and 20 per cent. The effort was noticeable in the degree of effort the subjects put into the tasks, rather than in accuracy, and there was a direct relationship between the increase in happiness and increased productivity. In Sgroi's later study, he found that subjects who had experienced a bad life event in the past three years, such as serious parental illness or bereavement, scored lower on the happiness ratings and were around 10 per cent less productive on the lab task, with the effect particularly noticeable if the event had happened within the previous year.

Shawn Achor demonstrated what can be achieved through practising a simple exercise on a regular basis. Working with a group of tax managers working for KPMG in New York, he asked them to practise just one of five activities that correlate with happiness ratings for a three-week period. The exercises included jotting down three things they were grateful for, meditating at their desks for two minutes, and keeping a daily journal of meaningful experiences. When the group who took part in the exercises were compared to a control group four months after the intervention period, the experimental group showed higher scores on optimism and life satisfaction. Their mean scores increased from 22.96 to 27.33 on a 35-point scale on a life satisfaction measure – one that is a strong predictor of productivity and happiness at work.

Boost your happiness baseline

So, are there things you could do to boost your happiness baseline? Read any article in popular magazines about happiness, and the gratitude exercise comes up. Count your blessings, take some time to reflect on how many things you feel grateful for today. This has become one of the biggest clichés in psychology, but it is worth trying from time to time – certainly better than counting all the people who have annoyed you or events that have frustrated you. But it would be hard to gain much from a gratitude exercise if all you are thinking about is a catastrophe that you believe is imminent because of some mistake you have made, or some setback.

The first step to increasing your happiness baseline might be to counteract the habits that are undermining your happiness. Those mental habits are acting like ballast, preventing the balloon from taking off.

Those habits could be day-to-day routines that are undermining energy, preventing you from getting balance in your life, and leaving you feeling overloaded by demands. Or they could be mental habits driven by perfectionism or by too great a sense of responsibility for things you can't control, or by a tendency to default to self-criticism if anything goes wrong.

It's difficult getting to happiness if those habits are constantly undermining you. You need to be in the good zone of the energy and resilience curve to be able to sustain feelings of happiness. You lose the potential for happiness the further down the curve you go. To be in the good zone, your physiology needs to be in balance – your neurotransmitters need to be primed for happiness. That needs balance and anchoring the routines that maintain your energy and stable mood.

Ten steps to happiness

1. Get the basics right

If you read descriptions of what it feels like to be happy, words like vitality, energetic and active come up repeatedly. It's difficult to feel happy about life if you are struggling with energy or feeling exhausted much of the time.

Similarly, it's hard to feel happy if your life is completely out of balance and you are feeling guilty about not seeing enough of your children or your partner or you are feeling resentful about having no time for yourself. And it's hard to feel good about life if your core relationship is falling apart and you are coming home to arguments, criticism, abuse, or long periods of silence. So we need to focus on the basics – back to the earlier chapters on creating some balance, building in slots of time for routines that reinforce energy and a handful of things that make for a happy, connected relationship. Doing some things to make your partner happy is likely to make you happier – it's difficult to be happier than your partner.

Getting the basics right

Which ones are anchored in your life, week by week? Which ones have you drifted away from?

- Exercise
- Relaxation time
- Sleep
- Good diet
- Time with your partner
- Time with friends

---

2. Develop mental flexibility

Develop greater mental flexibility to challenge some of the mental habits that might leave you feeling guilty or self-critical or undermine your peace of mind.

- The flexibility to see that although your head has gone to a potential catastrophe, the outcome is likely to be something manageable – a platform.
- The flexibility to resist seeing that you are the sole reason that something has gone wrong in your life – balance the causes.
- The flexibility to be kinder to yourself and recognise your flaws without being judgemental and losing sight of the qualities that you could feel good about.
- The flexibility to allow yourself some healthy selfishness, to take time for yourself to get balance in your life without feeling guilty.

3. See your impact

When you feel that life is going against you, when you feel close to overwhelmed – like many of the people we have met – it is important to see the impact you do have. This is about seeing what you are naturally good at and observing the effect it has. When I ask people like Hannah, Cath or Keith what they are good at – just naturally good at, without self-doubt – they often struggle to answer the question. They find it easier to tell me what they are not good at. But eventually they come up with a few things: 'I'm good at problem-solving', 'I'm a good communicator', 'I'm good at developing relationships', 'I'm good at taking the heat out of a crisis', 'I'm good at motivating people.'

You only need to get to a handful of skills, maybe two or three, but you do know you are good at them. Now try to see the impact of those qualities as often as you can to observe the impact as it is happening – let the room give you the feedback. Even when other things are not going well, this is a good way to cut through the noise and see what you do well, and the effect it has.

Now go beyond what you are good at and get to your core qualities – the characteristics that come close to defining you. Qualities like warmth, intelligence, likeability, decisiveness, reliability, supportiveness, humour, creativity. We should be grateful for those qualities; they have contributed to everything we have in life, everything we appreciate – our relationships, friendships, where we have got to in our work lives. Seeing those qualities express themselves day-to-day and seeing the impact of them can allow us to focus on what really matters and let go of other things that may not be going well. Seeing the impact of our core qualities can allow us to be kinder to ourselves when things go wrong – they can balance perfectionistic tendencies.

4. Acknowledge how you deal with life's random resilience tests

Most weeks, life will throw some random resilience tests at you. It could be an IT failure as you are about to send a document too close to the deadline, a transport failure on a day you have to be in early, somebody letting you down when they have promised you information you need, one of your children being sick on the most inconvenient day, your childcare not being available.

One characteristic of living in the good place in the curve is having the spare mental capacity to deal with those resilience tests. If we start to edge into the curve, beginning to feel overwhelmed, struggling, less confident, those random events can seem too much to handle – it is like life is conspiring against us. There is more likely to be an emotional reaction to them – anger, irritability, breaking down in tears, blaming someone who has nothing to do with it, all signs of exhausted mental capacity.

Underneath this reaction, of course, is the victim mindset: 'This should not be happening to me.' But these things happen to everyone: this is life. You need to get to the resilience mindset, starting with:

- **Acceptance** – focus on the problem, don't waste time blaming, step back and think: What needs to be done?
- **Finding flexibility** – make some changes to your plans for the day: What can I take control of here?
- **Prioritising** – determining what needs to be done and reorganising other things: What do I need to let go of?

Now see yourself handling it without getting overly frustrated or emotional, maybe even enjoying the sense of being flexible and getting through this resilience test.

There is evidence that the difference between people who get more distressed by day-to-day stressors is not in the number of events they have to deal with, but how they deal with them. Keeping a note about how you deal with life's random resilience tests can give you an added degree of detachment and can be very reinforcing.

5. Give support to others

The support you give to others is as important as the support you receive. Being part of a team where others are supportive – there for you when you need a helping hand or a sympathetic conversation – is well recognised for its effects on buffering people from the pressures of life. Less recognised is the impact of the support you give to others. At times when you are really busy, it is very easy just to try to get through the demands and cut out any interaction with others around you. The last thing you need is somebody coming to you with something they are struggling with. But those people who are supportive of others at work are likely to feel more engaged and happier at work than people who cut themselves off from others.

Shawn Achor, writing in *Harvard Business Review*, quotes a study he carried out with Phil Stone and Tal Ben-Shahar on over 1600

Harvard students, which found that social support was one of the most significant contributors to happiness at periods of high stress. Those participants who helped others cope with work demands and generally put themselves out for others were 10 times more likely to be engaged at work and 40 per cent more likely to be promoted than those who were less involved with others.

This links to the idea of the contribution you give beyond the role you do. Some people are content to do the role they are hired to do, but others make a contribution beyond the role and this contribution comes from their personalities – warmth, supportiveness, humour, helping out, taking the initiative. If you left your job, the role would be replaced, but the contribution might not be. It's the contributions that make up the personality of the team. It's the quality of the contributions that people think back on with a sense of fondness after they have left. So consider your contributions and day-to-day examples – like helping someone who was out of their depth, or sharing a humorous story, or teaching a junior person a skill they need – because those day-to-day examples of contributions beyond the role contribute to your overall happiness at work.

In the bigger picture, the quality of your relationships is a better predictor of your happiness than what you possess. Appreciate those relationships at home and at work. Occasionally express your appreciation. Make your work life social, have lunch or a coffee with colleagues, allow time in a meeting to chat about what's going on in your lives. At home, encourage the fun and humour in your relationships with your partner and your children. It's the closeness of the relationships that get to happiness, not the things you are aspiring to own.

6. Tackle what needs to be done
Most of us put off doing what we don't want to do. Many people keep themselves busy doing things they don't really need to do in order to avoid something they should tackle. We can waste hours procrastinating

rather than starting some task that appears to be too difficult, messing up our balance to life by forcing us to work late when we could have got on with it earlier. All that agonising, leading to avoidance. We can avoid a task like writing a report or starting a project, we can avoid going for a health check, we can avoid opening a letter that could contain some bad news, we can avoid making a phone call because of a fear of rejection, we can avoid a difficult conversation. Avoidance undermines our confidence and can depress our mood – it's certainly not a path to happiness.

Tackling something, on the other hand, gets closer to confidence and a stronger feeling of coping with life. A study by Maria Dijkstra and Astrid Homan of 543 people in the Netherlands, published in Frontiers of Psychology (2016), explored how people cope with stressful circumstances. It found that those who face up to the stressful events and confront them actively have a stronger sense of personal control, which in turn leads to better psychological health. Those who tend to avoid the issue or disengage from it have poorer scores on measures of psychological well-being. So make a list of those tasks you are likely to put off, schedule a slot in your diary, remove distractions and tackle them. Warm up to the more difficult ones by tackling some of the easier ones to get into a roll. Once you've got them done, give yourself a break and do something to reward yourself. But you'll feel a positive sense of accomplishment as you tackle them.

7. Develop a mindset of permission

We have looked at many examples of people with seriously unbalanced lives that ultimately took them down a pathway towards ill health, physically or mentally. Underlying their approach to life and work were rigid attitudes – about responsibility, conscientiousness, often perfectionism – that blocked the flexibility they needed to sustain their energy, their balance to life, and their effectiveness in demanding jobs. To make any change sustainable, they all needed to find a mindset of permission. The alternative is a constant feeling of guilt.

Consider this mindset: This is a very demanding job and I have many demands at home – anything I am doing that is not for work or my children is time away from my work or children, and that leads to guilt.

Consider this mindset: This is a very pressuring job and my home life is demanding, but if I am going to be effective into the long term, I need to prioritise time for looking after my energy and my effectiveness.

The first mindset is close to the way of thinking of many of the people we have looked at. Trying to persuade them to do anything for themselves, to create time for exercise or relaxation or to get to bed earlier, will all run up against the rigid mindset of guilt. Their mindset needs to change for greater flexibility, balance, and ultimately for a better life.

Hannah

Hannah recognised that her mindset had become too rigid and was constantly making her feel she was not up to the job. Looking at her background helped her to understand where this mindset had come from.

Hannah was the third child in a family of five children. Her parents were loving, but life was a struggle financially. She has good memories of playing on the family farm with her siblings, but as the oldest girl, a lot of responsibility was put onto her to look after the others. Her mother was seriously ill when Hannah was 12 and she took over her mother's role, making sure her brothers and sisters were cared for emotionally as well as physically. Academically, she grew up in the shadow of her two older brothers, both of whom went to good universities and into professional jobs. Hannah struggled at school, but she got a good degree. She was popular, played sports, got into drama and had a good time at university. She went into advertising, a good fit with her personality. She came to London, worked for a firm in New York, and then in the London office of an international agency where she was promoted to a senior job. She runs a major account and is recognised as a really good leader. In career terms, she has done better than her brothers. However, since her early years she has felt second best, and not bright enough, despite constantly achieving. She lives in the shadow of early disappointments. Although she recognises that she has come a long way in life, her perception of herself has not kept up with the rapid trajectory of her life. Her mindset is one of insecurity, blaming herself if anything goes wrong, anxious about failing or letting others down. Her long hours at work, constant availability, her neglect of time for herself are a natural consequence of this mindset.

As part of her approach to restructuring how she dealt with work pressures, rebalancing her life and changing how she prioritised her work and home demands, Hannah took a number of steps to change some of her mental habits. It started with a recognition of some of the things she was really good at – making good relationships, communicating well, running teams – and seeing the impact of those abilities day-to-day.

She started taking a few minutes before she went home to review her day: What has gone well today? Who have I helped? What did I tackle that I might have been tempted to put off? What have I progressed? Then she started deliberately finding an alternative way of seeing some circumstances when her head had automatically gone to self-criticism.

Gradually, she found an inner voice to prioritise time for herself, for exercise routines, for yoga, for doing what really mattered at work rather than being available to everyone, and occasionally pushing back on impossible demands and allowing herself to discuss timescales with her clients. She reduced her working day from 12 or 13 hours to nine hours. She was more focused, she delegated more effectively, and overall, she was more effective as a manager than she had been before. From time to time she found herself in meetings not leaning forwards as she used to do to take a problem, but instead advising on it, making a contribution but leaving it there. None of this was easy. As she put it, she often heard the voice of her old personality, but she pushed it back and deliberately chose a different path.

Keith

Keith found the voice of permission to let him let go of the legacy problems he had inherited when he took the management job, and to discuss a plan with his manager about how they could be tackled over a longer period. He found the permission mindset to let him go home by a reasonable time and prioritised time for his interests, for exercise, and for a social life again.

Nadia

Nadia started to give herself permission to leave some less important tasks to the next day, occasionally put her calls on hold to catch up on some of the admin tasks like her colleagues did, and not to visit her mother every night after her children were in bed. She recognised that her mindset of over-responsibility had taken her very close to the point where she was going to let everyone down.

Cath

Cath gave herself permission to create an email boundary after she got home, and not to work after her evening meal unless it was something she felt she had to do. Like Hannah, she stopped taking on other people's problems but advised on them instead. Without the mindset of permission, she would not have been able to rebalance her life. Then she began to see that it was working – that she had become more effective at work in fewer hours and more able to enjoy her home life. Guilt would occasionally hover in the background, but she was more able to let it go, seeing it as the ghost of an old mental habit.

8. Be curious

Curiosity has a number of close relatives – creativity, learning, flexibility, detachment. Curiosity allows us to step back from something that could lock us into a closed mindset and make us defensive or angry. Think about people you know who become visibly angry and adopt a rigid stance on some controversial topic. Their closed mindset rejects any other viewpoints.

Curiosity would take us to complexity, and we need complexity, not narrow-minded simplicity, to understand what is going on today. Jason went to curiosity to cope with his ultra-demanding client. Initially he had gone to defensiveness and anger. Curiosity took him to 'Why is he behaving this way?', 'What is it like being this person?', 'What is he really saying?' That took him to detachment and a more flexible way of coping with him.

Curiosity makes us challenge habits we have got into: are there other ways of doing this? It lets us adapt faster; we cling on to less inefficiency, we are more open to new ideas.

It is not the robots we should be afraid of, it's the humans who are behaving like robots – no longer curious, sticking to routines that are becoming inefficient, fearing change and ambiguity.

Francesca Gino, a professor at Harvard Business School, notes that curiosity leads to more open communication and better team performance; those who are high in curiosity are better listeners and are more willing to share information. She quotes a study by Spencer Harrison at INSEAD, the French business school, on workers in a call centre: those who scored highly on a survey on curiosity sought more information from colleagues and were more likely to be creative in addressing customers' concerns.

Curiosity is also associated with less defensiveness in stress situations and reduced conflict, with a greater willingness to put yourself in another person's shoes. Todd Kashdan, Professor of Psychology at George Mason University, notes that curiosity increases perseverance on complex tasks, by creating a deep engagement in what we are doing. When we are curious, we get more from life and we give more to what we are engaged in.

9. Reflect on the day

This is about developing mental filters to capture the day. What do you remember about the day: frustrations? People who let you down? Delayed trains? What you hoped to do but didn't get the time to do? A few things you managed to get done?

What you capture will determine your mood: frustration, disappointment, achievement, satisfaction, enjoyment, happiness. Here are a few questions that are worth reflecting on to develop a more positive mental filter:

- What did you do today that you feel good about (at work and at home)?
- What did you nudge along today? Every day we nudge things along and some days we complete them. Take credit for the nudging.
- Whose life did you touch today? Who did you help, or connect with, where did you make a contribution that affected someone? Where did you visibly make a positive impact on someone's mood?
- What did you tackle today that you could have been tempted to put off doing?

- Where did you deliberately find the voice of permission to break the mould and do something differently?
- What were the experiences that you genuinely appreciated about today? What did you have fun doing today?

Reflecting on some of these questions for a few minutes could lay down new mental habits that get closer to happiness.

10. A mindset for change

Everything we have looked at so far, in different combinations, makes up the balancing system that buffers us from the pressures and disruptions of life. This balancing system is essentially what our resilience is about. It is through our resilience system that we navigate life and it is when we have to face major changes in our life circumstances that our ability to navigate life is most keenly tested. The starting point for both Keith and Nadia gradually losing their mental equilibrium was change. In Keith's case, his promotion into a job for which he was not prepared, and in Nadia's case, the reorganisation of her work group, the loss of the administrative support and the expectation that the team absorb the administrative tasks on top of their existing work. Tom's life had gone so completely off balance that it culminated in a panic attack in a traffic jam on the way to work. The starting point for his life going off-track was the combination of a difficult divorce, and changes at work that left him feeling his life was out of his control.

Change has the potential to disrupt us and even destabilise us. Many people are now working in organisations that are constantly changing. Change is the norm for them; companies boast about disruptive change. We have an ambivalent attitude towards change. We can be anxious about the implications of change that is on the horizon, but on the other hand we recognise that a life without change would be too dull and predictable. We might recognise that some of the things we most appreciate in our lives have come about as the result of change – and not necessarily change that we planned.

As always, it is our mindset about change that is the key. If we see some anticipated change with a sense of threat, then, as we have seen, that perception of threat alone can destabilise our physiology, resulting in raised cortisol and other adrenal hormones, increasing anxiety and reducing mental sharpness and decisiveness, possibly spilling over into our home lives and interfering with sleep. But if you look at changes you have been through, you are likely to see that even though you were apprehensive about that change event, you adapted. You might even see that not only did you adapt, but something came out of that change experience that you did not anticipate but have come to appreciate in your life. Our ability to adapt is far greater than we anticipate and recognising our potential to adapt even to difficult experiences could help us be more accepting, rather than feeling threatened by change that may be on the horizon – it could give us a certain fearlessness about change and a faith that we will get through.

Michel

Michel works in an international organisation that has been struggling to maintain its market share for some years. This has resulted in several reorganisations, with the loss of many people with whom Michel has worked and got to know as good colleagues. He has been with the company for over 10 years. He is in his late 30s. Brought up in Lyon, he saw his father lose his job when he was a boy, and the disruption this brought to the family as he struggled to find another job. He remembers the anxious conversations between his parents and how his father lost his good humour and became withdrawn. The family moved to a town close to Marseille, where his father found another job. Michel moved schools but he found it hard to fit in and he missed his old neighbourhood. However, discovering he was good at football saved him; he made new friends, worked hard, and did well at maths and sciences. He enrolled for computer sciences at university. He joined a company in France, but then eagerly took the opportunity to move to London a few years later. His career progressed and he is now managing a group of six IT specialists.

There are many things about the company that Michel appreciates, including its emphasis on developing its people and the opportunities it has given him to learn new skills. He gets on well with his current manager – she is the fourth manager he has had in the last five years. The team is overworked following the last reorganisation, when two areas were brought together, resulting in a substantial number of his colleagues being made redundant. So far Michel has survived, but he lives with a constant sense of anxiety about losing his job.

Michel is married; his wife is a teacher in a school in north London. They have two young children, who go to local schools. He and his wife have a good relationship, but Michel knows he often comes home exhausted by his work. His hours have gone up to around 10 a day. He knows he has taken too much on, but he thinks it would be risky to push back, given the general insecurity in the company. Nevertheless, he often feels close to being overwhelmed by everything he has to do. He often wakes early and lies in bed with a sense of anxiety about going to work. For the past six months or so he has felt too tired to exercise and he is less involved with his family. He feels generally flat and life has become more of an anxious struggle. He has put off making any decisions that involve spending money; even planning a holiday seems too risky right now.

Ally

Ally is also facing some degree of disruption as a result of changes at work. Ally has worked for an energy company for 15 years in a small office in West Sussex, close to where she lives and not far from her husband's job at Gatwick airport. They have two teenage children in local schools, both approaching exams, which could have an impact on their future education. Ally was brought up close to where she now lives. Her mother lives close by; she has a variety of health complaints and is not coping that well with life since Ally's father died a few years ago.

Ally has a good social life. Her sister and family live close by. She goes to a keep-fit class in the local church hall once a week, and when the weather is good she enjoys spending time in her garden.

The company has gone through several significant reorganisations, including being acquired by a larger group. There have been headcount reductions, but so far the West Sussex office has largely been unaffected. Then, suddenly, the company announced that they would close the site by the end of the year. The entire function would be moved to a newly built high-tech office a few hours' drive away. Anyone who wanted to go would be guaranteed a job in the new office, and they would be given a relocation package. Alternatively, there was a redundancy process and some compensation. But jobs were not easy to find in this area, their mortgage was dependent on both of them working, and they did not have much in the way of savings. Suddenly, Ally's sense of security, her dream about refitting the kitchen and replacing the family car, evaporated and was replaced by a feeling of anxiety and anger about what was being imposed on them.

Both Michel and Ally are facing changes in their work lives as a result of corporate organisations and decisions made by remote senior managers who Michel and Ally have never met. But somehow the degree of change imposed on Ally seems greater. Her life is so finely balanced that the change she is facing could destabilise everything – her home life, her children's schooling, her social and family routines. Michel's circumstances could probably accommodate this disruption in his work life more easily. However, both are reacting badly to the circumstances.

What is it about some changes that make them harder to adapt to than others? Think about your own circumstances here. Take a few minutes to answer these questions:

How many changes have you been through in the last 18 months?

- At work (change of job, different role, change of boss, location move, increased uncertainty)
- At home (house move, relationship change, new child, changes in health status)

Rate those changes on a scale from 1 to 10 on how disruptive each one was, with 10 being highly disruptive. Now take the ones that you have rated more disruptive. What is it about those changes that make them more disruptive?

When I ask people these questions in workshops, the most common answers to why some changes are more disruptive include:

- I didn't have control over what was going on (true for Michel and Ally)
- Change affected many areas of my life (more true for Ally)
- It was a threat to the future (true for Michel but more so for Ally)
- It came on top of other changes
- It has greatly increased the demands on me (true for Michel)

The loss of control and the uncertainty it brings is usually far up that list. In my experience of helping hundreds of people whose lives have gone through periods of considerable uncertainty, I am convinced that we are not that well programmed, physiologically or mentally, to deal with uncertainty. Many people feel more equipped to deal with a bad thing in their life than living with the uncertainty that a bad thing might happen.

Acceptance

Acceptance is a useful mindset here. Accept that this change is happening and accept what your emotions are doing – anxiety or anger, completely understandable given the disruption and uncertainty you are facing. But try not to let these feelings dominate. Don't reinforce them by going over arguments that you will not be given a chance to express, like how this change is unnecessary or why you don't think it will work. Try to get to acceptance that this is happening and that you will adapt to it. Remind yourself about other difficult circumstances you have adapted to and what has come out of those changes. This is more helpful for your emotions than reinforcing anger.

But what can we take control of, even when we are surrounded by uncertainty?

Take control of your response

You may not be able to take control of the decision for this change in your circumstances, but you can decide what your response to it will be. Don't let it take more of the space than it should. Box it in. This unpredictability does not need to take over your home life. Michel should increase his exercise and the routines that help him balance life, rather than letting them drift. Put a priority on behaviours that stabilise the physiology of mental well-being and health. Keep the routines that make for good relationships with your partner and your children.

Live within a shorter time frame

If you are facing uncertainty, shorten the time frame to give you a greater sense of certainty in the short term. In Michel's case, he was responsible for a project that was due to be completed in six months' time. In all likelihood, his life is pretty secure inside that six months, so make that six months the time frame to live within for now. Make the most of what is in the present and the near future while you prepare for the longer term.

Conversations can change perspective

Talk it through with people you trust, people who are likely to be helpful, rather than with people who are stuck in resentment or resistance. Talk it through with your family and friends who have been through similar experiences and colleagues who are adapting to it. Listen to their perspectives. *Adapting comes about as you gradually change perspectives over time until you arrive at a view that is a long way from where you started out.*

Redirect your mindset

Try to take control of where your head has gone, to the mindset you have adopted about this change. Change is a set of facts with implications attached and these could be causing you the stress. The implications could be threatening – for some people, including Michel and Ally, it has gone beyond threatening to potentially catastrophic. Michel fears he may never get another job if he loses this one, that his skill set is too narrow, that he has been in this company for too long, that he may have to sell his house and downsize. Ally also fears she will not get another job, that the strain on their home life might undermine the family, that they might split up. Both feel they have failed their families as a result of these unavoidable events happening. Start to examine the potential catastrophe: get to a more likely platform, an outcome that is more probable. Examine the options and gather information. Try to get to the self-compassion mindset, that this has happened through no fault of yours, that you are doing what you can to deal with it.

Be prepared

Take control of what you can control. In Michel and Ally's case, update the CV, talk to potential recruiters, meet up with old colleagues who have moved on to other companies or are working for themselves. Be conscious of what you are putting off doing. Confronting all of this and confronting financial issues with personal budget planning will make you feel more prepared.

Use a visualisation technique

Imagery can be helpful in getting us to mental preparation. I have used this image with people who are going through major changes that carry a lot of uncertainty: Imagine your living room with a cupboard in one corner. The cupboard represents the area of uncertainty – the potential loss of a job or a divorce are good examples. Now, the cupboard can take as much space in the room as you let it – it could take the entire room, or you could contract the space it takes. Every now and again you need to open the cupboard and do something, but then close it and enjoy the rest of the room. Populate the room with good things – plans, people. You can't wish the cupboard away, and letting it fill the entire room won't get rid of it, but one day you will wake up and the cupboard will be gone.

Next, select some previous change experience you went through, one that is now behind you. Bring back the mental images of how you found out about that event, how you felt at the time, the steps you took to deal with it and what the outcome was. Remember the point where you started to adapt to it. Now visualise anything that came out of that change experience that was beneficial to you.

Have faith

Try to get to a mindset of faith. Let's face it, control can only take us so far. What happens when we reach the limits of control? This is where some people feel intensely uncomfortable. This is where we need faith, a strong belief that life will work out. Michel, after he has updated his CV or met up with old colleagues, needs to have faith that if the company asks him to go, he will find another job, possibly a better job – he needs to have faith in himself and in his experience. Ally needs to have faith that the family will pull together despite this disruption, that life will work out for them, even though at this point she does not know how.

Ultimately, we balance control and faith. Too much of a reliance on control can make us obsessive and anxious. Too much of a reliance on faith can make us passive, it can make us miss opportunities to take control of circumstances that might work out better for us.

One of the most inspiring writers on change and unpredictability, in particular, was a German development economist who was as much a psychologist of human behaviour as he was an economist. He believed we are at our best, our most creative and most innovative, when we encounter circumstances that are unanticipated – essentially, when our plans collide against the uncompromising realities of life.

Albert Hirschman was born in Berlin in 1915, not the most promising time or place to be born if you were Jewish. In his early life he was caught up in the inescapable realities of unpredictable changes as they unfolded across Europe. In a sense, his life was a preparation for the philosophical approach he would take to change in his later professional life. At the age of 18, after his father died, he moved to Paris and, as Europe collapsed into fascism, he came to London to study at the London School of Economics (LSE). In 1936 he enlisted in the Spanish Civil War, part of the first wave of volunteers. After his time in Spain, he moved to France, where he could pass as a French citizen after the Nazis invaded. He joined the

French army but after France was defeated, he moved to Marseille. There he met an American, Varian Fry, and together they helped hundreds of Jews escape from France across the Pyrenees to America. The obstacles were huge – the French police, France's border guards, informants – but Hirschman was an ingenious problem-solver, very resourceful, brave, with an open, friendly personality. As the authorities were closing in, at the last minute he escaped over the Pyrenees and took a liner to the US. He was only 25 years old.

His life is described in a magnificent, very readable and at times gripping biography, *Worldly Philosopher: The Odyssey of Albert O Hirschman*, by the Princeton historian Jeremy Adelman, who brings Hirschman to life: his openness to life experiences, his warmth, his optimism, his intellect, and his constant curiosity. Malcolm Gladwell's review of Adelman's book for *The New Yorker* captures the essence of Hirschman's approach to change and gives examples of how projects that at first appear to have failed turn out to create opportunities for unexpected success.

Hirschman's life was in constant motion, at times a consequence of decisions he made, at times due to events he would not have anticipated. At Berkeley he met Sarah, the daughter of Russian émigrés, who he was to marry. After the US went to war, many of his colleagues went to Washington to work for the government, but Hirschman enlisted and was posted to Algeria, and then to Italy. His daughter Katia was born when he was overseas; he saw her for the first time when she was two years old. When he returned to the US, it was not easy for him to get a job, despite his experience, a PhD, and a book he had written. Eventually he got a job with the government agency that was involved in European development after the war ended. But even then, life was not settled. By the late 1940s, the US was going through a chapter of paranoia, with McCarthy and Nixon accusing the government department in which Hirschman worked of being a nest of Communist sympathisers. Not for the first time in his life,

Hirschman saw the writing on the wall. He took a job with the World Bank to develop projects in Colombia. Bear in mind, he was married, now with two daughters, and Bogotá was lawless, with armed gangs on the streets; it was in political chaos. You could imagine the sort of conversations friends would have with him, advising him that going to Bogotá would be a terrible mistake. But Hirschman's philosophy was that you could not tell if a decision was a mistake until you had tested it out and there could be consequences of decisions – some good, some bad – that could develop over a long stretch.

His wife, Sarah, had a similar open-minded attitude to change. Adelman quotes a letter she wrote to her parents around the time of their move to Bogotá: 'We both realise that you should think about the future, make plans for the children, etc., but I think that we both somehow feel that it is impossible to know what is best and that the present is so much more important – because if the present is solid and good it will be a surer basis for a good future than any plans that you can make.' That is a statement of faith if ever there was one.

They spent four years in Colombia, which turned out to be a very productive time and a happy time for them as a family. No clear plan, not a lot of control, but a lot of faith that they could make it work. As you can imagine, for someone who had had to adapt to so much change and face circumstances over which he had very little control, Hirschman was outside the mainstream of development economists of his time. For them, projects were about precise plans and top-down control. If something went wrong, it represented a failure of the plan. For Hirschman, life was far more complex. Plans could take you so far but there are inevitably events that cannot be foreseen and cannot be planned for – and for Hirschman, that's when life got interesting. That's when a combination of curiosity, creativity and perseverance can take us to an outcome that might far exceed what the plan envisioned. He recognised that creativity needs special conditions to emerge: 'Creativity always comes as a surprise to us, therefore we can never count on it and we dare not believe in it until it has happened.'

Adelman makes the point that most economists saw equilibrium and stability as the goals, and disequilibrium and disorder as anomalies. Hirschman saw disequilibrium at the heart of change. Many of us facing some disruptive events in our lives, events we have been thrust into, have a similar expectation – that equilibrium and stability should be the goals and consequently periods of disorder and uncertainty give rise to anxiety and frustration. But if we accept that periods of change are disruptive and disordered, and if we have faith that that disorder could bring out qualities in us that we might not have anticipated, but will bring gifts into our lives that will take us by surprise, then we will become far less fearful of change.

Are you ready?

Consider these key questions to help prepare you for change:

Do you understand what this change is about, and why you have to go through it?

This gets closer to acceptance and understanding the rationale, rather than resisting it.

Who will you discuss it with?

Be selective; talk to people who have gone through similar change experiences and who are adapting to this experience – not those who are angry and resisting it.

What do you see as the implications of this change for you? Rationally, do you think you might have envisioned a potential catastrophe rather than a more likely outcome?

This is where you need a few conversations to check out what the reality is likely to be, rather than reinforcing the potential catastrophe.

What are you doing to box in this change experience? What can you do to contain it, so other areas of your life can be enriched and enjoyed, rather than overshadowed by this experience? What are

you doing to reinforce all the other areas of your life that are not directly impacted by this change?

This includes those routines that stabilise energy and mental well-being – your home life, relationship time, interests, and short-term plans, rather than drifting away from all of those.

What can you do to exercise some control over the effects of this change experience?

This includes gathering as much information as you can, negotiating for some things that would make the change situation work better for you, rather than going to a mindset of helplessness.

What might a good outcome of the change experience be for you? What could the opportunities be for you?

Allow your thinking to become optimistic rather than defaulting to how you will lose out in some way. Balance the pessimism.

Have you taken time to think about previous change experiences that might have been disruptive, but which you have adapted to? What came out of those experiences?

What do you have faith in that will help you get through this? Your abilities, your relationships, your network, your personality strengths – how life has worked out for you?

Be very specific here.

Finding happiness through disruption

In 2008, General Motors announced the closure of their giant assembly plant in Janesville, Wisconsin, throwing many thousands of people out of work. It was followed by the closure of other businesses that were closely linked to the automobile industry, like the Lear factory that manufactured car seats for General Motors. In Janesville, families worked for GM and had done so over generations. This was a traumatic blow for the community. Some families found that their entire income had collapsed.

Amy Goldstein, a writer for *The Washington Post*, immersed herself in the community for several years, getting to know families who had been affected by the closure and following up their stories. Her observations and conversations with the families are recorded with compassion and empathy in her book, *Janesville: an American Story*, published in 2017.

While politicians worked on a package of incentives to attract industries to the area and attempted unsuccessfully to persuade GM to use the plant for other operations, local people started charity initiatives to relieve the hardship around them. Over time, the closure took a heavy toll on families and on mental health. A few families abandoned their teenage children to live with grandparents or fend for themselves, while the parents left the area.

In 2010, over 400 students in the local schools did not have a fixed place to live. Many were 'couch-surfing' in friends' houses. Greatly touched by the reality of those kids' lives, a group of local people started a charity with the aim of opening two hostels for homeless young people and after several years of real struggle, they achieved their goal of opening one of the hostels. Some families pulled together, with their children taking on two or three jobs on top of their studies to get by financially. Some ex-GM employees found work in another GM plant hours' drive away and commuted back at weekends. Some took on study courses at the local Blackhawk Technical College. Many had not studied since they left school and found it so daunting they dropped out.

What comes across in *Janesville* is how some people have a relatively strong base of personal assets that make up their resilience, whereas others have a much more tenuous, fragile structure, determining who succeeds and who does not.

Two women who had worked at Lear doing manual work – Barb, who had dropped out of school at 16, and Kristi – enrolled for a course in criminal justice. They supported one another and graduated at the top of their class and then got jobs in the local prison, earning less than they got at Lear. They both disliked the job. It gave them very little satisfaction, and this is where their stories sharply diverged. Barb, with the complete support of her husband, Mike, left that job and enrolled for an advanced course, which potentially gave her greater job opportunities. Kristi's life veered dramatically off course. Her marriage disconnected and she had an affair with a man who had been a prisoner, as a consequence of which she lost her job. A few days after her suspension and close to her fortieth birthday, she took an overdose. Since the plant closure, the suicide rate in the Janesville county had doubled to 32 in a year for a time. Barb carried on with her studies on top of a full-time job paying less than half of what she was earning at Lear. She graduated and got a job working with developmentally disabled adults, which gave her considerable satisfaction and a new sense of identity.

'To her surprise,' Goldstein writes, 'Barb believes that Lear's closing was the best thing that could have happened. Its closing taught her that she is a survivor. It taught her that work exists that is worth doing, not for the wages, but because you feel good doing it. Working with developmentally disabled adults, who depend on her and call her day and night, often does not even seem like a job. It is a way of life. Barb has promised herself that, after the injuries to her shoulder and wrist on the Lear assembly line, after her brief and depressing stint at the County Jail, she will never again stay working anywhere that she is not happy. She does not look back at Lear. She looks forward to how her clients are growing and, with her help, becoming as independent as they can be.'

Her tenacity, optimism, sense of purpose, and the strength of her relationship with her husband, together with her connection with the challenge of doing something she has never done before, transformed her life and her beliefs about herself, following the loss of her job at the manufacturing company.

The path to happiness

We have come a long way from a discussion of happiness and how it affects our psychological health and our success in life. Clearly there are many routes to happiness and many things we can do to increase our happiness baseline, despite the circumstances in which we find ourselves. Protecting our physiological well-being and our energy, taking care of our close relationships and rooting out mental habits that interfere with stable positive emotions greatly help. Taking time to reflect on day-to-day life, seeing the effects of what you are good at, acknowledging those whose life you have touched in some supportive way and small things you are thankful for all have an impact on your ability to feel happy. Cultivating an open-minded curious mindset with faith that life will work out beyond what you are able to control can allow you to embrace times of unpredictability and change without becoming guilty or fearful, and could allow you to remain grateful for what remains stable and supportive in your life. In combination, all of these elements could take you closer to happiness, creating a more stable foundation for positive emotions than striving for more material possessions like a new car or a bigger house. But our happiness is also influenced by our circumstances at work: our relationships with our colleagues, the personalities of the people we report to and the culture of the organisation we are a part of. And similarly, decisions you make about the microculture you create can greatly influence the happiness baseline and the psychological well-being of anyone who reports to you.

9

The microculture you create

Nadia's manager saw how distressed she was by an overly pressurising customer call. She took the time to sit with Nadia while she talked about how she had been feeling as a result of the work demands and also about the pressures in her home life. She offered Nadia some practical advice about being more flexible in how she managed the demands of the job. For some time after that conversation, her manager would check on how Nadia was doing, sometimes just a few minutes or over a coffee – informal, but concerned and encouraging.

Similarly, Keith's manager, Jess, had seen that Keith was not his usual self. She had seen how his working hours had gone up, she could see in his facial expressions how tense and preoccupied he looked. When she talked to him about how he was managing the demands and the projects, she could see he had overloaded himself and she could hear the agitation in his voice when he talked about the deadlines and the client expectations.

Those are concerned managers. They are tuned in to how their teams are responding to the pressures of their jobs, they take an interest in their people, they are naturally supportive and helpful in practical ways.

If their managers had been too busy to take an interest, then both Nadia and Keith could have ended up on sickness absence as a consequence of the symptoms they were gradually developing. That, in turn, would have greatly added to the pressures their managers were under. As it was, the short conversations they had with their managers prevented that outcome and encouraged them to develop more flexible ways of dealing with the pressures. The manager or team leader can potentially have a very significant impact on the mental well-being of their teams.

This is a two-way relationship. If you manage others, and you want to stay in a state of good mental well-being, despite all the pressures and changes that may be going on in your life, then you need your teams to be in a state of good mental health and energy as well. If they start to drift down the curve, becoming increasingly tired, less confident and less effective in how they are working, inevitably that will affect you sooner or later. Remember, when people are in a good state of mental well-being, they are around three times more productive than when they drift into the overwhelmed side of the curve. Your team is your resource – not just for delivering results, but for protecting your own mental health.

With this in mind, it would not be unreasonable to assume that the organisation for which you work would be interested in helping you navigate life, rather than blowing you on to the rocks. There is now a real divide between organisations that give a lot of thought to the mental well-being of their people, and those that do not. But many people are blown on to the rocks, not by the demands of the job or by the hours, but by the thoughtlessness of their managers.

This is where some people turn their attention to the culture of the organisation. According to Boris Groysberg and colleagues at Harvard Business School, culture is a set of unwritten rules that are reflected in our behaviours, values and assumptions, and shared by the group as a whole.

Some cultures are more oriented to the well-being of their people and encourage behaviours like respect, openness and fairness, which, if they are strongly embedded, should strengthen the ability of employees to manage the pressures they are under. However, in my experience of talking with people about the culture of their organisation, it is rare to find people who can articulate what the corporate culture is about. And in many cases, what comes across are well-meaning abstractions.

The impact of microculture

What is definitely not an abstraction, however, is the microculture of anyone who is in a leadership position. Your boss, the person who runs the team you are a part of, creates a microculture that has a direc' impact on your resilience – on how you handle the pressures you are under, but also on your life more broadly, on your balance to life, and potentially on your mental health and energy.

Rory

Rory, a young lawyer I saw who was seconded to a financial organisation a few months earlier, found himself in an overworked team, out of his depth, and struggling with the workload. He knows his manager is not 'a people person'; she has not checked on how he is doing since he joined the team and she is quite inaccessible, but in desperation he sends her an email asking to meet to help him clarify the priorities. He receives an automated reply within a few minutes: 'Request for meeting declined.' What does this email tell us about the microculture of the team in which Rory is working? His manager is essentially conveying the message: 'Don't bother me, just get on with it.'

I've discovered that this mindset – 'just get on with it' – is by no means uncommon. It is often a mindset that has developed in team leaders who are themselves struggling with too much to do, often working long hours, neglecting themselves, their balance to life, and their energy, and are now neglecting their teams, leaving them to fend for themselves. Those managers have lost sight of the connection between the effectiveness and mental energy of their teams, and their own effectiveness and well-being.

Rory could see that he was going to get no support from his manager. He compensated as best he could by building a network of support among his colleagues. The experience also liberated him from his normal high standards through the realisation that he was essentially on his own, doing the best he could, and some mistakes would be inevitable. That is a managerial mindset of neglect, but some managers create microcultures that are toxic.

Jan

Jan has worked in a London-based consulting firm for seven years. Bright, organised, liked by her clients and colleagues, willing to work long hours when she has to, she is seen as having the potential to become a partner in a few years' time. She is sitting in her flat with her boyfriend, having got home late, she is in tears, her confidence undermined. It has been like this for several nights. This has been the worst assignment she has been on, not because of the client, not because of the complexity of the work, not because of the long hours, but because of the behaviour of her direct boss, Val. Val is critical, undermining, nothing is good enough, she is over-controlling and at other times unavailable; she is inconsistent in the approach she wants Jan to take, and recently she has been undermining her in front of colleagues. She interrupts her in meetings and cuts her off in conference calls.

Jan has tried to talk to Val about how she is behaving, she has asked whether she thinks she should be on this assignment, but those conversations have got nowhere. Val is clearly coping poorly with her own work demands, she deals with frustration badly, she can get angry in front of others, and she can make cutting, dismissive comments to people in her team. The last straw was when Val ripped up a document in front of her colleagues that Jan had spent several hours putting together. Jan left the room, went back to her desk, broke down in tears, and wrote her resignation letter. She was persuaded to stay in the firm; she moved to work for a more experienced partner who recognised her abilities and put her on another assignment that helped to rebuild her confidence. Val was strongly urged to have coaching on her management style.

Val is not unique. I see many bright, capable people, like Jan, who, for months, have been having difficulty sleeping, waking with feelings of dread about going to work, whose confidence has been undermined, often to the point of feeling depressed and worthless because of the behaviour of their boss. But how does this happen? How does someone whose work success depends on good people working for them end up demotivating and undermining bright, capable people?

The most likely explanation is not that Val is some type of psychopath, out to destroy the confidence of bright, aspiring juniors, but that she is herself struggling, coping badly, and has become completely disconnected from what it means to manage others. In doing so, she has developed a very destructive mindset about her junior colleagues – 'My people aren't good enough' – and her behaviour follows from that.

The impact of a positive microculture

Nadia and Keith, however, were working for managers who, despite having very demanding jobs themselves, remained thoroughly connected to what it means to be a manager of others. They had developed microcultures that were supportive and encouraging, where the well-being of their teams was as important as their work performance.

Over the years, when I have been brought in to support team meetings at large organisations, it has been very interesting having conversations about microculture. A senior manager in a trading group told me: 'We're a winning team. I try to make people feel special, proud to work here – it's my job to encourage them.' A partner in a law firm working on international deals said: 'We do great work and have fun doing it', and a partner in a consulting firm told me: 'I've created something people want to be part of; we can only succeed as a team.' A senior manager in a client service firm, who had recovered from being off work with anxiety and depression, said: 'I like to be encouraging and build trust – give people scope to do well, provide structure and guidance.' Then he added, reflecting on how he was just before he developed his illness: 'Previously, I wasn't even aware of how my behaviour was impacting on others.'

It's also interesting asking people about the kind of microculture their manager has created – comments range from 'My manager is indifferent, there's no sense of belonging, very little contact, no appreciation' to 'My manager is supportive; he trusts me, respects me, doesn't micromanage. I wouldn't ask to change to anyone else.'

Imagine, for a few moments, what it would be like to work for those positive team leaders – to work for someone who fosters fun in what they do, who makes you believe you are part of a winning team, who is encouraging and takes pride in bringing out the best in what you do. Imagine the sort of conversations there would be in those teams. Culture is about conversations. The conversations are an embodiment of the microculture and the mindset of the leader. Conversations can encourage, coach, motivate, support, help people flourish, overcome a sense of threat, make people believe in themselves, lift them out of disappointment, build trust and respect, help them go beyond what they believe they are capable of. Conversations can make you feel you matter – that you are more than a cog in the wheel.

Ten conversations to build a healthy culture

There are 10 conversations that can build a really healthy culture, which goes a long way towards enabling people to thrive in very demanding jobs, helping them to balance the pressures and stay in the good zone of the energy and effectiveness curve.

1. Check on how people are, tune in to red flags

Look out for small signs that a member of your team may be drifting away from the healthy zone in the curve. Some of those signs are obvious; others are more subtle indicators that the person is just not their usual self. And that can be a way into a conversation about how they are feeling: 'We've worked together for several months. I think I know you pretty well – you don't seem your usual self lately. How are things going – do you fancy a coffee?'

Red flags to look out for:

- How the person looks: the face tells you a lot about who has become exhausted, who is no longer sleeping well, who has become anxious or feels threatened by life, whose mood has dropped, who is no longer enjoying life – just as the face can tell you who is up for the challenge and excited about what they are doing.
- Irritability, impatience, intolerance and frustration showing in someone who is normally pretty patient and tolerant. And, of course, these indicators could come across in emails in a person who is normally fairly measured in what they send.
- Signs of the person withdrawing, going into their heads – the loss of short exchanges about the weekend, family, sport; the loss of humour, fewer contributions in meetings.
- Mistakes that are unusual for that person – very often quite small mistakes, like getting a number wrong or missing a deadline, rather than big judgement calls.
- Becoming less focused or coherent; more distracted.
- Emotional signs: becoming tearful or fighting to hold back tears.

Any of these signs can be an indication that the person is drifting off-track. A conversation at a really early point could help that person get back into the healthy zone. Many people are not particularly tuned in to how they feel. I have many examples where someone has been nudged in the direction of getting help by a colleague or manager who has had a sensitive conversation following on from seeing some of those red flags. This type of conversation could be from manager to team member; it could also be colleague to colleague if you see some red flags in someone you know reasonably well.

Could it be an upwards conversation? Someone I had previously seen came back to see me recently. I asked him what had brought him back. 'My PA,' he replied. I asked him what he meant. 'Well, my PA came into my office a few days ago and she said, "It's been a while since you've seen Bill, isn't it? Shall I make you an appointment?"' He said he thought about it for a few moments and agreed. She had seen he wasn't his usual self: more irritable, lower mood, disconnected. But obviously a conversation needs trust and respect, and that was the kind of relationship they had.

Ignoring the red flags is not an option. Gradually, over some months, the person might slip further into the curve, slowly spiralling into exhaustion, struggling, becoming increasingly overwhelmed, until eventually it develops into something that requires professional help and possibly time off work.

But why wait until you see red flags developing in members of your team? The examples we have seen are reactive to seeing some changes in the person, but some people regularly check in on how their teams are feeling. Some managers, as part of routine one-to-one meetings, ask the person how they are feeling about the pressures they are under – helped by being quite open themselves about times when they have been affected by too many demands, or life slipping out of balance. You know who has a particularly difficult assignment right now, you know who is dealing with an unusually demanding client, or who is facing changing circumstances at work. Empathising with them about the pressures they are facing and asking them how they are feeling about those pressures can get to a degree of openness before any actual red flags appear. And of course, if the person is coping well, you have created the conditions within that relationship that make it more likely they will be open with you if they start to feel overwhelmed in the future.

This is not about being a counsellor. You are simply giving the person an opportunity to talk about how they are feeling and where they feel temporarily overwhelmed. In many cases, just by giving them an opportunity to talk about the circumstances, they can see a way forward, how they could deal with the pressures differently. And there are many cases where you might be able to make a suggestion from your own experience that could be helpful to the person.

I would see this type of conversation as a key management or leadership skill. The manager should know his or her team well enough to see signs of the person drifting into the curve. This is a conversation for the manager to have – not something to be outsourced to HR or to the EAP (Employee Assistance Team). It's the manager who can make a real difference here.

2. Encourage conversations about how people balance the pressures they are under

If leaders realise that where their people are on the performance and well-being curve has to do with decisions they make about how they manage themselves and their energy, then leaders could have conversations that encourage healthy behaviours. The problem is that many managers see where people are on the curve as being due to nebulous qualities like resilience or coping skills, rather than due to choices and decisions people make about how they look after themselves.

Imagine you are part of a team that is about to embark on a demanding project that will run over several months, involve periods of long working hours, and occasionally run into weekends. The person leading the project kicks off a meeting by saying something like: 'This is going to be a tough assignment – it's going to last several months, there are going to be some weeks when the hours are going to be long. Now, I don't want you burning out. I want you to make your well-being a priority. I want to go around the table for each of you to say what things just aren't negotiable for you to look after your energy and to keep yourself in good mental shape.'

Some in the team might talk about exercise, others might talk about getting over seven hours' sleep, or Pilates on a Tuesday night, playing hockey one night a week, seeing their children before they go to bed. What would you say? The answer to that question – and sharing it with the team in a culture that is encouraging you to stick with those balancing behaviours, rather than drifting away from them when the demands increase – could make a real difference to how you come through that project.

That type of conversation, about what you are doing to look after your energy and mental well-being, could be one you have quite regularly with your team and with your manager – not just at the beginning of a new assignment – to embed the idea that balance matters in a demanding job.

3. Conversations about flexibility

Most of the people we have looked at in this book are working in jobs where there are no fixed hours. The demands can increase and the hours increase; they might be working over time zones and they are available for conference calls early or before going to bed; emails constantly come in throughout the time they are awake. These people are being hugely flexible, and their flexibility needs to be matched by the flexibility their organisations allow them. This could be crucial for the balance to life they are able to create.

If balance is seen as something that is essential for people's energy and effectiveness in their jobs, then managers should see the need for conversations about this. That could open up flexibility about working from home part of the time, having a zone of flexibility around the start of the day when people could take their children to school or go to the gym, flexibility to exercise during the working day, flexibility to get home to relieve childminders without feeling guilty.

These conversations could extend to questioning people about why they are working every evening after their children are in bed, or regularly working at the weekends, or why they are not taking a break at lunchtime. Some people would benefit from a conversation about not responding to emails on holiday or at weekends. Many people would benefit from a conversation about anything you have learned to do to create some balance in your life.

4. Conversations about focus and managing demands

As a manager, you can see who is really focused in how they work, who is constantly distracted, who is clear about priorities and who is just trying to get to the bottom of the to-do list. You can see who plans time in the diary to get things done. You can see who negotiates over deadlines and what they do to stay on top of their emails. You can see who stays in control of a demanding job and who gets overwhelmed. Could you have conversations to encourage more focused ways of working?

This might include encouraging your team to negotiate deadlines or push back when the demands are too great. It might include asking them what they are going to reprioritise before they take on another project. It might include how they delegate work. A conversation about how they manage the demands could give them more autonomy over how they respond to their email volume. What does it say about priorities if you are working on something that requires focus and analysis, and you are nagged by your manager because you didn't respond to an email he sent you 15 minutes ago?

A conversation with you could give them the confidence to negotiate demands or deadlines with their clients, or to push back about requests for meetings at unreasonable times. Conversations like these could develop a much more empowered attitude among your team, rather than them feeling helpless or beaten down by too many demands.

A junior person in a strategy firm told me this story: she had been working for a senior colleague for nine months or so, she was enjoying the job and learning a lot, and although there were times when she felt overloaded, she didn't mind working late. At the end of the assignment, her boss gave her some feedback: after commenting on her abilities as an analyst and her positive approach to the job, he wound up the review by saying, 'Look, I've really enjoyed you being part of my team, but not once in the time you have been working for me have you pushed back or tried to negotiate the demands. You need to learn to do this because if you don't, this firm could burn you out.' How's that for a green light for a really conscientious person to take control of the demands?

5. Encouraging the challenge mindset

You have asked a junior member of your team to take on a task they haven't done before, such as a more complex assignment, or leading a client meeting for the first time. You can see the person's head has gone to threat – 'how I could mess this up'. This is an opportunity to have a conversation about how he feels about doing this and an opportunity to show him how to cross the gap between threat and challenge.

Why did you ask him to take on this task? What qualities did you see in him that made you think he is capable of doing this? Help him to think about times in the past when he took on something and succeeded. Help him to break the task down into manageable pieces and discuss them with you. Giving the person the confidence that they can fulfil this unfamiliar task, while at the same time helping them to see that it is not the end of the world if it doesn't succeed, but hopefully they will have learned something from it, is what it takes to go from a sense of threat to a challenge. That can be one of the most confidence-building conversations a manager can have with a member of his or her team.

6. Notice the type of feedback you give

Closely linked to helping someone cross from threat to challenge is the sort of feedback you give when you see that something has gone well. When you acknowledge something, what are you acknowledging? Many managers praise the product. They might say: 'That's a good document', or 'That was a good meeting', or 'The client seemed happy with what you were saying.' These comments are encouraging and certainly better than saying nothing, but would you go a step further? Would you turn it into a comment about the person? Would you say: 'You're a really concise communicator', or 'You know how to run good meetings', or 'You know how to sell an idea to a client'?

Comments about the person, not about the product, are very rarely expressed, but when they are, they go right to confidence and are remembered for a long time. These types of comments can help the person see the impact of what they are good at, and help them to externalise rather than internalise when something goes wrong, protecting their confidence.

7. Conversations that rescue confidence

Things go wrong all the time: projects overrun, clients are dissatisfied, deadlines are missed, people are criticised. There is a real danger that inexperienced but conscientious people internalise those experiences, even feeling they have failed or believing they do not have the qualities to succeed in this type of work. They might catastrophise in their heads, anticipating losing their jobs.

Julie

Julie comes out of a meeting that she and her manager had run for a group of clients. Julie had presented some data to back up what her manager was proposing. The meeting had not gone well. The clients were not impressed, they had been challenging of the analysis and critical about some points. Julie felt defeated; she felt she had let her manager down and that she had been the weak link in the presentation. Sitting in a taxi on the way back to the office, with her manager, looking at her emails, Julie thought she should ask what her manager thought about the meeting, almost anticipating criticism and a confirmation that she had done a bad job. The conversation gave Julie a completely different perspective. Her manager pointed out that she had been in several meetings with those clients, they were very hard to please, they always found something to criticise or challenge, but she thought that Julie had put together a good presentation and came across well, even when she was challenged on some of the analysis.

Good marks to Julie's boss for helping her externalise the meeting. But full marks if she had anticipated that Julie might feel this way and probed herself, rather than potentially leaving Julie feeling that she had failed. As a minimum, try to get to what the person could learn from what has gone wrong and be willing to share what you have learned about similar events. Share your perspectives.

8. Conversations about change

In some organisations, change is such a constant that managers give little thought to how it is communicated. Change that might have a real impact – on how people work, their sense of security, their balance to life, or to the make-up of their team – could be communicated via an email by managers who are more caught up in the process of the change than in the reality that it will affect people's lives and emotions. Change nearly always carries areas of ambiguity or uncertainty and that can trigger feelings of insecurity, stress and anxiety in those who are affected. Inevitably, that can have an impact on their mood, their home lives, possibly their sleep and ultimately, their health. It would take a relatively small amount of empathy for a manager to put themselves in the shoes of people in their team and ask themselves: how might they be affected by this change proposal?

A conversation with the team could explain the rationale behind the change and the plans that have been made to minimise disruption or training proposals. It is also an opportunity to explain what the consequences might be in the longer term if things just stayed as they were – the long-term consequences of doing nothing could be more disruptive than the short-term consequences of this change project. A group discussion could also focus on problem-solving and encouraging innovative ideas to deal with some of the difficulties that might not have been anticipated by those who had instigated the change project.

Some of those change projects will, of course, affect the manager as well as the team. For the manager to share how he or she is feeling about it, and what they are doing to adapt to it, develops a 'we are in this together' mindset and sharing of perspectives.

People adapt at different speeds; some are more anxious than others. For a manager to recognise this and meet with their team members individually can also help people stay on a reasonably positive track, rather than drifting to helplessness or resentment.

Many change projects fail to achieve what was hoped – not because the strategy or the planning was faulty, but because people crucial to its implementation were not properly involved or informed. The time it takes to have helpful, practical conversations with the team and with people individually can pay off in greater commitment to the change project, as well as in stronger group cohesion.

9. Conversations that encourage openness, innovation and learning

Why wait for others to initiate change? With the right kind of conversation, ideas could develop in your team that are innovative and could have a wider impact for the business as a whole.

Inefficiencies and frustrations abound in all organisations. Over time, people adapt to them; they become desensitised to them. They might even cease to notice them. But conversations starting with 'what has frustrated you this week, and what could be done to change that?' could stimulate more innovative thinking. It could also foster a more empowered mindset about work, rather than the energy-draining effects of feeling there is nothing you can do about this.

In today's fast-moving work environment, where nothing remains as it is for long, organisations need people who are willing to think beyond the immediate tasks of answering emails and delivering short-term results. A leader encouraging curiosity and creative thinking could spur the sort of innovation that keeps an organisation moving forwards. But many people feel awkward and embarrassed about asking questions or making suggestions – it makes them feel exposed. Safer to say nothing than to invite ridicule or rejection.

This is where the idea of psychological safety comes in – that for a team to perform at its best, to be innovative in how it deals with problems, there has to be a high degree of respect and trust that ideas will not be rejected and the person who has put forward an idea will not be left feeling embarrassed or foolish.

Amy Edmondson, a Professor of Leadership at Harvard Business School, in a ground-breaking article published in 1999, describes psychological safety as a sense of confidence that a team will not reject, embarrass or punish someone for being open, for pushing forward an idea, or for reporting a mistake.

Her interest was in 'learning behaviour': how a team obtains and processes data that allows it to adapt and improve. This includes seeking feedback, sharing information, asking for help, talking about errors and putting forward new ideas. In some organisations, those behaviours are risky: a person could be punished for making a mistake, sharing information gives someone else in the team a competitive advantage over you, asking for help equates with weakness, and failing could bring your career to an end.

She studied 51 work teams in a manufacturing company, observing team meetings and collecting data on over 400 team members looking at the degree to which team members felt it was safe to talk about something that carried some degree of interpersonal risk. She found that where team members felt it was safe to take a risk, to be open about mistakes, particularly if they felt the information was going to be used to generate better ideas, then that greatly contributed to high-performing, innovative teams.

In 2015, Google reported on an internal study on what makes a team effective. Conducting interviews on over 200 people and looking at more than 250 attributes, they concluded that five key attributes set successful teams apart from the rest:

1) Psychological safety
2) Dependability
3) Structure and clarity
4) Meaning of work
5) Impact of work

Psychological safety – 'where team members feel safe to take risks and be vulnerable in front of one another' – was the front runner of the five variables and underpinned the other four. Individuals who work in teams with high levels of psychological safety are less likely to leave the company, they bring in more revenue, and are more highly rated by senior colleagues.

Researchers at the Singapore Management University Raymond Smith and Valerie Tan make the point that in the face of rapid and often disruptive change, companies need to become more team-focused, continually striving to improve how they work. In seeking to answer the question of why some teams outperform others in a 2018 study, they found that psychological safety had 10 times the impact on teamwork, relative to other organisational climate factors combined – more than remuneration, development opportunities and recognition. So how can leaders foster psychological safety in teams?

The first step is to eradicate the blame culture: the energy-sapping, defensive, back-protecting, passing the buck attitude that pervades many teams and organisations. Leaders should take the lead by making it clear that mistakes are opportunities to learn; they should talk about mistakes they have made and what they learned from them. They should encourage sharing of information. If a team member goes on a training course or attends a conference, they should share what they have learned with the others. Encourage team members to share what customers are telling them and regularly review how you are getting information about what your customers are looking for. Encourage people to talk openly in meetings and to confront difficult topics, rather than remaining silent and then complaining either about frustrations or about other team members after the meeting.

But none of this will be effective without developing trust – trust is at the heart of a psychologically healthy team. To what extent is trust a key component of the microculture you try to foster?

10. Developing trust and openness

Without trust, none of the conversations that make up a healthy microculture would have any credibility. Why should someone trust you?

You can see a member of your team is slowly drifting into the zone of red flags. You approach them with good intentions, hoping they will share what they are struggling with. Why should they be open with you? They might see this conversation to be a huge risk to their credibility or to their career opportunities. What have you done to encourage trust and openness?

If they are struggling with too many deadlines, they might tell you about that. But suppose they fear that a project they have taken on might fail – might they tell you about that? Suppose they are preoccupied about a relationship that is falling apart, that has badly affected their sleep – would they tell you about how that is affecting their concentration? Suppose they had recently been diagnosed with depression and were struggling with the side effects of medication – would they be open with you about that?

Trust, crucial for openness, develops from conversations that go deeper than those that make up more transactional relationships. What kind of relationship do you have with your people? What do you know about them? I know many people working in corporates or professional service firms who have more open conversations with clients than they have with colleagues or with their bosses.

Do you know about relationships your people are in, about what's going on with their children? Do you know if they have children? Do you know who has an elderly relative whose health has declined? Do you know who is struggling to get a mortgage or with school problems? Do you know what they enjoy doing at weekends? And what do they know about you? If you know a lot about them, but they know very little about you, that feels more like an interview than a relationship.

What sort of model are you? Why would someone trust a conversation with you about drawing tighter boundaries around the job – not working after the children are in bed, or at weekends – if you are regularly working late or are clearly sending emails on Sundays?

Why should they trust your intentions if you run a meeting about how the team could work more effectively and have tougher conversations with clients about deadlines if you then agree a deadline that is going to really pressure the team over a bank holiday weekend? For trust, you need to be a credible model.

And for trust you need to be authentic. Some people, less confident of their ability, play a role of being a manager, almost as if they are afraid of being themselves. Trust yourself and let yourself be yourself.

Paul

Every now and then, I see someone in my clinic who makes a point that stays with me because of what it could teach others. I had seen Paul for a few sessions to help him recover from a depression that had developed following a relationship falling apart. The relationship had floundered because of his work hours, which had left his girlfriend feeling she would never be a priority to him if he carried on in this job. The demands were certainly heavy: he travelled regularly to other European cities, his hours were unpredictable, he often worked late. There were definitely decisions he could have taken that would have helped him manage his life better, and conversations he could have had with his managers about expectations and deadlines that would have given his relationship more of a chance. But the conversation he knew would have helped would have been one with his manager about life at home not being easy right now, that he needed to give more time to his relationship. But he couldn't have that conversation because he felt his managers would not have understood.

Then he told me: 'If I worked a 9 to 5 day then what goes on in my home life is basically my affair. But I don't work a 9 to 5 day, I work often 11 hours or more. I think that what goes on in my home life should therefore be of interest to my managers. But do they ever ask me: how are things at home with all the hours you are working? No – they don't even ask me how I am. But just that question would show me they cared and would make it far easier for me to have a conversation if something was going wrong.'

How comfortable would you be about having a conversation with your boss on the following issues?

- Having difficulties with a client/customer
- Having made a mistake on a work matter
- Feeling insecure about meeting your targets this year
- Having difficulty with a colleague
- Having difficulties in your home relationship or in your family
- Changes to your health, including your psychological health
- Concerns about how a colleague is treating a junior person

How comfortable would you want your team to be about having those conversations with you? Every leader and manager has to make a decision about that. Their answer will determine the degree of trust and openness there will be in their team, and that will shape the microculture they create for their people.

Keith and Nadia were working for managers whose microcultures encouraged sufficient trust for them to be open about what they were struggling with. Those conversations and the support that went with them helped Keith and Nadia regain control of their lives and mental well-being. Rory was less fortunate, working for a disconnected, inaccessible person, who in no sense was managing the team he was in. Jan's manager had created a microculture with no trust or openness, but that was instead destructive and undermining of her confidence and mental health.

A psychologically healthy culture needs frequent conversations in group meetings and in one-to-one reviews, discussing expectations about openness on issues that are both work-related and personal, that people might feel inhibited about, backed up with questions that invite openness. Crucially, it needs the leader to be open about why this matters, which might include him or her sharing what they have experienced that makes greater openness and trust a priority for them.

10

Navigating life

The times in which we are living may not be best suited to our mental health. Our culture reinforces competitive individualism, which has developed into perfectionistic goals and models of how life should be. The plastic world of social media magnifies the imperfections of our lives. The global working culture for many people lacks any constraints in how they work, making it very difficult for committed, conscientious people to draw any boundaries around their day.

Rates of anxiety are increasing. We have good reason to be anxious. Political systems on which many people hold faith are breaking down. Narcissistic leaders, even in democratic societies, are engaged in highly risky projects that could endanger the livelihoods and security of millions of people. Low rates of economic growth, escalating inequality and mounting debt undermine the foundations of health and educational systems on which millions of families depend. Random killings, mass shootings, cars driven into groups of innocent people underscore the unpredictability of life. Radical, disruptive change in your work life could wipe out your job and make your skill base obsolete, all decided by a group of strategists and senior decision-makers whom you will never meet. And, of course, there are huge existential threats, like the global pandemic which has ripped through Europe, the US and Asia like a wildfire, with governments desperately trying to control it through lockdown measures. These measures themselves have massive implications for all our futures. Yes, we have reason to be anxious.

We have looked at several people in these chapters who are struggling with the demands of their lives. They cover a wide range of occupational groups, from senior managers and partners in professional service firms to people on the front line in telesales jobs. They have a lot in common: committed, conscientious, fearful of letting themselves down, anxious about failing, their lives have drifted out of balance as they struggle to live up to the expectations they are under. They have all drifted into a pathway that has taken them further and further from good levels of energy, happiness and mental flexibility. Some have tipped into states of anxiety or depression; others have completely lost their energy and burned out. Many have never experienced these symptoms before, but they have an impact on every aspect of their lives. It is impossible to estimate how many are on this pathway but have not yet developed symptoms that take them to healthcare professionals, but it is likely to be many millions, because this is how we live today.

It is quite obvious from the people we have looked at that taking it for granted that you will get through difficult times because you always have is a dangerous assumption. Most of these people coped well with life – until the point when circumstances overwhelmed them. They have not been helped by their tendency to drift away from prioritising their own well-being when they most need to take care of it. They have not acknowledged the importance of routines like exercise, diet, sleep and ways of relaxing or how they balance the pressures they are under. In most cases, they haven't even recognised the red flags of having drifted off-track until they became too serious to ignore.

We need to actively navigate life, starting with a recognition of when the weather is changing, storm clouds gathering. We may be managing life adequately when we are not particularly challenged, when everything seems reasonably in control, but how much capacity do we have to deal with unexpected pressures?

Many people's lives are finely balanced – too finely, there's not enough capacity to absorb a change in their circumstances. The combination of constant work demands, children, all the domestic things we have to do, sometimes a relationship that has drifted and is no longer giving us the happiness or the encouragement that it used to do, then something changes, it creates a new demand, and there may not be enough flexibility in the system to accommodate this additional pressure.

The sort of circumstances that could easily overload a finely balanced life could be:

- Being promoted
- Changing job
- A sudden increase in work demands
- A geographical move
- Returning to work after having a baby
- About to take on a tough assignment
- A job change that involves overseas travel
- A change in domestic circumstances
- Taking on a house renovation
- A change in health of a relative

These are all circumstances that could lead some people to drift into the pathway that eventually leads to ill health. And almost inevitably, as they start to feel over-pressurised, they drift away from their balancing routines. They become disconnected from some aspects of their lives that had a balancing function without them recognising it. Not everyone allows this drift to happen – however, they are more successful at navigating through difficult times.

Jake

For the past couple of years, Jake has been under more pressure than he can remember. He works for a financial services company; the pressures have always been high, but since the company was acquired by a larger organisation the pressures he has been under have greatly increased. On top of his management job he has also become responsible for introducing a new IT system, which is a bigger project than he has done before. At home, he and his wife have taken on a renovation project and until the renovations are completed they are living in a small rented flat. He and Sam have been married for eight years. They have two children, a daughter who is five and a son who is aged two. Sam was diagnosed with depression a few years ago. She takes an antidepressant, but the relationship has suffered as a consequence. Jake feels he has to be careful about what he tells Sam in case it upsets her or makes her feel anxious. He misses the open conversations they used to have. The building works have greatly stretched them financially, and the combination of the work and home pressures weigh on him. There are times when he worries that he has overextended himself, or that the IT project might fail and he might lose his job.

Nevertheless, despite the pressures, Jake recognises that overall he is feeling reasonably good about life. He is in the good zone of the energy and effectiveness curve. He sleeps pretty well, his mood is generally positive, most of the time he feels quite optimistic about life. He has a demanding schedule, he typically works a 10-hour day and the deadlines can be difficult, but overall he feels in control of the demands. He worries about Sam and he worries about how the children might be affected by her depression, but he is optimistic that she will recover.

Others could have slipped into the pathway that leads to ill health under similar pressures. They might have difficulty sleeping, at times feeling overwhelmed. They might have become irritable or withdrawn; they might have struggled with the work pressures, resentful of the increased targets and frustrated at being let down by the IT contractors. Their concentration and decisiveness could have been affected. They might have drifted to working longer hours. They might have started to drink more as a way of relaxing after they got home. Their ways of thinking about themselves and their circumstances might also have subtly changed to self-doubt or self-criticism or to helplessness, which would have further undermined their ability to manage the pressures.

But Jake has not gone down that path. Looking at Jake's day-to-day behaviour shows that he is taking nothing for granted as far as his mental well-being is concerned. He makes good decisions about many of the things that relate to good mental health. Despite the pressures from his job, he maintains routines that help stabilise the physiology of mental energy and well-being.

Jake runs a tight day. He gets up early, usually around 6 a.m., and goes for a run most mornings. He has breakfast with his children, and a couple of days a week he takes his daughter to school. On his way to work he stops off at a cafe for a coffee and to review emails and plan his day. He is very focused, prioritises well, does emails in blocks and delegates well. He tries to get home twice a week to be involved with the children before they go to bed. He enjoys the peace of reading them a story before they go off to sleep and he often sits in their room for a little while listening to them sleeping before going downstairs to have supper with Sam. They eat together in the kitchen, chatting about the day. He prioritises his sleep. He knows he needs about seven and a half hours; he gets to bed about 10.30 p.m. and has an hour or so before he goes to bed when he doesn't look at emails.

What is also interesting are the routines that Jake has developed to keep himself emotionally grounded. A few times a week he writes in a journal, making a note of what has happened that he would like to remember, and he reflects on four or five things a day that he feels grateful for. He sees the impact of what he does, and he thinks about the meaning of what he does at work in being a supportive manager of the team, and his relationships with his clients, who are often having difficulty in their businesses, and at home with Sam and his children. He gives a lot of thought to what it means to be a good dad. He has a spiritual belief; he occasionally steps into a church and spends a short time in the peaceful atmosphere, reflecting on his life. He has an underlying faith that life will work out, that life brings its challenges – but they will pass, and as a family, they will be alright.

Creating a balancing system

What we are looking at here is a set of skills that Jake has developed to balance the pressures he is under. This collection of skills makes up his resilience – his balancing system. Many people have a good balancing system when life is going well, but when the pressures increase they automatically give more and more time to the demands and they let go of the balancing routines as a consequence. This can include drifting away from balancing ways of thinking that help to ground our emotions, as well as routines that help to stabilise our physiology and energy. These balancing routines organise themselves into building blocks that become integrated and reinforce one another.

There are four building blocks:

1. Maintaining a physiological balance

Anything we do to maintain stable physiological systems that underpin our energy, stable mood and anxiety, and protect our mental well-being, make up one core building block. This includes recognising the impact of exercise, ways of relaxing, good sleep routines, our diet, keeping alcohol moderate, our social life, time in nature for our energy and mental effectiveness. It also includes treating some of them as non-negotiable so that they do not drift out of our life when the demands increase. They are anchored on a week-by-week or day-by-day basis, regardless of how busy our life has become. You certainly don't need to do all of these – doing just a few of them could be enough to stabilise the physiology of energy and mental well-being – but crucially, don't drop all of them when life gets busy.

2. See what you can control

Decisions we make about the choices we have and what we can take control of to make life work for us make up the second building block. This might include challenging ourselves to look at habits that might be limiting our flexibility to take greater control of our lives; habits that might be preventing us from having a reasonable balance in our lives. This might include questioning why we are working through the day with no breaks, working after the children are in bed, or looking at emails constantly. It might include questioning our travel schedules, to make life less exhausting. This allows us to create boundaries in day-to-day life to protect balance in life, our relationships, time with our children and some time for ourselves against the relentless pressures of overly busy lives. These decisions resist the pressure of work from taking more and more of the space. This is also about taking control of our work lives – seeing where the choices are to be more effective in how we work so that we do not become overwhelmed by too many demands, and helping us stay focused on our longer-term goals. This might include challenging ourselves to take more control of our diaries, blocking time for key things we want to get done. For some, it might include being more willing to ask for help or negotiate demands or push back when there is just too much to do. For others, it might involve setting a limit to how many meetings they have in a day, and reducing their length. It also includes taking more control of interruptions, doing emails in blocks rather than when they come in. Bearing in mind the people we have met who have become completely overwhelmed by work demands that never end, we need to think about what we are doing to prioritise what really matters.

3. Establishing support

The third building block is to establish good supports, so that we do not feel we are on our own in the face of life's challenges, and to think about the time we give to sustaining and enriching these relationships. These supports could be at home, in our families and relationships and friendships. And they should also be at work, in the network of supportive colleagues who we trust and with whom we can be open when life gets difficult and we feel out of our depth.

4. Developing a flexible mindset

The fourth is the mindset building block, which includes anything we do to reinforce strong attitudes linked to self-acceptance and openness rather than perfectionism; an enduring sense of purpose and meaning in our lives; and a belief that, regardless of the difficulties we are facing, we are not helpless – there are choices to take control of some aspects of the situation we are in. Then there are the mental skills we have learned to navigate difficult circumstances without falling into mental habits that could undermine confidence and mood and make us feel needlessly anxious or guilty.

These four building blocks are completely interconnected. If our physiology is stable, it is more likely we will be able to exercise mental habits that keep mood and confidence stable. And we have looked at many examples of how the way we think directly influences cortisol and neurotransmitter responses.

In navigating life, we need to do something in each of these building blocks; we should also recognise that when we drift away from any of these balancing routines, we raise the risk that we will drift away from others.

Underpinning all of this is a mindset of permission – or perhaps it is a mindset of self-protection or duty – that essentially says, 'I've got a demanding life at work and at home – I want to be really effective at work and be a great mum/dad to my children. For me to sustain this, I need to prioritise time to take care of my energy and my well-being into the long term.'

And that's the mindset that gets to navigating life skilfully and thoughtfully.

A checklist for navigating difficult circumstances

Let's take a few minutes to consolidate your resources for navigating life.

1) Are there any storm clouds gathering? What's ahead of you that could be challenging or disruptive?

2) Where would you say you are in the energy and effectiveness curve? Any red flags?

- Feeling more tired than usual
- Sleeping less well
- Feeling irritable and moody
- Less confident
- Not looking forward to things – everything feels an effort
- Demands feel overwhelming
- More emotional, close to tears some of the time
- Becoming more withdrawn
- Feeling more anxious and worried than usual

3) How solidly anchored are the routines that stabilise the physiology of emotional well-being? Which ones are non-negotiable? Which ones have you drifted away from?

Track yourself for a week on the following behaviours to arrive at your baseline score:

	Day						
	1	2	3	4	5	6	7
Exercise (Yes/No: 1/0) *Approx. 30 minutes*							
Relaxation time (Yes/No: 1/0) *Yoga, meditation, listening to music, breathing exercises*							
Sleep (7+ hours: 1; less than 6 hours: -1)							
Diet (blood-sugar stabilising: 1; blood sugar destabilising: -1) *See Chapter 2*							
Alcohol (125ml+: -1)							
Time in nature (Yes/No: 1/0)							
Time with friends (Yes/No: 1/0)							
Time with your partner (Yes/No: 1/0) *Time just for the two of you*							
Daily score							
Score for the week							

You could track how you are doing week by week or for one week every month.

Try to keep your scores in the moderate positive range, with one or two items you hold as non-negotiable. Use the tracker to navigate, not letting a good positive score drift to a negative score when life becomes more demanding.

4) What boundaries do you have? What are you doing to protect your balance to life to get time for your partner, your children, the things you enjoy doing?

5) What are you doing to stop work from taking over? Are you setting email boundaries, taking breaks in the day, limiting working in the evenings, keeping weekends free?

6) How tightly are you managing your workday? Are you planning and using tough prioritising, discussing demands, limiting interruptions, emails and meetings?

7) How are you protecting time for you and your partner? Are you getting home early enough to do something together? Do you have routines that you both enjoy? Are you making plans together?

8) What are you doing on a regular basis to keep yourself emotionally grounded? For example, reviewing the day with these questions in mind:

   - What have I done today that I feel good about?
   - Who have I helped today?
   - What did I tackle that I might have put off doing?
   - What do I feel grateful for today?
   - What has given me a sense of meaning and purpose today?

9) Which mental habits do you need to be aware of for their potential to disrupt your emotions (see Chapter 5)? How will you challenge them? For instance, the tendency to see a catastrophe rather than a platform; the tendency to internalise when something goes wrong; the tendency not to ask for help when you need it; the tendency to be self-blaming rather than accepting when something goes wrong.

10) What perspectives will you hold on to when the waters get choppy? What has your experience of getting through difficult circumstances taught you? Be very specific here.

Learning from experience

Many people who have gone so far down the pathway that they have collapsed into ill health, and have then recovered their emotional well-being and energy, develop a commitment to themselves never to go there again. They emerge from the whole experience stronger than they were before it all went wrong. For them, keeping in mind the structure of the curve, with its accumulation of red flags and the building blocks that make up the balancing system, can allow them to navigate their lives more successfully.

Andrew

Andrew had lost all balance in his life as a result of working on an unusually demanding combination of assignments at a point in his career when he was coming up for partnership in the firm he had been working in since coming to the UK five years ago. He had found himself working on both a UK and US assignment at the same time and he gradually slipped into the habit of working in both UK and US time zones. He had always given a great deal to his job, but on these assignments there were no constraints other than any that he could provide for himself. He was enthusiastic, committed and he enjoyed the work and his relationships with his team and clients. It was rare for him to work fewer than 13 hours a day, but recently his hours had gone to unsustainable levels, occasionally 18 hours or more. He had been struggling to sleep for several months but now he was waking after two to three hours, feeling very alert and unable to get back to sleep, his mind racing with everything he had to do. He had developed uncomfortable symptoms of anxiety, including butterflies in his stomach and times when he could feel his heart racing. Sometimes he felt so tired he could hardly think; he was often close to tears and there were times when he just felt like running away from this job. But he felt trapped – he had two young children, and he didn't want to let himself or his team down. He felt in a permanent state of high arousal: times when his head raced, over-breathing and the occasional panic attack.

Long before the circumstances came to a head, Andrew's life had slipped out of balance. He often found himself racing to catch the last train home; his earlier habit of getting home for the children's bath routine one or two nights a week had gone, and most nights he ate on his own after his wife had gone to bed. Andrew got to the point where he was so exhausted he could hardly concentrate. He went to his GP and was signed off work. In all, he was off for two months. In that time, he restructured his entire balancing system using the building blocks as a guide. He got into a regular exercise routine of running for half an hour daily, he improved his diet, and he added a relaxation technique to help him sleep. He got back to playing the piano, which he had not done for over 10 years. This combination reduced his anxiety and improved his sleep, and eventually he lost the feelings of exhaustion.

By the time he got back to work he had decided on working with stronger boundaries, aiming for a 10-hour day and an email boundary in the evening, something he had never done before. He committed to being home for the bath routine a couple of times a week and to having times when he and his wife could spend time together. He took much more control of how he worked, moving away from a list-driven approach to much tougher prioritising, more effective delegating and a greater willingness to negotiate demands.

Over all of this were some significant changes to his attitude about work and balance in his life, starting with the realisation that only he could take control, that every day was a choice between the old way of no boundaries or clarity as to what the day was about; that he owed it to himself and to his family to prioritise his health.

Three years later, Andrew is still maintaining this balanced approach to his work life. He monitors himself on the key building blocks and keeps a diary of what he is doing to maintain physiological stability and of how well he is sticking to family commitments. There have been times when he has struggled to maintain the structure, but as soon as he starts to experience red flags, particularly disturbed sleep, he pulls back and considers how he will navigate himself through these demands.

Andrew is working for the same organisation, he has been promoted, and the demands are no less, but he is maintaining his energy and the balance to his life. He has kept his boundaries; he sleeps seven hours a night and he feels good about life. He is much more actively involved in his family life. Going down the curve into exhaustion and paying a heavy price left him with the determination never to go there again.

Others might recognise that they have gone a long way into the curve but have not yet developed symptoms of ill health. They realise it has been many months since they felt really good about life. They might be conscious of feeling tired most of the time and struggling to stay on top of a demanding job, irritable, distracted, less connected to friends and family. It has all become joyless. You may recognise some of yourself in these characteristics.

Many of these people, having been introduced to the building blocks that make up our balancing system, go on to make a handful of changes that allow them to navigate back into the good zone of energy, effectiveness and more positive mood, and sustain that despite times of increased pressure.

Jasmin

Jasmin is a head teacher in an Outer London school. She has been in this job for two years. She loves teaching, having wanted to be a teacher since she was a young girl. She is warm, outgoing, caring;

she exudes a natural enthusiasm for what she does. Jasmin had inherited a troubled school; it had had a poor inspection report, staff were demoralised, and there were many dissatisfied parents. Jasmin had not recognised how these pressures were affecting her until she attended a workshop I ran for head teachers in her area. Then she realised how far down the curve she had drifted, well beyond her zone of elasticity. She saw that she had gradually accumulated more and more red flags, including sleeping poorly, feeling constantly tired, occasionally breaking down in tears and feeling agitated about everything she felt responsible for and the uphill road she felt she had in front of her. She recognised that it had been two years since she was in a good zone of emotional stability and energy. Initially she had been excited about taking on the head teacher role, but within six months she felt overwhelmed by the pressures she was facing.

In the workshop, she also recognised how much she had drifted away from nearly everything that used to enrich her life and keep her in balance. Because she had been waking early, she typically got up around 5 in the morning and started working at home between 5.30 and 6 a.m. She rarely finished work before 8 at night, struggling to get through her emails and admin work. In the evening, by the time she had made supper and cleaned up, there was practically no time for herself. She had always been a moderate social drinker, but now she was drinking about half a bottle of wine in the evenings. More worryingly, she recognised that she was looking forward to that first glass of wine to help her relax.

First, Jasmin recognised that unless she prioritised time for looking after herself and her energy, she was eventually going to fail in this job. As she put it: 'This is not just about me – I need to get back in good shape to give my best to my school.' Jasmin made a number of changes. She stopped drinking midweek and only drank moderately on weekends. She recognised that in her previous job she had had a half-hour walk to work, whereas in this school she drove to work. She realised she missed the effects of the walk in helping her close the day and clear her head. She got back into the habit of daily walks and would occasionally go for walks at lunchtime. She deliberately structured better sleep routines, getting to bed earlier and relaxing herself back to sleep if she woke in the night. As far as rebalancing life was concerned, she made a commitment to get home earlier two nights a week, brought her Pilates classes back, and determined to see more of her friends and sisters than she had been doing over the last few months.

One of the most significant realisations that Jasmin had was in seeing that she had taken practically all the responsibility for the changes that needed to be made in the school on her shoulders. She reorganised her immediate leadership team, and developed a more open, sharing approach with them, working with them and delegating many of the projects that she needed to put in place.

By the time I saw her for a follow-up meeting a few months after the workshop, all of these changes were part of her restructured approach to week-by-week life. Recognising that she needed to prioritise time for herself for the sake of the school was the main source of motivation for Jasmin to sustain those changes. She was feeling much more effective, she had regained her energy, and her self-confidence was boosted by seeing some of the tangible effects in her school. She also tried to integrate some of the learning points she had introduced to her own life into her style of managing her team. She regularly checked on how they were coping with the pressures they were under and encouraged much greater openness. She also encouraged her team to think about their balance and how they were working, to create a healthier culture in her school.

The crucial point that both Andrew and Jasmin came to see is that this is not about following a list of healthy behaviours. It is about seeing the system of the four building blocks – maintaining physiological balance, taking control of what we can, building our supports and developing flexible ways of thinking – and making some changes in each one. If you are already overloaded, being urged to exercise, sleep well and improve your diet will only make you feel more overloaded. And in any case, we all know we should be exercising, eating healthily and getting more sleep. It starts with a mindset that you matter: if you are not in the equation, it is likely you will not be able to cope with the demands and you could fail. Commitments to exercise, to improve sleep or to take on other routines that stabilise our energy require us to take control of our over-pressurised lives – where we set boundaries, decisions we make about the best use of our time and what we negotiate, recognising that the demands never end and we must define how we prioritise those demands, rather than simply doing more. It includes investing time in our relationships for our happiness – at home, but also at work, as Jasmin did to build a more supportive team to share the load and to make her feel less isolated with all the demands on her shoulders. And none of this can be achieved without subtle changes in our attitudes and our mindset about work to create the flexibility and willingness to experiment with a different approach. This is a system, not a list of things to do.

As I write this, we are in the middle of the lockdown that the UK government imposed to limit the spread of the coronavirus, which has threatened to overwhelm our health services. This, of course, is hugely disruptive to day-to-day life. Most of us cannot go to our workplaces; we are disconnected from friends, family and colleagues; the normal places we go to for exercise and entertainment and our social lives are closed. On top of that we are living with greater levels of uncertainty than most people have experienced before. So how are people navigating themselves through these circumstances?

Let's look at two examples of people I have been working with during lockdown, to see how they have adapted to the current challenges they face.

Lucy

Lucy works in a professional service firm, and lives on her own in a London flat. The lockdown in the UK allows her to go out of her flat for an hour a day to exercise, but she otherwise has no contact with anyone other than through technology. She has developed a strict structure to her day with a good walk in a local park for an hour early in the morning. Her workday is well defined with a clear sense of purpose for her team and for her clients, who need her advice now more than ever. She checks in on her team as a group and individually, conscious of some of the difficulties they might be having. She is aware of how easy it could be for her day to be taken up entirely by video meetings, so she deliberately blocks time for the work she wants to get done that day. She has learned that if she doesn't do that, her day inevitably runs into the late evening. She closes her day with a yoga session from an app, and connects with her family every evening and with friends a few times a week. She takes care of her diet and is conscious of the risks of snacking.

Interestingly, Lucy is now doing some things that she would not have had the time to do before, but are giving her a sense of being grounded in where she is right now, like baking and needlework. She has also developed some mental habits that allow her to feel a degree of security in the present, deliberately preventing her head from darting off into an uncertain future. She reminds herself that today she is well, her family are well, and there is purpose in what she is doing right now. She has also developed a strong sense of thankfulness for what she has in her life that she might previously have taken for granted. She goes through a routine of making a note of those things at the end of each day.

You can clearly see what Lucy is doing through the perspective of the resilience-building blocks. She has given a strong priority to looking after her physiological well-being through exercise, yoga, a good diet and sleep. She has taken control of the structure to her day and how she is working. She is compensating for the loss of her social life and exercise classes rather than giving up or feeling helpless. Her mindset is strong, anchored in purpose and her sense of relevance to her team and her clients and a perception of thankfulness rather than just seeing what she is not able to do, the frustrations of the present circumstances and feeling disconnected or lonely. At times it can be stressful, but overall, she is feeling pretty good with this balancing system helping her to manage the pressures she is under right now.

Holly

Holly is a mother of two young kids, living with her husband in London. She also is in a highly demanding job for an international company. Her children's schools are closed, but the schools have provided online lessons which run for the duration of a normal school day – 9 a.m. to 3 p.m. The potential for getting overwhelmed by the combination of demands is huge.

She and her husband are dividing the day with Holly looking after the kids in the mornings, and her husband looking after them in the afternoons. Holly is ruthlessly prioritising work demands, accepting there are many things she doesn't have time for now, and she discusses the priorities with her boss on daily calls. Normally quite perfectionistic, she has learned from conversations with friends that many are conscientiously following the home-school programme and trying to do a full day at work as well, and have ended up exhausted, working late into the evening, not getting to bed until after midnight. She recognises that that is not a good approach. Instead, Holly has adopted a more pragmatic mindset – what could we achieve in three hours with the kids? Three hours is better than nothing, and realistically, they will be back at school before long, and they will catch up. She takes her kids to the park every day, and three times a week she goes for a 20-minute run. She keeps in touch with her friends and family via Zoom; she and her husband try to make time together after the kids are in bed. Some evenings she has to work late, but she is tough in what she prioritises, and she has broken the habit of randomly looking at emails in the evening. She knows she needs seven hours sleep and she makes that a priority, although the kids occasionally wake her in the night. Overall, she is managing the demands; she recognises she needs to prioritise some things for her energy, she is taking control of priorities and she is consciously trying to replace her perfectionism with a pragmatic mindset for her work and homeschooling demands. She has times when she feels like she is failing, especially when she talks to other parents who are not working or colleagues who do not have kids, but she is able to push these thoughts aside, with a recognition of what she is managing to do in very unusual circumstances.

Both of these women have similar busy work lives, but their circumstances are completely different. They are struggling with different realities and challenges but with similar personality pressures. They have both successfully and helpfully adopted mindsets of 'regardless of the circumstances I will make it work . . . there are choices I can make, including choices about how I see the circumstances I am in . . . I'll get through it a day at a time'.

11

Planting the seeds

When I run workshops on resilience and mental well-being, people often come and say 'How could we pass this on to our children?' or 'I would really have benefited from learning about this early in life'. When I told my daughter, Becky, who has three young children, that I was going to write a book, she immediately asked: 'Are you going to include a section on bringing up kids?'

Planting the seeds of resilience in our children could be one of the most valuable things a parent can do. There is certainly a lot of concern right now about the mental health of children. A comprehensive paper published in 2018 titled 'Mental Health of Children and Young People in England' reports that one in eight young people between the ages of 5 and 19 had at least one mental disorder. The most common conditions were anxiety and depression, with 16.9 per cent of girls in the 17 to 19 age range having an emotional disorder.

Much of the discussion around this focuses on providing counselling in schools. Many schools are taking the mental health of their students seriously. Some have introduced classes in mindfulness. Other interventions have focused on adolescents, recognising that that age group faces particularly difficult challenges, including difficulties regulating emotions and being hypersensitive to exclusion, which increases the risk of depression in this age group. Others have focused on preventing bullying and helping children who have been bullied so that they do not develop longer-term difficulties as a consequence.

All of this is, of course, about stepping in when some difficulties have been identified. But could we create a stronger base of resilience early on?

There is a good body of evidence on what contributes to resilience in children. Some of this focuses on the child – their personality, empowerment, intelligence; some focuses on the family – relationships with parents, conflict or harmony at home; and some focuses on the environment – the extended family and school experience.

There are some impressive longitudinal studies on childhood resilience, including the Kauai Study in Hawaii, which followed 700 infants through to the age of 40. A team of mental health workers, paediatricians and other specialists monitored the children at regular intervals, assessing how they handled setbacks and adversity in their lives. A third of the group had experienced adverse circumstances in life, including poverty, domestic conflict and parental drug abuse. But only one in six had a mental health issue by the time they were 40. The good news is that most children are pretty resilient, even in the face of early adversity. The researchers, Emmy Werner and Ruth Smith, called those children 'vulnerable but invincible'. Despite their adverse circumstances, 'they grew into competent, confident and caring adults. They did not develop any behaviour or learning problems during childhood or adolescence'.

They identified several protective factors that contributed to resilience, including a belief in the controllability of their lives rather than feeling helpless. Their sense of control over life events led to greater planning and anticipation than was evident in less resilient children. Many of them sought out people or opportunities that could influence their circumstances rather than passively reacting to constraints.

Other factors included being good problem-solvers and the ability to draw meaning from adversity. A religious belief also helped provide stability and meaning in their lives. The resilient children tended to be responsive to people, had good communication skills and had the ability to focus their attention and control emotional impulses. As a consequence, they developed faith, optimism and self-confidence.

Other studies have identified proactivity – a belief in their own effectiveness, rather than being passive observers – as contributing to resilience. Mary Alvord and Judy Grados, American psychologists writing in the *Journal of Professional Psychology* in 2005, review the characteristics of apparently resilient children who do well despite adverse circumstances in their lives. They point to self-regulation as a crucial skill for children to learn – i.e. the ability to manage their emotions and behaviour, to 'self-sooth' and calm themselves, which is more likely to gain positive attention from others and can lead to developing healthy social relationships. They say that children who have developed a proactive approach to life, who take the initiative and believe in their own effectiveness, cope better with life. They can have an impact on their environment, rather than being passive observers. They argue that having social competence and building positive connections with peers, family and other adults is significantly related to children's ability to adapt to life's stressors.

They go on to describe individual and family clinical interventions, including teaching problem-solving skills, encouraging children to express their feelings, developing self-esteem through offering children responsibilities that encourage a sense of accomplishment, and teaching relaxation techniques.

Robert Brooks, a psychologist at Harvard Medical School, has developed an approach to fostering self-esteem in children using 'islands of competence'. An island of competence is a specific area of strength. In developing this strength in a child, the confidence ripples out to other parts of their life. He said that all children have unique strengths and courage, and so if we can find and reinforce these areas of strength, 'we can create a powerful "ripple effect", in which they may be more willing to venture forth and confront situations that have been problematic'. He developed this idea after seeing many children in clinical practice who were struggling and experiencing frustration and failure in their lives, with a sense of inadequacy, helplessness and hopelessness. He thought: 'If there is an ocean of inadequacy, then there must be islands of competence – areas that have been or have the potential to be sources of pride and accomplishment. We must help children and adults to identify and reinforce these islands so that at some point they become more dominant than the ocean of inadequacy.' He wanted to shift the focus from weaknesses to strengths, from pessimism to optimism. Asking parents to identify their children's islands of competence shifts their energy from 'fixing deficits' to 'identifying and reinforcing strengths'.

A sound platform

Creating a sound platform to help your children navigate life is about planting the seeds of resilience through the day-to-day conversations you have with them. Start early, don't wait until they hit adolescence. Starting early could give them a stronger base for dealing with adolescence.

Dr Ann Masten, a psychologist from the University of Minnesota, who has studied resilience for 40 years and directs the Project Competence Programme on Risk and Resilience, argues that resilience stems from a healthy operation of learned adaptational systems. She says: 'The skills you need at one age are the platform for building future skills. If you establish a sound foundation early, you can build forward.'

Planting seeds of resilience

Use the framework of the stress curve and the four building blocks as a structure for thinking about family conversations.

1. Where you are on the mental well-being/stress continuum is going to affect your children

If you come home irritable, frustrated or stressed, that will carry over to your children, which could lead to a more difficult evening for you as they play up. So before you enter your home, ask yourself: 'What mood is walking in?' Very often, just asking that question can modify your mood. But on other occasions, if you are stressed or frustrated by your day at work, use it as an opportunity to tell your children how you are feeling and why. This can do a number of useful things:

- It can help your children develop a better ability to articulate emotions, which does not come easily to some children. In fact, some adults have real difficulty expressing and articulating emotions.
- It can normalise emotions – that frustration, disappointment, feeling overloaded, are normal day-to-day feelings, and they will pass.
- It can also explain the cause – work difficulties, a bad commute, or an unanticipated last-minute demand that means you will have to work this evening. The cause is not about them.

2. Establish routines that encourage happy conversations

As often as you can, have supper with your children. Use it as an opportunity for everyone to chat about their day. No phones, no television. And don't turn it into something unpleasant, like reprimanding someone or discussing the school report. Make it light and humorous. Everyone around the table, regardless of how young they are, has their say. And no phones applies as much to the adults as to the children. Homes need digital boundaries. Use the time around the table to encourage humour – an invaluable skill for children to learn. It detaches you from stressful circumstances, it encourages self-acceptance, it instantly connects.

3. Doing things together is more effective than telling your children to do it

For example, exercising together is fun. When my children were little, I used to go for a run in the nearby park with them on their bikes – and the biggest motivator for me to stay fit wasn't for the health of my arteries, it was to be fit enough to play really active games with my children. Cooking together is a great way to get children thinking about good nutrition – go shopping together for fresh food, let them decide what they are going to cook. It takes longer, it's messier, but it plants seeds about what a good diet is, and there is a sense of accomplishment at the end of it.

If they've had a tense day, wind down together. Don't give them a mindfulness app. Sit on the bedroom floor with your child and take her through a relaxing slow breathing exercise. Add a relaxing image for the last few minutes. This could become a lasting skill to help them manage emotions.

4. Develop an attitude of being empowered rather than helpless

Have conversations to help children feel they are in control of life circumstances – skills such as anticipating, planning, problem-solving. Planning how they will manage a school project, or revise for an exam, or planning how they will cook a meal, are all great opportunities. And think about what could go wrong and how you could plan for that, rather than getting emotional or giving up.

5. Encourage negotiating

Children negotiate from a very young age. It's really fun watching it happen. Encourage it – you are helping them develop an invaluable resilience skill. Many people never learn to negotiate; they feel embarrassed, or they don't feel they have the right to do it. Negotiating can prevent you from getting overloaded as an adult; it can get you the support or resources you need. It contributes to a more successful life. Negotiating contributes to happy relationships.

For negotiating, you need to be flexible. All children need clear lines about what's not acceptable, but try to keep them wide, with scope for discussion. If you are inflexible about your rules, they won't learn to negotiate. But equally if you are too lax, they get their way anyway – no need to learn to negotiate. You could even coach them in how to do it better – what they need to say to persuade you, how to listen, how to compromise. Negotiating is a skill for life.

6. Encourage your children to have a balanced life
Some children are over-scheduled – schoolwork, extra studies, music lessons, sports practice, drama. What are they learning from all this scheduling? That they have to be constantly busy; it might get to the point where they feel uneasy if they are not doing something that's been planned for them. It doesn't take much imagination to see what this could lead to later in life. Encourage balance, time when they can wind down and do some relaxing things, like playing with their Lego or whatever they enjoy doing. And have a digital cut-off a couple of hours before bed – that should apply for the whole family, not just the children.

7. Play together, laugh together, have fun together
Playing imaginative games encourages a child's imagination and acts as a release. Playfulness lightens the burden of intensity. There can be too much heaviness and intensity about constantly performing. Children need a release from this, and perspectives about other things mattering.

If you are in the swimming pool with your children, play an imaginative game with them – don't coach their swimming style. This will be tense and frustrating, and if everything they do with you is intense, that feeling will define how they see time with you. When I look at some dads with their children – and it's usually boys – they might be kicking a ball together. Well, it's better than not being involved, but there's not a lot of fun in that. Children are not projects, they are unique characters – enjoy their individuality, their fun and their energy. Let play be something you value as a family and then it develops into the relationship you have.

8. Encourage self-acceptance, rather than perfectionism
Children have different strengths – some things they are just not good at. Allow them not to be good at something. If they have given it their

best shot, that's what matters. Don't have a conversation about where they have lost marks in an exam, but encourage them to feel good about the effort they put in. If they have been messing about, weren't prepared, or didn't work, that's a different matter.

If they want to improve something that doesn't come easily to them, that should be encouraged in whatever way you can. Never turn a setback into a negative generalisation, such as 'You just don't try hard enough' or 'You're just not motivated'. Encourage a plan to help them achieve what they want to do. And turn successes into positive generalisations: 'You make up really good stories', 'You really work at it when you set your mind to something.' Generalisations turn into confidence and into the basis of identity.

9. Contain and manage worries
If your child is anxious about something, normalise it, help them break it down into manageable, flexible chunks to make it less overwhelming. Help them persist if they get discouraged. You could also try taking them through a simple relaxation exercise, visualising succeeding at whatever it is they have got anxious about – planting a seed of how to turn a threat into a challenge.

10. Review the day together
From time to time, around the supper table, ask one or two of those questions about reviewing your day (see Chapter 6). 'What have you done today that you feel good about?', 'What did you feel grateful for?', 'What are you looking forward to tomorrow?' – these are questions for all of you, not just the children. Asking them develops the habit of consolidating the day and for developing a lens to see the day positively.

On other occasions, ask: What frustrated you today, and how did you deal with that frustration? Mum and Dad answer this as well. Think about the messages here: about how to articulate what frustrates you, listening to adults talk about how they manage those events and the sense of acceptance and equality that comes from that conversation.

This is life – it trips us up in different ways. Make the best of it, share the experience, turn it into humour and carry on.

11. Spend time individually with your children

If your life is overly busy, struggling to get everything done, there is a tendency to do things as a family: you all go for a walk in the park, or over to the swings. One thing I really learned as a dad is how much children value individual time with you, even if it's not that long. A bike ride together, reading a story, going to the shops, or a visit to a museum. But it's got to be equal. From a very early age, children have a sense of injustice if someone is getting more time with you. I think if children are getting individual time with you, it reduces attention-seeking behaviour as well.

12. Encourage and celebrate accomplishment

Encourage small areas of responsibility that your children can take pride in and give them a sense of accomplishment. It could be helping to look after their younger brother, or planting vegetables in the garden, or baking a cake for a birthday, or helping you do the supermarket shop, or making jam for the grandparents. And always encourage self-acceptance if something doesn't work out, and ideally highlight what you might learn from it.

A proactive approach

Anthony Seldon, Vice-Chancellor of the University of Buckingham, writing in *The Times* in January 2020, notes the epidemic level of mental health difficulties, especially among students and young people. He criticises the reactive approach of only addressing the problem when serious symptoms emerge.

Seldon advocates a plan involving health and education departments working together to build the capacity of young people to help themselves deal with life's challenges, by encouraging them to take greater control of their lives and their emotions and helping them to lead fulfilling lives rather than falling victim to psychological ill health. He lays out a plan to help schools educate students about how to achieve these goals and he is optimistic that this proactive approach will achieve much more than simply putting more money into mental health services.

We certainly need to be more proactive when it comes to the psychological health of our children. Yes, schools can help lay the foundations for good mental health through fostering self-respect and coping skills. But relying on health services and our education system to address the issue of psychological health in our children could leave many parents feeling disempowered. Family life centres around the conversations we have with our children and the activities we share with them. With a reasonable understanding about what resilience is about, it doesn't take a lot of imagination to see how family conversations could encourage children to understand and manage difficult emotions like frustration or anxiety, how small changes to day-to-day routines can have an effect on how we feel, how we could take some degree of control over difficult circumstances and how we could encourage balanced attitudes – like self-acceptance, humour, perseverance and responsibility – that form the foundations of self-esteem and psychological health.

12

Seventy million prescriptions

Hannah, Keith and Tom had all gone to their doctors to talk about how they had been feeling: tired and lacking in joyfulness in Hannah, and sudden, alarming panic attacks in Keith and Tom. All three had been offered antidepressants, although none of them were clinically depressed. They hadn't gone to their doctors to get an antidepressant. Hannah had gone because she was worried about how tired she felt, Keith was concerned about the panic attack he had had at work, and Tom was seeking reassurance about his heart, having experienced a panic attack in a traffic jam on his way to work. They all felt strongly, however, that medication was not the route they wanted to take. They wanted to regain control of their lives.

Nearly 71 million prescriptions for antidepressants were handed out in England in 2018, according to the UK NHS Digital Data. That compares with 36 million in 2008, with a steady increase year on year. One in six of the UK population aged between 18 and 64 were prescribed antidepressants in 2018. According to an article published in *Pharmaceutical Journal* in 2017, between April 2015 and June 2016 over 160,000 under 18-year-olds were prescribed medication typically used to treat depression and anxiety. A report from the American Psychological Association in 2017 reports that 13 per cent of the US population over the age of 12 take antidepressant medication. There was a 64 per cent increase in antidepressant usage between 1999 and 2014 in the US.

Many of these prescriptions would have been handed out to people who are not depressed but who are anxious or stressed or not sleeping well as a result of life circumstances. For about one person in three, antidepressants are effective. For a similar proportion, they have little effect. The most common antidepressants target neurotransmitter balance, serotonin in particular, named the SSRIs (selective serotonin reuptake inhibitors). But as we have seen, there are many potential pathways that can lead to depression, and serotonin depletion is only one of them.

How effective are antidepressants?

It is not easy getting an accurate picture of how effective antidepressants are, partly because of selective reporting of results of experimental trials. Those who prescribe antidepressants rely on published data to tell them about the effectiveness of different medications and it is crucial that what appears in the journals is an accurate representation of what researchers have found, particularly in studies that compare the effects of antidepressants with placebos. However, there is a much greater likelihood that studies that have found a positive result for antidepressants will get published than studies that have found they are no more effective than placebos.

Erick Turner, research psychiatrist at Oregon Health and Science University, and colleagues, reporting in the prestigious *New England Journal Of Medicine* in 2008 in an article titled 'Selective publication of antidepressant trials and its influence on apparent efficacy', make the point that evidence-based medicine needs unbiased reporting of results of drug trials. Otherwise there can be unrealistic estimates of a drug's effectiveness. They looked at research reports sent to the U.S. Food and Drug Administration (the FDA) on 12 antidepressants to see how many of these reports ended up being published in journals to which medical practitioners would have access. They found that approximately one in three of the reports were not published. Significantly, more of the published results were reporting positive results of antidepressant effectiveness than negative or questionable results. According to the published articles, it looked like 94 per cent of the trials on antidepressant effectiveness were positive, whereas the total picture reported to the FDA showed only 51 per cent to be positive. They calculated that this resulted in an inflation of antidepressant effectiveness by 32 per cent.

Two large-scale reviews of the effectiveness of antidepressants, one reported in *The Lancet* in 2018 and one in the *Journal of Psychotherapy and Psychosomatics* in 2010, found antidepressants to be only moderately more effective than placebos.

Withdrawal and side effects

Many people have taken antidepressants for years and many have found that coming off them has not been as easy as they had hoped. Withdrawal reactions or 'discontinuation syndrome', as it has been called, can include headaches, fatigue, sleep disturbances, agitation and anxiety, and slowly tapering the patient off the medication does not necessarily prevent these withdrawal effects from happening. There is also evidence that, for some patients, the long-term use of antidepressants could lead to a loss of drug efficacy and result in their condition becoming worse.

Medications have side effects and the side effects of some commonly prescribed antidepressants include weight gain, loss of sex drive and often sexual functioning, sleep disturbance and fatigue, which obviously could add to feelings of discouragement and could reduce the closeness of relationships that are so important for good mental health.

The action of antidepressants on our bodies is not properly understood. A 2017 study led by researchers at McMaster University in Canada looked at the effects of SSRIs and another class of antidepressants – tricyclics – on mortality rates. They conducted a meta-analysis of 16 studies made up of approximately 375,000 participants. Controlling for other possible variables, they found that those taking antidepressants had a 33 per cent higher mortality risk than people who were not taking the drugs. Those taking antidepressants were also at a higher risk of a cardiovascular event such as a heart attack or stroke.

Getting it in perspective

We need to get medication in perspective. If you are really struggling to get out of bed, barely able to function as a parent, not able to concentrate or make decisions at work, feeling completely worthless and contemplating taking your life, then you are most likely depressed, and medication is a very sensible choice. Similarly, if you are suffering from a primarily physiological disorder, such as bipolar disorder, or a psychotic condition, medication can help you manage it. But Keith, Tom and Hannah were definitely not in that category. If they had started on a course of medication, they could have felt even more disempowered. They could have moved to a mindset of: 'I am ill, I need to wait until the medication makes me better.' It could have made it less likely that they would look at what they could take control of to manage their lives more effectively. With this illness mindset, they might have moved even further away from a well-balanced life.

In many cases, how the person is feeling is *perfectly understandable* given the circumstances of their lives – over-pressurised, struggling, exhausted, working longer to compensate, neglecting sleep, no time to unwind, disconnected from their emotional lives. This is not about depression, this is about an unbalanced life.

But they chose not to take medication – they chose to take greater control of their lives, to rebuild a strong system to get their lives physiologically and mentally back in balance. They could see an immediate connection between what they were doing and how they were feeling. The choices they were making made them feel more empowered, gave them a far better understanding of how they worked, physically and mentally, and left them with a determination not to slip down that pathway again. They got back on track and were much more self-aware, with a stronger base of resilience than they had had before.

A complex system of resilience

All of the people whose stories we have looked at have come to a more empowered understanding about what it means to be resilient. Resilience is basically our mental strength. Many people see it as a quality we have. A quality like intelligence; for instance: 'I've always been bright. I always will be bright. I don't need to think about it.' Similarly, for resilience: 'I've always coped with life, I always will cope with life. I don't need to worry about it.' But suppose it is not a quality, suppose it is a collection of things we have learned to do – a collection of *skills*. Then we certainly wouldn't take it for granted. We would respect it, be curious about it, and motivated to add new skills to perfect it.

The slow pathway that goes from really good mental well-being – energised, feeling reasonably in control of life, emotionally in balance, feeling confident and good about life – all the way down to ill health, anxiety or burnout is a pathway of gradually drifting away from our framework of resilience skills. We drift away from routines around exercise, sleep, how we wind down, many even drift away from ways of managing work demands, becoming less focused and decisive; we lose the boundaries that separate work from our home lives. We gradually lose our attitudes and mindsets that keep us feeling effective and confident. The whole system that balances the pressures gradually falls away.

Resilience is a complex system of interconnected elements, with each part having an effect on all the others. Our diet can affect energy and mood via our neurotransmitters, as can exercise and time spent with good friends in a humorous conversation. Our neurotransmitters have an effect on our relationships, our ability to empathise, and our sleep. Poor sleep can undermine our mood, disrupt cortisol and the energy we have for an engaged home life, and our motivation to exercise and see friends. Exercise can have an impact on our sleep, how much we drink, our sex life, and the quality of our core relationships. All of these elements have an effect on how we see life, on our happiness and confidence, and how we view life has an immediate effect on our emotions and motivation. Exercise, diet, sleep, the quality of our relationships and friendships have an impact on our work performance, which in turn has an impact on how attentive and engaged we are at home, how we sleep and whether or not we exercise and maintain a good diet. We are one physiological and emotional system.

Balance: the critical element

To keep this system strong enough to keep us in the good zone of energy and well-being even in pressurised times, we need to make conscious decisions about balance. Energy, resilience and balance come up repeatedly in this book, but balance is critical to the other two. If we lose balance in our lives, we will lose energy sooner or later and that will undermine our resilience. We will then find ourselves heading into the pathway that takes us to ill health, physically or mentally.

Everyone we have met in this book has struggled with balance. But what is balance about? It is not about that out-of-date phrase 'work-life balance'. Today, work and our non-work lives are much more integrated. Our work lives can give us the variety, recognition, support, scope for creativity, friendships and fun that others get from their lives outside of work. Many organisations allow flexibility for merging work time with working from home, family demands, attending school events and sports, while keeping on top of what is going on at work. But working fixed hours doesn't necessarily prevent life from slipping out of balance, as we have seen with Keith and Nadia. Working flexibly can give you some advantages, but we need to be conscious of decisions we make to prevent work demands from taking more and more of the space until everything we need for energy and balance drifts away.

What makes life particularly challenging today is that there are no constraints on how we work or the hours we do. This contrasts with how life was just one or two generations ago. Then there was a rhythm to the day. Work stopped at a predictable time, home life was distinct from work. There was a closer connection to friends, many of whom you might have known all your life, and to the wider family. Church attendance and a sense of community belonging were stronger. There was an easier pace to the day.

A sense of belonging, solid friendships and relationships, and an easy ability to balance life go a long way to providing a foundation for mental well-being. Today, we have to navigate life with its relentless pressures, unpredictable changes and ambiguities, and we do not know how strong the foundations are until they are tested.

Balance is about making decisions about the hours we work and how we create time for other areas of our life that we value, like being a parent or someone's partner. Balance is about recognising the pressures we impose on ourselves, like perfectionism, conscientiousness and competitiveness, and keeping them in perspective, with some ways of thinking that hold those pressures in check. It is about finding attitudes like self-acceptance, pragmatism, and a strong sense of purpose to allow us to bounce back from setbacks, which could otherwise create feelings of self-blame, undermined confidence or a sense of failure.

Balance is about hour-by-hour decisions we make at work, about what priorities really matter out of an endless list of what we could be doing. And of course, balance is about protecting the physiological systems that underpin our energy and mental fitness – without that, the whole system is weakened.

Navigating life is about having the self-awareness to see where you are as soon as you drift off-track. When you really have no time to breathe, it's time to change course rather than just doing more. It is about genuinely respecting and safeguarding the system of skills, including ways of thinking that keep the pressures in balance – taking nothing for granted. It is about taking every opportunity to add skills to your system and challenging yourself about what you could control and what you need to let go of. It is about sharing your insights about navigating life with your team, creating a healthy microculture so that you are all in a stronger position to support one another. And it is about having warm conversations with your children, sharing stories and your ideas about managing life to plant the seeds for them to navigate their lives successfully and happily.

References

Chapter 2: Drifting off-track

Baker, C. (2018). 'Mental health statistics for England.' House of Commons briefing paper No. 6988. Available at: https://www.parliament.uk/commons-library

Financial Times (2019). 'The trillion-dollar taboo: Why it's time to stop ignoring mental health at work.' Available at: https://www.ft.com/content/1e8293f4-a1db-11e9-974c-ad1c6ab5efd1.

Freudberger, H. & Richelson, G. (1980). *Burnout: the high cost of high achievement.* New York: Bantam Books.

HSE. (2019). 'Work-related stress, anxiety or depression statistics in Great Britain, 2019.' Available at: https://www.hse.gov.uk/statistics/causdis/stress.pdf

Lastovkova, A. et al. (2018). 'Burnout syndrome as an occupational disease in the European Union: an exploratory study.' *Second Health.* Vol. 56, No. 2, pp.160–165.

Maslach, C. & Jackson, S.E. (1981). 'The measurement of experienced burnout.' *Journal of Occupational Behaviour.* Vol. 2, No. 2, pp.99–113.

Maslach, C. & Zeiter, M.P. (2016). 'Understanding the burnout experience: recent research and its implications for psychiatry.' *World Psychiatry.* Vol. 15, No. 2, pp.103–111.

World Health Organization. (2017). 'Depression and Other Common Mental Disorders Global Health Estimates.' Available at: https://apps.who.int/iris/bitstream/handle/10665/254610/WHO-MSD-MER-2017.2-eng.pdf?sequence=1

Chapter 3: Running on empty

Basso, J.C. & Suzuki, W.A. (2017). 'The Effects of Acute Exercise on Mood, Cognition, Neurophysiology, and Neurochemical Pathways: A Review.' *Brain Plasticity.* Vol. 2, No. 2, pp.127–152.

Blackburn, E. & Epel. E. (2017). *The Telomere Effect: A Revolutionary Approach to Living Younger, Healthier, Longer.* New York: Grand Central Publishing.

Bratman, G. et al. (2015). 'Nature experience reduces rumination and subgenual prefrontal cortex activation.' *Proceedings of the National Academy of Sciences.* Vol. 112, No. 28, pp.8567–8572.

Brown, K.W. et al. (2003). 'The benefits of being present: mindfulness and its role in psychological wellbeing.' *Journal of Personality and Social Psychology.* Vol. 83, pp.822–848.

Bullmore, E. (2018). *The inflamed mind: a radical new approach to depression.* New York: Short Books.

Campbell, J. et al. (2018). 'Debunking the Myth of Exercise-Induced Immune Suppression: Redefining the Impact of Exercise on Immunological Health Across the Lifespan.' *Front Immunology.* Vol. 9, p.648.

Chatzi, C. et al. (2019). Exercise-induced enhancement of synaptic function triggered by the inverse BAR protein, Mtss1L. *eLIFE.* Vol. 8, e45920.

Chekroud, S. et al. (2018). 'Association between physical exercise and mental health in 1.2 million individuals in the USA between 2011 and 2015: a cross-sectional study.' *The Lancet Psychiatry*. Vol. 5, No. 9, pp.739–746.

Childs, E. et al. (2014). 'Regular exercise is associated with emotional resilience to acute stress in healthy adults.' *Frontiers in Physiology*. Vol. 5, p.161.

Coates, J.M. et al. (2008). 'Endogenous steroids and financial risk taking on a London trading floor.' *Proceedings of the National Academy of Sciences*. Vol. 105, No. 16, pp.6167–6172.

Colzato, L. et al. (2012). 'Meditate to Create: The Impact of Focused-Attention and Open-Monitoring Training on Convergent and Divergent Thinking.' *Front Psychology*. Vol. 3, p.116.

Cooney, G.M. et al. (2013). 'Exercise for depression.' *Cochrane Systematic Review*. Vol. 9.

Crust, L. et al. (2011). 'Walking the walk: a phenomenological study of long-distance walking.' *J. Appl. Sport Psychol.* Vol. 23, pp.243–263.

De Young, R. (2007). 'Walking for mental vitality: Some psychological benefits of walking in natural settings.' Available at: https://www.researchgate.net/publication/251940530_Walking_for_Mental_Vitality_Some_Psychological_Benefits_of_Walking_in_Natural_Settings

Erikson, K.I. et al. (2010). 'Physical activity predicts gray matter volume in late adulthood.' *Neurology*. Vol. 75, No. 16, pp.1415–22.

Erikson, K.I. et al. (2011). 'Exercise training increases size of hippocampus and improves memory.' *Proceedings of the National Academy of Sciences*. Vol. 108, No. 7, pp.3017–22.

Firth, J. et al. (2018). 'Effect of aerobic exercise on hippocampal volume in humans: a systematic review and meta-analysis.' *Neuroimage*. Vol. 166, pp.230–238.

Goldin, P.R. (2010). 'Effects of Mindfulness-Based Stress Reduction (MBSR) on Emotion Regulation in Social Anxiety Disorder.' *Emotion*. Vol. 10, No. 1, pp.83–91.

Harvey, S. et al. (2018). 'Exercise and prevention of depression: Results of the HUNT cohort study.' *Am. J. Psychiatry*. Vol. 175, No. 1, pp.28–36.

Hunter, M. et al. (2019). 'Urban nature experience reduces stress in the context of daily life based on salivary biomarkers.' *Frontiers in Psychology*. Vol. 10, p.722.

Jacka, F. et al. (2017). 'A randomised controlled trial of dietary improvement for adults with major depression (the SMILES trial).' *BMC Medicine*. Vol. 15, No. 1, p.23.

Kandasamy, N. et al. (2014). 'Cortisol shifts financial risk preferences.' *Proceedings of the National Academy of Sciences*. Vol. 11, No. 9, pp.3608, 3613.

Kasso, J. et al. (2017). 'The effects of acute exercise on mood, cognition, neurophysiology and neurochemical pathways: A review.' *Brain Plasticity*. Vol. 2, No. 2, pp.127–152.

LeChance, L. et al. (2018). 'Antidepressant foods: an evidence-based nutrient profiling system for depression.' *World Journal of Psychiatry*. Vol. 8, No. 3, pp.97–104.

Maddock, R. et al. (2016). 'Acute modulation of cortical glutamate and GABA content by physical activity.' *The Journal of Neuroscience*. Vol. 36, No. 8, pp.2449–2457.

Maro, H. et al. (2016). 'Why sleep matters – the economic costs of insufficient sleep.' *Rand Health Q.* Vol. 6, No. 4, p.11.

Marselle, M. et al. (2014). 'Examining group walks in nature and multiple aspects of wellbeing: a large-scale study.' *Ecopsychology*. Vol. 6, No. 3.

Masashi, S. et al. (2017). 'Gardening is beneficial to health: A meta-analysis.' *Preventive Medicine Reports*. Vol. 5, pp.92–99.

Miller, J.C. & Krizen, Z. (2016). 'Walking facilitates positive affect (even when expecting the opposite).' *Emotion*. Vol. 16, No. 5, pp.775–85.

Miller, R. et al. (2018). 'Running exercise mitigates the negative consequences of chronic stress on dorsal hippocampal long-term potentiation in male mice.' *Neurobiology of Learning and Memory*. Vol. 149, pp.28–38.

Moore, S. et al. (2012). 'Leisure time physical activity of moderate to vigorous intensity and mortality: a large pooled cohort analysis.' *PLOS Medicine*. Vol. 9, No. 11, e1001335.

Ocean, N. et al. (2018). 'Lettuce be happy: A longitudinal UK study on the relationship between fruit and vegetable consumption and wellbeing.' *Soc Sci Med*. Vol. 222, pp.335–345.

Oppezzo, M. & Schwartz, D. (2014). 'Give your ideas some legs: The positive effect of walking on creative thinking.' *Journal of Experimental Psychology*. Vol. 4, No. 4, pp.1142–1152.

Osorio, C. et al. (2016). 'Adapting to stress: understanding the neurobiology of resilience.' *Behavioural Medicine*. Vol. 43, No. 4, pp.307–322.

Pareja-Galeano H. et al. (2016). 'Biological rationale for regular physical exercise as an effective intervention for the prevention and treatment of depressive disorders.' *Current Pharmaceutical Design*. Vol. 22, No. 24, pp.3764–75.

Park, B-J. et al. (2007). 'Physiological Effects of Shinrin-yoku (Taking in the Atmosphere of the Forest) using salivary cortisol and cerebral activity as indicators.' *Journal of Physiological Anthropology*. Vol. 26, No. 2, pp.123–8.

Park, B-J. et al. (2010). 'Physiological Effects of Shinrin-yoku (Taking in the Atmosphere of the Forest) in an Old-Growth Broadleaf Forest in Yamagata Prefecture, Japan.' *Environ. Health Prev. Medicine*. Vol. 15, No. 1, pp.18–26.

Puterman, E. (2010). 'The power of exercise: buffering the effects of chronic stress on telomere length.' *PLOS One*. Vol. 5, No. 5, e10837.

Puterman, E. (2018). 'Aerobic Exercise Lengthens Telomeres and Reduces Stress in Family Caregivers: A Randomized Controlled Trial.' *Psychoneuroendocrinology*. Vol. 98, pp.245–252.

Roe, J. & Aspinall, P. (2011). 'The restorative benefits of walking in urban and rural settings in adults with good and poor mental health.' *Health & Place*. Vol. 17, pp.103–113.

Schoenfeld, T. et al. (2013). 'Physical exercise prevents stress-induced activation of granule neurons and enhances local inhibitory mechanisms in the dentate gyrus.' *Journal of Neuroscience*. Vol. 33, No. 18, pp.7770–7777.

Smith, D.G. et al. (2019). 'Identification and Characterization of a Novel Anti-Inflammatory Lipid Isolated From Mycobacterium Vaccae, a Soil-Derived Bacterium With Immunoregulatory and Stress Resilience Properties.' *Psychopharmacology*. Vol. 236, No. 5, pp.1653–1670.

Soga M. et al. 'Gardening is beneficial for health: a meta-analysis'. *Preventive Medicine Reports* 2017, pp.92–99.

Suwabe, K. et al. (2018). 'Rapid stimulation of human dentate gyrus function with acute mild exercise.' *Proceedings of the National Academy of Sciences*. Vol. 115, No. 41, pp.10487–10492.

Chapter 4: When relationships disconnect

Amati, V. et al. (2018). 'Social relations and life satisfaction: the role of friends.' *Genus*. Vol. 74, No. 1, p.7.

Appelberg, K. et al. (1996). 'Interpersonal conflict as a predictor of work disability: a follow-up study of 15,348 Finnish employees.' *Journal of Psychosomatic Research*. Vol. 40, No. 2, pp.157–67.

Berkman, L.F. & Syme, S. L. (1979). 'Social networks, host resistance, and mortality: A nine-year follow-up study of Alameda county residents.' *American Journal of Epidemiology*. Vol. 109, No. 2, pp.186–204.

Cohen, S. et al. (2011). 'Does Hugging Provide Stress-Buffering Social Support? A Study of Susceptibility to Upper Respiratory Infection and Ilness.' *Psychological Science*. Vol. 26, No. 2, pp.135–147.

Comte-Sponville, A. (1995). *A Short Treatise On The Great Virtues: The Uses of Philosophy in Everyday Life*. New York: Vintage Publishing.

Eng, P. et al. (2002). 'Social Ties and Change in Social Ties in Relation to Subsequent Total and Cause-specific Mortality and Coronary Heart Disease Incidence in Men.' *American Journal of Epidemiology*. Vol. 155, No. 8, pp.700–709.

Franke, S. & Kulu, H. (2018). 'Mortality Differences by Partnership Status in England and Wales: The Effect of Living Arrangements or Health Selection?' *European Journal of Population*. Vol. 34. No. 1, pp.87–118.

Holt-Lunstad, J. et al. (2008). 'Is There Something Unique about Marriage? The Relative Impact of Marital Status, Relationship Quality, and Network Social Support on Ambulatory Blood Pressure and Mental Health.' *Annals of Behavioural Medicine*. Vol. 35, No. 2, pp.239–244.

Holt-Lunstad, J. et al. (2010). 'Social Relationships and Mortality Risk: A Meta-analytic Review.' *PLoS Med*. Vol. 7, No. 7, e1000316.

Holt-Lunstad, J. et al. (2015). 'Loneliness and Social Isolation as Risk Factors for Mortality: A Meta-Analytic Review.' *Perspectives on Psychological Science*. Vol. 10, No. 2, pp.227–237.

Kiecolt-Glaser, J.K. & Newton, T. (2001). 'Marriage and Health: His and Hers.' *Psychological Bulletin*. Vol. 127, No. 4, pp.472–503.

Kiecolt-Glaser, J.K. et al. (2003). 'Love, Marriage, and Divorce: Newlyweds' Stress Hormones Foreshadow Relationship Changes.' *Journal of Consulting and Clinical Psychology*. Vol. 71, No. 1, pp.176–88.

Keicolt-Glaser J. & Wilson S. (2017) 'Lovesick: how couples relationships influence health.' *Annual Review of Clinical Psychology*. Vol. 13, pp.421–443.

Keicolt-Glaser J. et al. (2005) 'Hostile marital interactions, pro-inflammatory cytokine production and wound healing.' *Arch. Gen. Psychiatry*. Vol. 62, pp.1377–1384.

Kurtz, L.E. & Algoe, S.B. (2015). 'Putting laughter in context: Shared laughter as behavioral indicator of relationship well-being.' *Personal Relationships*. Vol. 22, No. 4, pp.573–590.

Lavner, J.A. & Bradbury, T.N. (2012). 'Why Do Even Satisfied Newlyweds Eventually Go on to Divorce?' *Journal of Family Psychology*. Vol. 26, No. 1, pp.1–10.

Leavitt, K. et al. (2017). 'From the Bedroom to the Office: Workplace Spillover Effects of Sexual Activity at Home.' *Journal of Management*. Vol. 45, No. 3, pp.1173–1192.

Marjoribanks, D. & Bradley, A.D. (2017). 'The Way We Are Now – The state of the UK's relationships.' *Relate*. March 2017 issue.

Markman, H.J. et al. (2010). 'The premarital communication roots of marital distress and divorce: the first five years of marriage.' *Journal of the Division of Family Psychology of the American Psychological Association*. Vol. 24, No. 3, pp.289–98.

McDaniel, B.T., & Coyne, S.M. (2016). '"Technoference": The interference of technology in couple relationships and implications for women's personal and relational well-being.' *Psychology of Popular Media Culture*. Vol. 5, No. 1, pp.85–98.

Pines, A. (1996). *Couple Burnout: Causes and Cures*. England: Routledge.

Robinson, S. et al. (2017). 'Privileging the Bromance: A Critical Appraisal of Romantic and Bromantic Relationships.' *Men and Masculinities*. Vol. 22, No. 5, pp.850–871.

Robles, T.F. et al. (2014). 'Marital quality and health: a meta-analytic review'. *Psychological Bulletin*. Vol. 140, No. 1, pp.140–187.

Rutledge, T. et al. (2004). 'Social Networks Are Associated With Lower Mortality Rates Among Women With Suspected Coronary Disease: The National Heart, Lung, and Blood Institute-Sponsored Women's Ischemia Syndrome Evaluation Study.' *Psychosomatic Medicine.* Vol. 66, No. 6, pp.882–8.

Shirom, A. et al. (2011). 'Work-Based Predictors of Mortality: A 20-Year Follow-Up of Healthy Employees.' *Health Psychology.* Vol. 30, No. 3, pp.268–275.

Tavistock Relationships. (2020). 'Relationships and Mental Health'. Available at: https://tavistockrelationships.ac.uk/policy-research/policy-briefings/689-couple-relationships-and-mental-health-a-policy-briefing-from-the-relationships-alliance

Vaillant, G.E. (2012). *Triumphs of experience: The men of the Harvard Grant Study.* Cambridge, MS: Belknap Press of Harvard University Press.

Various. (2010). *Simple Pleasures: Little things that make life worthwhile.* London: Random House.

Yim, J. (2016). 'Therapeutic Benefits of Laughter in Mental Health: A Theoretical Review.' *The Tohoku Journal of Experimental Medicine.* Vol. 239, No. 3, pp.243–9.

Chapter 5: Taking control of your life

Bailey, B.P. & Konstan, J.A. (2006). 'On the need for attention-aware systems: Measuring effects of interruption on task performance, error rate, and affective state.' *Computers in Human Behavior.* Vol. 22, No. 4, pp.685–708.

Dewan, P. (2014). 'Can I Have Your Attention? Implications of the Research on Distractions and Multitasking for Reference Librarians.' *The Reference Librarian.* Vol. 55, No. 2, pp.95–117.

Gonzalez, V.M. & Mark, G. (2004). 'Constant, constant, multi-tasking craziness: Managing multiple working spheres.' *Conference on Human Factors in Computing Systems – Proceedings.* Vol. 6, pp.113–120.

Hofman, W. et al. (2013). 'Yes, But Are They Happy? Effects of Trait Self-Control on Affective Well-Being and Life Satisfaction.' *Journal of Personality.* Vol. 82, No. 4, pp.265–277.

Loh, K. & Kanai, R. (2014). 'Higher media multi-tasking activity is associated with smaller gray-matter density in the anterior cingulate cortex.' *PLoS ONE,* Vol. 9, No. 9, e106698.

Mark, G., Gonzalez, V.M. & Harris, J. (2005). 'No Task Left Behind? Examining the Nature of Fragmented Work.' *CHI,* pp.321–330.

Mark, G. et al. (2008). 'The Cost of Interrupted Work: More Speed and Stress.' *Conference on Human Factors in Computing Systems – Proceedings,* pp.107-110.

Newport, C. (2019). 'Was e-mail a mistake? The mathematics of distributed systems suggests that meetings might be better.' *The New Yorker.* Available at: https://www.newyorker.com/tech/annals-of-technology/was-e-mail-a-mistake

Ophir, E. et al. (2009). 'Cognitive control in media multitaskers.' *Proceedings of the National Academy of Sciences.* Vol. 106, No. 37, pp.15583–7.

Chapter 6: Glimpses of reality

Crum, A.J. & Langer, E.J. (2007). 'Mind-Set Matters: Exercise and the Placebo Effect.' *Psychological Science.* Vol. 18, No. 2, pp.165–71.

Crum, A.J. et al. (2011). 'Mind over milkshakes: mindsets, not just nutrients, determine ghrelin response.' *Health Psychology.* Vol. 30, No. 4, pp.424–429.

Crum, A.J. et al. (2013). 'Rethinking Stress: The Role of Mindsets in Determining the Stress Response.' *Journal of Personality and Social Psychology.* Vol. 104, No. 4, pp.716 –733.

Kim, E.S. et al. (2017). 'Optimism and Cause-Specific Mortality: A Prospective Cohort Study.' *American Journal of Epidemiology*, Vol. 185, No. 1, pp.21–29.

Kuper, H. & Marmot, M. (2003). 'Intimations of mortality: perceived age of leaving middle age as a predictor of future health outcomes within the Whitehall II study.' *Age Ageing*. Vol. 32, No. 2, pp.178–84.

Levy, B.R. et al. (2002). 'Longevity Increased by Positive Self-Perceptions of Aging.' *Journal of Personality and Social Psychology*. Vol. 83, No. 2, pp.261–270.

Levy, B.R. et al. (2004). 'Preventive health behaviors influenced by self-perceptions of aging.' *Preventive Medicine*. Vol. 39, No. 3, pp.625–629.

Matthews, K.A. et al. (2004). 'Optimistic attitudes protect against progression of carotid atherosclerosis in healthy middle-aged women.' *Psychosomatic Medicine*. Vol. 66, No. 5, pp.640–644.

Robertson, D.A. & Kenny, R.A. (2016). 'Negative perceptions of aging modify the association between frailty and cognitive function in older adults.' *Personality and Individual Differences*. Vol. 100. pp.120–125.

Zahrt, O.H. & Crum, A.J. (2017). 'Perceived Physical Activity and Mortality: Evidence From Three Nationally Representative U.S. Samples.' *Health Psychology*. Vol. 36, No. 11, pp.1017–1025.

Chapter 7: Our mental foundations

Abelson, J.L. et al. (2008). 'Effects of perceived control and cognitive coping on endocrine stress responses to pharmacological activation.' *Biological Psychiatry*. Vol. 64, No. 8, pp.701–707.

Chen, S. (2018). 'Give Yourself a Break: The Power of Self-Compassion.' *Harvard Business Review*. September–October 2018 issue.

Curran, T. & Hill, A. (2019). 'Perfectionism Is Increasing Over Time: A Meta-Analysis of Birth Cohort Differences From 1989 to 2016.' *Psychological Bulletin*. Vol. 145, No. 4, pp.410–429.

Dickerson, S.S. & Kemeny, M.E. (2004). 'Acute stressors and cortisol responses: a theoretical integration and synthesis of laboratory research.' *Psychological Bulletin*. Vol. 130, No. 3, pp.355–91.

Ferrari, M. et al. (2018). 'Self-compassion moderates the perfectionism and depression link in both adolescence and adulthood.' *PLoS ONE*. Vol. 13, No. 2.

Frankl. V. (2004). *Man's Search for Meaning*. UK: Rider.

Hill, P. & Turiano, N.A. (2014). 'Purpose in Life as a Predictor of Mortality Across Adulthood.' *Psychological Science*. Vol. 25, No. 7, pp.1482–1486.

Kozela, M. et al. (2015). 'Perceived control as a predictor of cardiovascular disease mortality in Poland. The HAPIEE Study.' *Cardiology Journal*. Vol. 22, No. 4, pp.404–412.

Maier, S. (2015). 'Behavioral control blunts reactions to contemporaneous and future adverse events: Medial prefrontal cortex plasticity and a cortico-striatal network.' *Neurobiology of Stress*. Vol. 1, pp.12–22.

Seligman, M.E.P. (1972). 'Learned Helplessness.' *Annual Review of Medicine*. Vol. 23, pp.407–412.

Shapira, L.B. & Mongrain, M. (2010). 'The benefits of self-compassion and optimism exercises for individuals vulnerable to depression.' *The Journal of Positive Psychology*. Vol. 5, No. 5, pp.377–389.

Sherman, G.D. et al. (2012). 'Leadership is associated with lower levels of stress.' *Proceedings of the National Academy of Sciences*. Vol. 109, No. 44, pp.17903–17907.

Shim, S. et al. (2015). 'The Grace of Control: How A Can-Control Mindset Increases Well-Being, Health, and Performance.' Available at: https://mbl.stanford.edu/sites/g/files/sbiybj9941/f/control_mindset_intervention_updated_1123_2015_ajc.pdf

Steptoe, A. & Fancourt, D. (2019). 'Leading a meaningful life at older ages and its relationship with social engagement, prosperity, health, biology, and time use.' *Proceedings of the National Academy of Sciences.* Vol. 116, No. 4, pp.1207–1212.

Chapter 8: Mindset at work

Achor, S. (2010). 'Why a Happy Brain Performs Better.' *Harvard Business Review.* Available at: https://hbr.org/2010/11/why-a-happy-brain-performs-bet

Achor, S. (2012). 'Positive Intelligence.' *Harvard Business Review.* January–February 2012 issue, pp.100–102.

Adelman, J. (2013). *Worldly Philosopher: The Odyssey of Albert O. Hirschman.* Princeton: Princeton University Press.

Boehm, J. K. & Lyubomirksy, S. (2008). 'Does Happiness Promote Career Success?' *Journal of Career Assessment.* Vol. 26, No. 2, pp.199–219.

Dijkstra, M.T.M. & Homan, A.C. (2016). 'Engaging In Rather than Disengaging From Stress: Effective Coping and Perceived Control.' *Frontiers in Psychology.* Vol. 21, No. 7, p.1415.

Gino, F. (2018). 'The business case for curiosity.' *Harvard Business Review.* October–November 2018 issue, pp.48–57.

Goldstein, A. (2017). *Janesville: An America Story.* London: Simon & Schuster.

Gladwell, M. (2013). 'The Gift of Doubt: Albert O. Hirschman and the power of failure.' *The New Yorker.* Available at: https://www.newyorker.com/magazine/2013/06/24/the-gift-of-doubt

Kashdan, T. et al. (2018). 'The five dimensions of curiosity.' *Harvard Business Review.* October–November 2018 issue, pp.58–61.

Lyubomirksky, S. et al. (2005). 'The benefits of frequent positive affect: does happiness lead to success?' *Psychological Bulletin.* Vol. 131, pp.803–855.

Seligman, M. & Schulman, P. (1986). 'Explanatory style as a predictor of productivity and quitting among life insurance sales agents.' *Journal of Personality and Social Psychology.* Vol. 50, pp.832–838.

Sgroi, D. (2015). 'Happiness and Productivity: Understanding the Happy-Productive Worker.' *SMF-CAGE Global Perspectives Series.* October 2015.

Spreitzer, G.M. & Porath, C.L. (2012). 'Creating Sustainable Performance.' *Harvard Business Review.* January–February 2012 issue.

Walsh, L.C. et al. (2018). 'Does Happiness Promote Career Success? Revisiting the Evidence.' *Journal of Career Assessment.* Vol. 26, No. 2, pp.199–219.

Chapter 9: The microculture you create

Edmondson, A. (1999). 'Psychological Safety and Learning Behavior in Work Teams.' *Administrative Science Quarterly.* Vol. 44, No. 2, pp.350–383.

Google: re:Work. (2015). 'The five keys to a successful Google team.' Available at: https://rework.withgoogle.com/blog/five-keys-to-a-successful-google-team/

Groysberg, B. et al. (2018). 'The Leader's Guide to Corporate Culture.' *Harvard Business Review.* January–February 2018 issue.

Smith, R.R. and Tan, V. (2018). 'The making of successful teams: A study on psychological safety and great workplaces in Asia Pacific: 2018 Asia insights.' *Research Collection Lee Kong Chian School Of Business*, pp.1–20.

Chapter 11: Planting the seeds

Alvord, M.K. and Grados, J.J. (2005). 'Enhancing Resilience in Children: A Proactive Approach.' *Journal of Professional Psychology: Research and Practice*. Vol. 36, No. 3, pp.238–245.

Brooks, R. (2007). 'The Search for Islands of Competence: A Metaphor of Hope and Strength.' *Reclaiming Children and Youth*. Available at: http://www.drrobertbrooks.com/pdf/0506.pdf

Masten, A.S. and Barnes, A.J. (2018). 'Resilience in Children: Developmental Perspectives.' *Children*. Vol. 5, No. 7, p.98.

NHS Digital (2018). 'Mental Health of Children and Young People in England.' Available at: https://digital.nhs.uk/data-and-information/publications/statistical/mental-health-of-children-and-young-people-in-england/2017/2017

The Times. (2020). 'We must teach students to look after their own mental health.' Available at: https://www.thetimes.co.uk/article/we-must-teach-students-to-look-after-their-own-mental-health-7hjww9w35

Weir, K. (2017). 'Maximizing children's resilience.' *American Psychological Association*. Vol. 48, No. 8, p.40.

Werner, E. & Smith, R. (1992). 'Overcoming the Odds: High Risk Children from Birth to Adulthood.' Ithaca and London: Cornell University Press.

Werner, E.E. & Smith, R.S. (2001). 'Journeys from childhood to midlife: Risk, resilience, and recovery.' Ithaca and London: Cornell University Press.

Chapter 12: Seventy million prescriptions

American Psychological Association. (2017). 'By the numbers: Antidepressant use on the rise.' Available at: https://www.apa.org/monitor/2017/11/numbers

Cipriani, A. et al. (2018). 'Comparative efficacy and acceptability of 21 antidepressant drugs for the acute treatment of adults with major depressive disorder: a systematic review and network meta-analysis.' *The Lancet*. Vol. 391, No. 10128, pp.1357–1366.

Lacobucci, G. (2019). 'NHS prescribed record number of antidepressants last year.' *BMJ*. Available at: https://www.bmj.com/content/364/bmj.l1508

Maslej, M.M et al. (2017). 'The Mortality and Myocardial Effects of Antidepressants Are Moderated by Pre-existing Cardiovascular Disease: A Meta-Analysis.' *Psychotherapy Psychosom*. Vol. 86, pp.268–282.

Piggot, H.E. et al. (2010). 'Efficacy and Effectiveness of Antidepressants: Current Status of Research.' *Journal of Psychotherapy and Psychosomatics*. Vol.79, pp.267–279.

Sandoiu, A. (2017). 'Antidepressants may raise death risk by a third.' *Medical News Today*. Available at: https://www.medicalnewstoday.com/articles/319462#:~:text=A%20new%20study%20suggests%20that,States%20take%20medication%20for%20depression.

Turner, E.H. et al. (2008). 'Selective Publication of Antidepressant Trials and Its Influence on Apparent Efficacy.' *New England Journal of Medicine*. Vol. 358, pp.252–260.

Acknowledgements

This book incubated over a long period, coming out of the many conversations I had with people who were struggling with over-pressurised lives, as I helped them to regain their emotional well-being and health. The insights I gained through my clinical work developed into my thoughts about resilience and how we can maintain our psychological health in challenging times. That led to sharing those ideas in practical ways in talks and workshops for a very wide range of audiences. But somehow the idea of writing a book seemed so much more daunting – it felt like a very big leap.

There are a number of people whom I would like to acknowledge who have helped me to make this leap. First, my daughter, Becky, whose excitement and enthusiasm helped to create a bridge over this chasm that I was perceiving, by introducing me to Bloomsbury.

Second, my psychologist daughter Penny, who has been my research assistant throughout this project. I have very much enjoyed working with her and I have greatly appreciated our interesting conversations and her views on this challenging topic.

I am hugely appreciative of how Karen, my wife and partner in our practice, has encouraged and supported me throughout this project and how she has been immensely tolerant of my working on this book through weekends and my breaks from work last year. Our many conversations have helped shape ideas that have been blended into this book.

A big thank you to my daughter Toria and my son Henry for their enthusiasm and genuine interest in how this book was developing. They would certainly not have let me off the hook if the project had just petered out. All of these wonderful people contribute to my ability to let go of the pressures of my job and have helped me navigate the challenges of my own life with their perspectives and humour.

It has been an enormous pleasure to work with Charlotte Croft and Zoë Blanc of Bloomsbury, with their encouragement, impeccable professionalism and judgement at all times. Zoë read the manuscript so many times I wouldn't be surprised if she could recite whole chapters from memory.

Finally, I would like to thank the thousands of people whom I have met in my years of clinical work who have given me many more insights into human psychology than any conference talk or research paper has ever done.

My warmest thanks to you all.

Index